Accessing and Analyzing DATA
with Microsoft® EXCEL

→ Drill into Microsoft Excel, Access, Data Analyzer, and Office Web Components

→ Capture, analyze, and present data for business decision making

→ Covers Microsoft Office XP and Office 2000

Paul Cornell

PUBLISHED BY
Microsoft Press
A Division of Microsoft Corporation
One Microsoft Way
Redmond, Washington 98052-6399

Copyright © 2003 by Paul Cornell

Library of Congress Cataloging-in-Publication Data
Cornell, Paul, 1968-
    Accessing and Analyzing Data with Microsoft Excel / Paul Cornell.
       p. cm.
    Includes index.
    ISBN 0-7356-1895-X
    1. Microsoft Excel (Computer file) 2. Business--Data processing. 3. Business--Computer programs. I. Title.

HF5548.4.M523C675   2003
005.369--dc21   2002044877

Printed and bound in the United States of America.

1 2 3 4 5 6 7 8 9   QWE   8 7 6 5 4 3

Distributed in Canada by H.B. Fenn and Company Ltd.

A CIP catalogue record for this book is available from the British Library.

Microsoft Press books are available through booksellers and distributors worldwide. For further information about international editions, contact your local Microsoft Corporation office or contact Microsoft Press International directly at fax (425) 936-7329. Visit our Web site at www.microsoft.com/ mspress. Send comments to *mspinput@microsoft.com*.

Acquisitions Editor: Alex Blanton
Project Editor: John Pierce

Body Part No. X09-35333

Table of Contents

Foreword

At no time in the past have organizations had the capability that they do today to gather and store such vast amounts of data: customer information and operational data are collected routinely, flowing into an enterprise from multiple sources with increasing speed. More than ever before, organizations are turning to business intelligence as the means to derive value from the volumes of data warehoused in their computer systems.

Organizations use business intelligence to interpret the data they've collected, providing them with insights that are critical to competing in the new economy: a deeper understanding of customer and partner relationships, key performance indicators, and a consistent view of the organization from the executive level to the front lines. These insights have a direct impact on profitability, increase a business's agility, and can lead to better accountability by providing an accurate view of an organization to all its employees.

A successful business intelligence initiative requires significant investment in software applications, tools, and technologies for reporting, querying, and analysis. It also requires the infrastructure to collect and manage large volumes of business data. Now that business intelligence is a competitive requirement, organizations aren't focusing on whether to invest in it, but on ways to obtain maximum value from their investment. To lower the cost of entering the business intelligence arena, or to stretch their current investment in business intelligence, companies need to leverage the systems and infrastructure they already have and extend the reach of their business intelligence solutions by making analysis tools and skills available to a wider base of users.

Many organizations discover that even with a data management infrastructure in place, business intelligence remains out of reach of the greatest segment of their users—the information workers on the front lines of the company. Traditionally, analysis and reporting of enterprise business data has been the realm of dedicated analysts. With increasing pressure to shorten decision cycles and decrease expenses, these tasks are becoming part of the daily routine of information workers in every facet of an organization. The information workers who are called upon to make fast and accurate decisions can benefit most from access to business intelligence. Access to information empowers users; by extending access to business intelligence to all employees, an organization realizes a higher return on its investment in data management and business intelligence as well as an increased competitive advantage through faster, more informed decision making at all levels.

Analysis solutions that are tailored to meet specific business needs help these employees be productive, allowing them to focus on their line of business rather than on learning or implementing new technologies and tasks. The Microsoft business intelligence platform includes the building blocks for flexible solutions designed to meet the needs of a company or a subset of users within a company. These tailored solutions deliver intuitive tools that enable information workers on the front lines to blend advanced decision-making processes into their daily routines. This approach delivers rapid benefits as employees identify and respond to trends in product performance, respond to marketing campaigns, and take account of other patterns in customer behavior.

The purpose of this book is to enable organizations to realize the full potential of their investments in Microsoft technology. Many of the capabilities of Office tend to be ignored by the majority of users, yet they offer significant business value to an organization. Companies spend thousands of dollars on specialized data analysis tools when the majority of the capabilities they seek are already available in the productivity applications on their users' desktops.

This book covers the core business analysis capabilities of the Office products and demonstrates how you can go beyond traditional reporting to deliver sophisticated data analysis solutions to your organization. You will learn not only about the features available in the products but, more important, how to apply those features in real business scenarios.

The book starts with a clear overview of the key capabilities for data analysis in Microsoft Office. The features are clearly explained so that you can quickly use them for your own analysis needs. It then moves on to more advanced topics to cover enterprise-wide analysis solutions that will enable you to spend more time solving business problems and less time writing reports for every user request.

Paul Cornell has spent the last few years demystifying the capabilities of Microsoft Office to make them more useful to the broad set of users in an organization. He's done a great job of explaining the features and how to apply them. He uses these same skills in this book to introduce the data analysis features in Office and explain how to use them in day-to-day situations. Having this information will enable you to deliver rich analysis solutions more quickly and with a higher rate of success.

I sincerely hope that you enjoy this book and use it to realize the full potential of your investment in Microsoft Office.

Francois Ajenstat
Senior Product Manager, Business Intelligence
Microsoft Corporation

Acknowledgments

I want to thank my team at Microsoft, especially Jean Philippe Bagel, for allowing me to write this book. I'd like to thank Frank Rice for answering my Microsoft Access questions, Colin Wilcox for producing the Microsoft Data Analyzer tutorial included on the book's CD, and Francois Ajenstat for writing the book's foreword.

Thanks to the team at Microsoft Press, especially Alex Blanton and John Pierce, for their enthusiasm, helpfulness, and attention to detail as they guided this book through to print.

I want to thank my family: my wife, Shelley, for giving up a lot of our together time; my daughters, Zoe and Bailey, for giving up some play time with Daddy; and my parents for always encouraging me while I pursued my dreams. I love all of you.

Finally, I want to thank God for giving me the knowledge and opportunity to write this book.

Introduction

Many business computer users spend a majority of each working day analyzing data in a variety of electronic formats, whether the data is in spreadsheets, in databases, or on the Web. These users need to do more than just look at data; they need to make important business decisions based on this data—decisions that affect their individual workgroup, their own businesses, or their entire organization.

Finding an organization these days, large or small, that does not record facts and figures about its operations, products, services, and customers is rare. Perhaps you have encountered one of the following scenarios in your own organization or business:

■ Part of your role within your organization involves basing business decisions on the products or services that your customers purchase. By analyzing your customers' purchasing trends, you know that if you take the right actions, you can increase sales and thereby increase your own value to the organization. Perhaps you aren't quite sure how to determine these purchasing trends, or you've been analyzing purchasing trends but suspect that there's a better way. Or maybe you're using software applications from a company other than Microsoft to analyze these trends and you want to see what Microsoft has to offer to make your data analysis tasks easier.

■ Your manager has asked you to create some reports for her, summarizing the in-stock levels of your organization's product over the last year. You're not sure how to use your organization's data analysis software to translate her request into the report format she prefers. Or maybe you frequently create your manager's reports, but the process is always tedious, and you think there might be an easier way to do it.

■ For the first time, your organization's chief operating officer (COO) asks you to present to him an analysis of your western region's sales figures for the last fiscal quarter. You want to do a great job, but you're a little nervous. You want to include compelling charts, callouts, highlights, recommendations for improvement, and footnotes to guide you in your presentation—and to guide your COO's business decisions—but you're not sure how to do all this with your data analysis software.

- The business you started five years ago is reaching its stride and now it's time to really get a hold of the financial numbers. You've increased the number of employees, struggled through several peak shopping seasons, and acquired a loyal customer base. Your current financial software applications are great for keeping track of your general ledger, but they fall short when it comes to really helpful data analysis. You purchased a copy of Microsoft Office at your local office supply warehouse and you've been using it to write and send out business letters, but you know there's a lot more you can use it for, if you just knew how.

- You develop software solutions for your organization, but you've never developed data analysis solutions before. Or perhaps you've developed software solutions but never any that use Microsoft applications. Or maybe you're just looking to improve your overall skills for developing data analysis solutions with Microsoft software.

- You are an information technology (IT) specialist, and you have just been put in charge of training users to increase their skills with Microsoft Office data analysis tools. You want to increase your own skills in this area as well as understand which skills you should incorporate into the training.

If you have experienced similar scenarios, then *Accessing and Analyzing Data with Microsoft Excel* will show you how to increase your skills with Microsoft data analysis software, which in turn will help you or your organization make smarter and faster business decisions. This introduction will help you further understand the purpose of this book, who the book is written for, and the topics it covers.

About This Book

Microsoft Excel provides valuable tools such as spreadsheet formulas, PivotTable reports, and graphs to present and analyze data. Other Microsoft Office applications—Microsoft Access, the Microsoft Office Web Components, and Microsoft Data Analyzer, to name a few—provide the means to store, present, and analyze data. This book will help you master the skills you need to use this suite of products to analyze business data, thereby enabling you to make better informed business decisions more quickly. Software solutions developers and IT specialists will also find useful information that can enhance their Microsoft data analysis solution development and system administration efforts.

Many books provide lists of a software application's features and describe how to use them. This book, however, takes the model one step further by applying these features to the subject of data analysis. You will learn about the advantages and the drawbacks to several data analysis techniques, and you will learn many data analysis skills as you practice using Microsoft Excel and other Microsoft data analysis software.

Who This Book Is For

The audience for this book can be divided into four main groups of business computer users: data browsers, data analysts, business decision makers (including small business owners), and solution developers. This book provides helpful information to members of all four of these audiences.

- Data browsers generally need read-only access to data. Data browsers view, sort, and filter existing data in spreadsheets, PivotTable reports, charts, and other deliverables created by data analysts. Data browsers don't need to worry about connecting to data or creating new reports based on existing data. Data browsers make business decisions, but only as these decisions affect their individual workgroups or individual customers. Examples of data browsers include hotel front-desk clerks, bank tellers, retail cashiers, manufacturing shift workers, customer service representatives, sales representatives, and administrative assistants.

- Data analysts create reports and other data analysis presentations for both data browsers and decision makers. Data analysts connect to original data sources and build spreadsheets, PivotTable reports, charts, and other deliverables from scratch. While data analysts occasionally field report requests from data browsers, much of a data analyst's day is spent creating ad hoc data analysis reports at the request of business decision makers. Data analysts add richness to reports through callouts, footnotes, formatting, and comments. Data analysts frequently create new reports based on existing reports and advise business decision makers by providing preliminary data analysis. Examples of data analysts include actuaries, accountants, marketing representatives, human resource personnel, researchers, paralegals, and financial analysts.

- Business decision makers guide organizations by making far reaching decisions based on data. Business decision makers might create their own reports, but they might also work closely with data analysts to define and refine key reports. In larger organizations, business decision makers educate data analysts on trends, key performance indicators, and other data facts associated with the business. They also educate data browsers to make good decisions, based on data, through business goals and objectives. Examples of business decision makers include small business owners, regional and district managers, unit managers, shift managers, chief financial officers, chief executive officers, chief operating officers, corporate vice presidents, and boards of directors.

■ Solution developers program Office applications and features in order to automate data reporting and analysis. Solution developers do not create reports or make business decisions, but they work throughout an organization to understand business and reporting requirements. They translate these requirements into programs that make the creation of reports—and the decisions that rely on those reports—faster, easier, and more predictable. Examples of solution developers include in-house software engineers, contract programmers, independent software vendors, and systems analysts.

> **Note** Academic researchers, physical and theoretical scientists, mathematicians and statisticians, and so on have their own unique data analysis needs. The needs of these professions are not specifically addressed in this book.

Organization of This Book

This book contains 12 chapters and 2 appendixes. The following is a brief summary of these chapters and appendixes. Understanding the book's contents will help you go to specific parts of the book that interest you, or you can just start with the earlier chapters to gain general knowledge and then move to the later chapters to build on your skills.

■ Chapter 1, "Making Sense of Data," introduces you to the field of data analysis, helps you understand what types of data you can and cannot analyze with Microsoft software applications, helps you understand the various data formats and how Microsoft Office applications handle these data formats, and describes how to troubleshoot data compatibility issues.

- Chapter 2, "Basic Data Analysis Techniques," introduces you to techniques such as sorting, filtering, formatting, importing, exporting, querying, creating charts, and pivoting data. This chapter also introduces how to work with data lists, relational and multidimensional data, and Extensible Markup Language (XML) data.

- Chapter 3, "Analyzing Data with Microsoft Excel," goes into detail about the features in Excel that can be used to sort, filter, format, import, and query data. This chapter describes how to work with charts and Web-based data and how to use the Analysis ToolPak and the Solver Add-In.

- Chapter 4, "Analyzing Data with PivotTable and PivotChart Reports," makes sense of PivotTable report and PivotChart report basics and describes how to use these tools for more advanced data analysis tasks.

- Chapter 5, "Analyzing Data with Microsoft Access," helps you understand the differences between relational and nonrelational data; how to use Access to get at external data; how to sort, filter, and query data; how to create reports; and how to analyze data by using Pivot-Table and PivotChart views in Access.

- Chapter 6, "Analyzing Data with the Office Web Components," introduces you to the features of the Spreadsheet Component, the Pivot-Table Component, and the Chart Component—tools you can use to present and analyze data on the Web.

- Chapter 7, "Introducing Online Analytical Processing," describes what online analytical processing (OLAP) is, why OLAP is important in the data analysis field, and how OLAP can be used to make better decisions. The chapter also includes an introduction to online transaction processing (OLTP) systems and the OLAP features in Microsoft Office.

- Chapter 8, "Analyzing OLAP Data with Microsoft Excel," continues the discussion of OLAP by demonstrating how to connect to, query, and work with OLAP data. The chapter describes how to create offline OLAP data cubes and in which scenarios this is helpful.

- Chapter 9, "Analyzing OLAP Data with Microsoft Data Analyzer," introduces Microsoft Data Analyzer and how you can use it to connect to and view OLAP data in a relatively new graphical application.

- Chapter 10, "Working with XML Data in Excel and Access," provides an overview of the Extensible Markup Language (XML) and its purpose, how to read an XML document, and how to use Excel and Access to analyze XML data.

- Chapter 11, "Extending Office Data Analysis Features with Code," describes how to program and automate Microsoft Office data analysis applications and features. Specifically, the chapter explains terms such as macros, procedures, and object models. You will learn the basics of how to program Excel, Access, the Office Web Components, and Microsoft Data Analyzer to build data analysis solutions

- Chapter 12, "Maintaining Data Reporting and Analysis Systems," introduces the requirements for maintaining Microsoft SQL Server and Microsoft Access databases to ensure the availability of your data storage systems and to foster data analysis.

- Appendix A, "Data Analysis Quick Reference," provides condensed procedures for working with the data analysis features of Excel, Access, the Office Web Components, and Data Analyzer.

- Appendix B, "Additional Tools and Resources," describes the data analysis tools provided on the CD accompanying this book and tools available on line at Microsoft's Web site (*http://www.microsoft.com*).

Where to Go From Here

While you can read this book from cover to cover, you will get faster results by focusing on the types of data your organization uses and the role or roles you serve in analyzing that data.

- All users should read Chapters 1 and 2.

- Users of Microsoft Excel and the Microsoft Office Web Components should read Chapters 3, 4, and 6.

- Microsoft Access users should read Chapters 5 and 6.

- Microsoft SQL Server users should read Chapters 3 through 6.

- Users of XML data should read Chapter 10.

- Readers who need information about OLAP and Microsoft Data Analyzer should read Chapters 7 through 9.

- Data browsers, data analysts, and business decision makers should read Chapters 3 through 6.

- Solution developers should read Chapters 3 through 6 and Chapter 11.

- System administrators should read Chapter 12.

Features of This Book

While you can certainly learn more about a given subject by reading a book about it from cover to cover, studies show that you can learn concepts more quickly and retain information longer by putting your newfound knowledge into practice. Throughout this book, you will see special sections with the headings *Your Turn* and *Putting It Together*. These sections provide opportunities for you to perform exercises to reinforce what you read. To perform these exercises, you must have access to the sample files that are included on the CD that accompanies the book, as well as a computer that meets the system requirements described later in this introduction. Notes, tips, cautions, warnings, and additional sidebars appear throughout the text to give you extra or important information.

Many of this book's procedures work the same in Microsoft Office XP and Microsoft Office 2000 applications. However, for ease of reference, this book's procedures follow the steps you would perform in Office XP. If you are using Microsoft Office 2000, you might need to follow slightly different steps, and these differences are often noted in the book's text. Procedures that work only in Office XP are identified with a note.

Using the Accompanying CD

The CD that accompanies this book contains the sample files and templates that are used in the exercises in the Your Turn and Putting It Together sections. The CD also contains some extra data analysis samples that you can use when you are finished reading this book. (For details about the CD extras, see Appendix B, "Additional Tools and Resources.") The CD also includes a fully searchable electronic version of this book.

To install the sample files and other content on the CD, follow these steps:

1. Insert the CD into your CD-ROM drive. The CD's autorun feature should display a welcome page from which you can install the sample files, data analysis extras, and the electronic book.

   If the CD does not start automatically, open the folder for your CD-ROM drive and double-click StartCD.exe.

2. Click the link for the content you want to install to run the setup program.

   By default, the sample files will be copied to *C:\Microsoft Press\Excel Data Analysis\Sample Files*. The setup program will create a folder for each of the book's chapters that use sample files; for example, Chap02, Chap03, and so on. The setup program will copy the data analysis extras to *C:\Microsoft Press\Excel Data Analysis\Extras*.

Microsoft Internet Explorer 5.01 or later and the proper HTML Help components are required to view the electronic book. If your computer does not have Microsoft Internet Explorer 5.01 or later, you can install Microsoft Internet Explorer 6 from the CD-ROM. For more details about the installation of the electronic book, see the readme.txt file included on the CD.

To remove the sample files, extras, or electronic book from your computer, use Add/Remove Programs in Control Panel.

System Requirements

To perform the procedures in the Your Turn and Putting It Together sections and run the samples, templates, and extras on the CD that accompanies this book, your computer must meet these minimum requirements:

- Internet Explorer 5.5 or later.

- Microsoft Office 2000 Professional or Microsoft Office XP Professional. (The Professional edition of Office includes Microsoft Access.)

- Microsoft FrontPage 2000 or Microsoft FrontPage 2002 (to work with exercises in Chapter 6).

- Microsoft Data Analyzer (to work with exercises in Chapter 9 and Chapter 11).

- Microsoft SQL Server 2000 Analysis Services (to work with exercises in Chapter 11).

- CD-ROM drive

- Enough memory and hard disk space to install the sample files, extras, and electronic book. The sample files and data analysis extras require approximately 9.5 megabytes (MB). The default installation of the electronic book requires approximately 10 MB.

Support

Every effort has been made to ensure the accuracy of this book. Microsoft Press provides corrections for books through the World Wide Web at the following address:

http://www.microsoft.com/mspress/support

To connect directly to the Microsoft Press Knowledge Base and enter a query regarding a question or an issue that you might have, go to

http://www.microsoft.com/mspress/support/search.asp

If you have comments, questions, or ideas regarding this book, please send them to Microsoft Press via post mail to

Microsoft Press
Attn: Accessing and Analyzing Data with Microsoft Excel Editor
One Microsoft Way
Redmond, WA 98052-6399

or via e-mail to

MSPINPUT@MICROSOFT.COM

Note that product support is not offered through the above mail address. For product support information, visit the Microsoft Product Standard Support Web site at *http://support.microsoft.com/directory.*

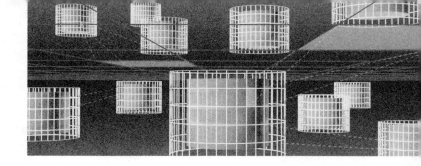

1

Making Sense of Data

Data is of no real business use if you don't use it to improve your or your organization's business decisions. For example, a business might track its customers' purchasing behaviors, but if it doesn't analyze these behaviors to determine which products to stock, discontinue, discount, cross-sell, or up sell, it could miss significant revenue opportunities.

In this chapter, you'll learn about the types of data you can analyze with Microsoft software applications; you'll understand how the formats in which an organization stores data can affect its approach to data analysis; and you'll learn how to use data analysis methodologies. Finally, you'll read about data analysis tools and applications developed by Microsoft and about the situations in which you should use them.

Objectives

By the end of this chapter, you should

- Understand what types of data you can analyze by using Microsoft software applications and features.

- Understand the sorts of business decisions data analysis can improve.

- Understand the differences among some common data formats and what effect these differences might have on your organization's approach to data analysis.

- Know how to troubleshoot data format compatibility issues.

■ Understand the differences among Microsoft file-based and server-based data storage software applications.

■ Know the key features of Microsoft Excel, Microsoft Access, the Microsoft Office Web Components, Microsoft SQL Server, the Microsoft SQL Server Desktop Engine, Microsoft SQL Server 2000 Analysis Services, and Microsoft Data Analyzer.

The Types of Data That You Can Analyze

Data analysis is the general term used to encompass activities related to the examination, interpretation, synthesis, and summarization of data. In real-world computing, these activities translate to people using software to make sense of—and making smarter business decisions based on—their business' or organizations' data. This definition of data analysis frames the rest of this book's contents.

All About Data

At its core, *data* is about using groups of letters, numbers, and other characters to represent *facts* in the real world. For example, the string of characters *Seattle 64°F 10/14/2002* most likely represents the fact that the temperature in the city of Seattle on the date 14 October 2002 was 64 degrees Fahrenheit. Similarly, the string of characters *MSFT 45.35 7/26/2002* most likely represents the fact that the closing price of one share of Microsoft stock on the date 26 July 2002 was US$45.35.

Each individual component of the fact represented is known as a *field*. In the previous example, the letters *MSFT* could constitute the Company field, the numbers *45.35* could constitute the Closing Price field, and the date *7/26/2002* could make up the Date field. A group of related fields are known as a *record*. To continue this example, two stock records might include the following: *MSFT 42.83 7/25/2002* and *MSFT 45.35 7/26/2002*. Related records that use the same field names are commonly grouped and stored together in electronic *data files* or *databases*. The software applications used to create and store these data files and databases usually include features that you can use to perform data analysis tasks.

Organizations use many types of data files and databases to store data, including

■ Text files, in which each field is commonly separated by a character such as a comma or a semicolon and each record is commonly separated by a carriage return.

■ Spreadsheets, in which each field occupies a single spreadsheet cell and each record is stored in a horizontal row of cells. Spreadsheets are usually discrete collections of individual records, and the records are usually not related to records in other spreadsheets.

■ File-based databases or server-based databases, in which groups of records (known in the database world as *tables*) are commonly related to each other in some way—for example, a table of customer names and a table of those customers' orders. Server-based databases usually provide more robust data storage and administration features, and they also support more concurrent data analysis tasks than do file-based databases.

Understanding these data formats and how they promote (or prohibit) data analysis will help you to better formulate your approach to analyzing data. This understanding is important because your organization likely has structured data such as tables inside Microsoft Word documents or Microsoft PowerPoint slides, e-mail messages in Microsoft Outlook folder views, or data stored in files created with other software applications that are not primarily designed for data analysis. An explanation of how to use Microsoft data analysis software features with these types of data is outside the scope of this book.

Note   You can still use Microsoft data analysis software to work with data stored in these formats. To do so, you should first export the data to a Microsoft data analysis software application such as Excel or Access. Consult your specific product's documentation to see whether exporting data for this aim is possible, and if so, how to do it.

The following table lists the Microsoft software applications you should use to analyze data in a specific format. Later in this chapter, I'll cover specific uses and features of these applications in more detail.

Data Formats	Data Storage Applications	Data Analysis Applications
Delimited text (for example, a comma-separated value file) or single or multiple unrelated row-and-column spreadsheets or data tables	Microsoft Excel Microsoft Access Microsoft SQL Server 2000	Microsoft Excel Microsoft Access Microsoft Office Web Components
Multiple related row-and-column data tables	Microsoft Access Microsoft SQL Server 2000	Microsoft Access Microsoft Office Web Components
Online analytical processing (OLAP) data	Microsoft SQL Server 2000 Analysis Services	Microsoft Excel Microsoft Office Web Components Microsoft Data Analyzer

Note The concepts defining OLAP data and data analysis strategies are covered in Chapters 7, 8, and 9.

Using Data to Make Decisions

Collecting and storing data in text files, spreadsheets, or databases has little benefit if you don't take any actions based on that data. For example, retail sales organizations can use information gained from analyzing their sales data to

- Introduce new product lines.
- Discontinue poorly selling product lines.
- Mark up or mark down product sales prices.
- Provide an adequate level of products during peak seasons.
- Up sell or cross-sell products to specific customers.
- Conduct discount sales promotions.

Manufacturing organizations can use their data to

- Decrease the amount of rejected products.
- Increase product quality.
- Adequately allocate human and mechanical resources.
- Purchase proper quantities of raw materials and machinery.

Insurance organizations can use their data to

- Introduce new lines of coverage.
- Discontinue high-risk lines of coverage.
- Set overall policy premiums.
- Reward customers holding multiple lines of coverage with overall reduced premiums.
- Up sell or cross-sell specific lines of coverage to customers.
- Deny or restrict coverage to high-risk groups.

Customer service organizations can use their data to

- Match services to customer preferences.
- Improve service levels offered to customers.
- Introduce new service offerings.
- Discontinue poorly performing service offerings.
- Set overall service pricing.
- Up sell or cross-sell services to specific customers.
- Conduct service discount promotions.

Throughout this book, you'll gain the skills you need to analyze data to make these types of business decisions and make them in a smarter way.

Developing a Data Analysis Strategy

Your organization should already be collecting and storing the data that you need to make good business decisions. If your organization does not have a data collection and storage plan, it is at a serious business disadvantage. You should regularly assess your organization's data collection and storage procedures or make recommendations to others in your organization who are responsible for establishing data collection and storage procedures. If you do not collect or store the right data, you might make less valuable business decisions.

Once collection and storage procedures are in place, an effective data analysis strategy can help an organization unite under a common vision, mission, or financial goal. For example, your organization might want to increase profits by 5 percent next quarter, add 750 new customers next month, or sell 1 million product units next year. This effectiveness can be achieved when representatives from across the organization come together to decide questions such as the following:

■   Which data facts should we record about our business?

■   Which data facts do we record now and are they sufficient?

■   How often should we record the data?

■   How should we record, collect, and store the data?

■   How will we present the data?

■   How will we make future business decisions based on the data?

Depending on the answers your organization comes up with, you may decide that you are collecting the wrong data, not collecting enough data, collecting data at the wrong times, and so on.

To help answer these questions, you should assemble your organization's key business decision makers, which might simply be you, or might involve your business managers or department heads, or even corporate officers (CEOs, CFOs, COOs, and the like). Without an understanding of business goals and how performance against these goals will be measured, those who implement data capture and analysis strategies within an organization could actually be working counter to the organization's overall goals.

You should also understand information technology (IT) requirements. What are the budgetary constraints in terms of computer hardware and software? If you have an IT department, knowing whether it has spent its budget for the rest of the fiscal year or whether a large purchase is right around the corner will affect your data gathering and analysis plans. Can you afford any computer upgrades for data storage and other hardware, software, and support?

For certain organizations, you could also assemble the following individuals:

- In a retail sales organization or customer service organization, you could assemble product and service developers, product purchasers, marketing specialists, sales and service managers, and sales and service trainers.

- In a manufacturing organization you could gather operations managers, materials buyers, resource planners, plant managers, safety supervisors, supply managers, warehouse managers, and shipping managers.

- In an insurance organization, you could meet with your actuarial managers, policy line developers, insurance agent managers, and insurance agent trainers.

Last but not least, don't forget to include your customers' points of view through focus groups, interviews, or informal surveys. Do they perceive your current data collection efforts as too intrusive? Does the data collection experience detract from your customers' purchasing behaviors? For example, if you visit a local retail store and the cashiers ask you for your complete address and phone number at every sales transaction, would you return there?

In answer to the question about which data facts to record, let's say your organization's representatives decide to start by recording facts only about your customers' purchasing behaviors and demographics. After an intense planning meeting, here are the areas the group decides to focus on:

- What products and services do our customers purchase most often?

- In what quantities do our customers purchase our products and services?

- At what times of the year, month, or day do our customers make purchases?

- Which combinations of products and services do our customers purchase together?

- Which of our discount promotions result in the most customer visits and purchases?

- Where do our customers live?

- What are our customers' ages?

- Are our customers married?

- Do our customers have children, and if so, how many and of what ages?

- What are our customers' professional and personal interests?

- Are our customers retired?

- What products and services do our customers purchase from other organizations?

In order to record data about your customers' purchasing behaviors, you determine that your sales receipt system needs to be modified slightly. To gather demographic data about your customers, you decide to offer a one-time 5 percent discount off a future purchase if a customer fills out a brief survey and turns the completed survey in at the point of purchase. You decide also to combine this survey data with personal information collected from your customers' credit applications.

> **Caution**   If you collect your customers' demographic or personal data without their consent, you could expose your organization to unwanted legal actions. Be certain that you understand any legal issues that affect customers' rights to privacy before you begin collecting their demographic or personal data. If you do collect customers' demographic or personal data, a good practice is to allow customers to *opt in* (choose to give you their data). This approach is preferable to making customers *opt out* (tell you to stop collecting their data).

Recording Data

The way that your organization records data facts is just as important as the data itself. Some approaches you can take to record data facts include

- Automated data capture devices such as turnstile counters, infrared beam interruptions, or other automated machinery.

- Observational data capture by means of people taking physical counts with tally sheets or hand clickers or manually reading scales or measures and recording the results.

- Transactional data capture at cash registers, bank teller windows, or other online transaction processing (OLTP) systems.

- Voluntary data submission through questionnaires, surveys, or application forms.

At a small retail store, for instance, you could take just a few simple actions to collect data to improve sales:

- Install an infrared beam at the store's entrance. Whenever the beam is interrupted, a counter is triggered. This measures customer traffic, which you can then compare to the number of sales transactions on a specific day. You can determine how many of your customers are just browsing versus how many are purchasing your products.

- Place a simple tally sheet at each telephone. Divide the tally sheet into one-hour time blocks, and divide each hourly block into subject blocks to record whether a caller inquired about store hours, directions to the store, whether a particular product was in stock, whether an order was still on layaway for that customer, and so on. Every time a customer calls on the telephone, the employee answering marks the tally sheet in the correct subject block and time block. This information will measure how many customers called, during which hours of the day they called, and for what reasons. Analyzing this information, you could determine whether you should add answers to frequently asked questions to your organization's automated telephone greeting (your hours and location, for example), whether you need to hire more salesclerks for certain days of the week or times of the day to handle phone calls, and so on.

- Make sure your cash registers record not only product names, quantities, and sales prices for each transaction, but also the date and time of the sale, payment method, the salesclerk's ID, any promotion codes, and any available customer information such as ZIP code, phone number, address, and so on. If you can't modify your current sales receipt system, consider purchasing or upgrading to a new system.

Troubleshooting Data Compatibility Issues

Perhaps your organization has data stored in a format that's not compatible with a particular Microsoft data analysis software application. Or maybe your data is stored in a format created with a Microsoft application that was not designed primarily for data analysis, such as PowerPoint. The following table provides some possible solutions to foster data analysis in these situations.

Problem	Solutions
The data is stored in a non-Microsoft electronic data file or database, such as on a mainframe computer.	To analyze these types of data with the techniques described in this book, you should export the data into text files, Excel spreadsheets, Access databases, or SQL Server databases. Consult the documentation for your specific software application or database to see whether exporting your data to one of these formats is supported.
The data is "ragged" (one or more of the records are missing values in one or more of their fields), which may lead to unexpected data analysis results.	Depending on the values allowed in the data file or database, use values such as 0 (zero), NULL, EMPTY, NONE, or N/A in each field with a missing value.
Unrelated data records are stored on the same electronic spreadsheet, which makes the data hard to manage.	Consolidate groups of related data records in separate spreadsheets. You can store multiple Excel spreadsheets (also called *worksheets*) in a single file, called a *workbook*, for organizational purposes.
You want to use the features of Microsoft Data Analyzer to analyze non-OLAP data.	Use the tools included with Excel to convert the non-OLAP data into an offline cube file, or use Microsoft SQL Server Data Transformation Services to import the data into SQL Server database format. Then use the tools included with Microsoft SQL Server 2000 Analysis Services to convert the data into OLAP cubes. See the specific product's documentation for instructions on how to do this.

Understanding Microsoft Data Analysis Software and Features

With today's complex computer software, the people who decide what information technology a business or an organization will use frequently look for software suppliers with complete, end-to-end solutions for their business needs. In the following sections, I'll describe in more detail the Microsoft software applications you can use for storing and analyzing data and the situations in which you would use a specific product. First, let's review some of the requirements and methods of data storage.

Data Storage

Before you can fully understand how to use the Microsoft data analysis software applications, you should understand the differences between *file-based* data storage applications and *server-based* data storage applications.

File-based data storage applications such as Excel and Access provide graphical data analysis features in addition to lightweight data storage capabilities. Excel is better suited to storing nonrelational data lists (groups of data records that stand on their own), while Access is designed to store relational data tables (groups of data records that rely on other data records to describe business facts) and can also store a larger number of records than a single Excel worksheet. Excel can store only about 65,000 records per worksheet, while Access can handle up to 2 gigabytes of data per database file.

Server-based data storage applications such as Microsoft SQL Server 2000 provide additional database management features such as enhanced data recovery, faster data retrieval, distribution of data analysis requests among groups of networked computers, and the ability to store and manage multiple databases at the same time. SQL Server 2000 can store about 2 terabytes of data per database that it manages.

You may want to use a nonrelational file-based data storage application such as Excel when

- You need to store only a relatively small amount of data (a few hundred megabytes or less).

- You want to store nonrelational data.

- You are not necessarily concerned about recovering your data should a disaster such as a power failure, a computer hardware failure, a computer virus, or electronic file corruption occur.

- Only a few business computer users (a couple of dozen at most) will be entering data into the data source or accessing the data from the data source at any given time.

On the other hand, you should use a relational file-based storage application (such as Access) or a server-based storage application (such as SQL Server 2000) when any of these conditions apply:

- You want to store a moderate to a relatively large amount of data.

- You want to store relational data.

- You are concerned about recovering your data if a disaster occurs.

- A moderate to relatively large number of users (a couple of dozen or more) are entering data into the data source or accessing the existing data from the data source at any given time.

Microsoft data analysis tools such as the Office Web Components and Data Analyzer do not store data at all; they connect to sources of data and then display data in a number of different ways, depending on the data analysis task you're trying to accomplish.

Over the next several pages, I'll introduce you to these data storage and data analysis applications and their features.

Microsoft Excel

Microsoft Excel is used by millions of computer users around the world. Chances are that you, your employees or coworkers, or the people who will join your organization in the future are familiar with Excel. There's an even greater chance that most computers in your organization already have Excel installed. It makes sense, then, for you and others in your organization to build on your basic skills and use Excel to store and analyze data.

Excel can be used not only to store data on worksheets, but also to analyze and share that data with others. Many organizations that once relied on expensive mainframe computers or outsourced their data analysis tasks can now assign many of these tasks to the average business computer user. Excel has a wide range of data analysis functions, a large variety of chart types, and specialized add-ins that encompass data analysis capabilities that used to be understood only by corporate financial analysts or executive financial specialists.

In addition to its analysis of simple lists of facts and figures, Excel also integrates with a pair of potent data analysis tools: PivotTable reports and PivotChart reports. The reports these tools generate offer summarized, interactive, highly graphical analyses of large amounts of data. PivotTable reports and PivotChart reports allow users to switch from one view of their summarized data to another by rotating rows and columns, in many cases with just a few quick mouse and keyboard actions. Better yet, the skills learned in using PivotTable reports and PivotChart reports to analyze nonrelational data can be applied to relational and hierarchical data as well.

Excel also allows you to work with many sources of data that are available on the Web. Excel can query Web data and import it into a worksheet that can be stored for analysis and reference. Excel can also be set up to query a Web data source at specified time intervals and import any data that has changed. You can use Excel with Office Web Components to expose the business data stored in worksheets to the Internet or an intranet.

Excel 2002 has built-in support for Extensible Markup Language (XML) data, a data format that transcends the binary formats used by specific software applications. (For more information about XML, see the section "Working with XML Data" in Chapter 2.) And, of course, Excel, as part of Microsoft Office, can be used with applications such as Word, Access, PowerPoint, and Outlook to create complete business data analysis solutions.

Microsoft Access

Although Access does not have the same number of analytical and statistical functions and add-ins as Excel, Access is uniquely qualified to handle relational data.

Relational data refers to groups of discrete data records that cannot fully describe business facts on their own. For example, a group of records might describe information about customers who purchase goods, but the details about the goods purchased are contained in another group of records. The groups of records are related to each other by a unique identifier called a *key*. In this case, the key could be a unique customer ID; each record in the group of goods purchased records is related to the customer information records by the unique customer ID. By using these keys, Access has the built-in ability to record, relate, look up, and analyze data by cross-referencing several groups of data at once.

Access also has these features:

- Built-in data views such as Datasheet view, PivotTable view, and PivotChart view. You can switch between these views with just a few mouse clicks.

- The ability to filter data by selection or by form, which provides more filtering options than the built-in filtering features of Excel.

- The ability to create Web pages (known as *data access pages*) that enable you to publish highly customizable graphical user interfaces for your data, which can then be viewed through a Web browser.

- The ability to script automated data access and analysis routines, known as *macros*, without needing to learn a programming language such as Microsoft Visual Basic for Applications.

- Several relational data wizards that can help you build simple data entry and data analysis applications.

Microsoft Office Web Components

Microsoft Office Web Components are used to build Web-based data analysis tools that have the familiar look of Excel spreadsheets, PivotTable reports, and PivotChart reports. The components can be embedded in Web pages or Web-based applications that you can then use to publish interactive data over an intranet, analyze data in a Web browser, or retrieve data from an intranet for local storage in an Excel spreadsheet.

There are three Office Web Components:

- The Spreadsheet Component includes Excel features such as loading XML data files, worksheet functions, multiple worksheets, and wrapped text. You can also publish worksheets from Excel to the Web, hosting the information in a Spreadsheet Component.

- The Chart Component includes features such as three-dimensional chart types, graphing multiple charts within the same Chart Component, conditional formatting, and custom annotations inside a chart.

- The PivotTable Component looks and behaves much like its Excel counterpart, and it supports features such as filtering and live data updating.

The Office Web Components can access not only nonrelational data, but also relational and multidimensional data. This provides you with access to almost all of your data without having to learn a suite of unfamiliar software application features.

You will learn more about the Microsoft Office Web Components in Chapter 6.

Microsoft SQL Server 2000

Microsoft SQL Server 2000 is a group of high-performance, server-based data software applications. These applications are very fast, can store lots of data, can recover from disasters and downtime quickly, and expose their features to a wide variety of data analysis applications. Because many of the SQL Server 2000 applications can be installed only on network computer servers, SQL Server 2000 takes advantage of server features such as enhanced security, ease of access from multiple computers, and centralized application management and control.

SQL Server 2000 features include

- The ability to access SQL Server 2000 databases over the Web.

- English query, which enables you to frame business questions in plain English phrases instead of in a complicated computer language.

- Distributed views, which allows an organization to balance data analysis tasks over several computers running SQL Server 2000 in a computer network.

- Enhanced indexing, which organizes data so that it can be located much more quickly (similar to looking up telephone numbers in a directory or speed dialing.)

- Automatic database management tools that take a lot of the time and guesswork out of performing database backups, fine-tuning database indexes, and alerting database administrators when problems occur.

- Data Transformation Services, which allows for a wide variety of data from different formats to be imported and translated into a format that SQL Server 2000 can understand.

For hosting business data analysis solutions on individual computers that are not network servers or that communicate only with a small workgroup of computers, Microsoft SQL Server 2000 Desktop Engine (often referred to as MSDE 2000) provides a low-cost, lower-resource alternative. For more information about MSDE, see the next section.

For analyzing larger amounts of data, Microsoft SQL Server 2000 Analysis Services is designed to summarize groups of data fields prior to a request for that information. Rather than you asking for a specific data summarization and waiting while the data analysis application calculates the results, SQL Server 2000 Analysis Services most likely has the result figured out already. This provides very fast performance, even with millions of data records.

Although the SQL Server 2000 family of applications supports business data analysis, the user interfaces these applications include for performing data analysis can be somewhat difficult to learn. Because applications such as Excel and Access perform almost all of the data analysis tasks that the features built-in to SQL Server 2000 can, this book will not cover SQL Server 2000 data analysis features. For more information about SQL Server 2000 data analysis features, go to the Microsoft SQL Server Web site at *http://www.microsoft.com/sql*.

Microsoft SQL Server 2000 Desktop Engine

The Microsoft SQL Server 2000 Desktop Engine is a lightweight version of Microsoft SQL Server 2000. Its system requirements are less stringent, and it has fewer features than SQL Server 2000.

MSDE 2000 is ideal for individual computer users who need SQL Server 2000 features—for example, faster application performance and better disaster recovery options than are available in Access—but who do not want to learn a new suite of database management tools.

Because MSDE 2000 is a subset of SQL Server 2000, MSDE 2000 supports only as many as five simultaneous database actions at a time. It also supports databases only up to 2 gigabytes in size. However, this capacity is more than sufficient for most business data analysis solutions running on individual computers or on a computer serving a small number of connected workgroup computers.

Solution developers can also include MSDE 2000 in the applications they distribute. MSDE 2000 provides an ideal offline data storage application for many solutions.

MSDE 2000 can be installed from any media that includes Microsoft Access 2002 or any Microsoft Office XP software application suite that includes Microsoft Access 2002. Check the MSDE 2000 end-user license agreement (EULA) for additional installation and distribution requirements.

For more information on MSDE 2000, go to the Microsoft SQL Server 2000 Desktop Engine Web site at *http://www.microsoft.com/sql/techinfo/development/2000/MSDE2000.asp*.

Microsoft SQL Server 2000 Analysis Services

Microsoft SQL Server 2000 Analysis Services is designed to perform data analysis tasks on large amounts of data in less time. Microsoft Office data analysis applications support SQL Server 2000 Analysis Services, so you or members of your organization can get answers to data analysis questions faster and without a lot of additional training.

Analysis Services provides access to data by creating multidimensional data storage units called *cubes*. Analysis Services calculates summarizations from cube data ahead of time, which means that getting results from data managed by Analysis Services takes less time than making such a calculation without a cube already prepared.

You will learn more about multidimensional data in Chapter 7 through 9. For more information on Analysis Services, go to the Microsoft Analysis Services Web site at *http://www.microsoft.com/sql/evaluation/bi*.

Microsoft Data Analyzer

Microsoft Data Analyzer, part of Microsoft Office, can display interactive bar charts and pie charts along with conditional color formatting, quickly compare similar data distributions among hierarchical slices of data, synchronize data views across multiple data slices, drill up and down through data cubes to locate specific data summarizations, and more.

Data Analyzer can export the data that it is analyzing to an Excel spreadsheet or an Excel PivotTable report for further in-depth analysis. Data Analyzer can also export a data view to a PowerPoint slide for integration into a presentation.

Data Analyzer is designed to work only with hierarchical data that is stored in a Microsoft SQL Server 2000 Analysis Services cube or in an offline cube (*.cub) file. Fortunately, Excel lets you grab data from many other data sources and turn it into an offline cube file format that Data Analyzer can use. Offline cube files are also helpful in situations such as when you are using portable computer on an airplane, when you are analyzing data in a hotel room without a connection to you network, or when you want to display a view of your data to a customer when you're in the field and you have no connection to live data via a wireless computer network.

You will learn more about Data Analyzer in Chapter 9.

Summary

From this chapter, you should understand the following:

■ Text files, spreadsheets, and file-based and server-based databases are the primary data sources that organizations analyze to make better business decisions. Although text files and spreadsheets are easy to create and share, they lack robust data storage and administrative features such as disaster recovery and concurrent data analysis task requests.

■ The quality of business decisions can be improved when an organization improves its overall data gathering and analysis strategies. Be sure to include the right people from your organization and your customers as you design these strategies.

■ To use Microsoft data analysis tools effectively, you might have to convert or import your existing data into a compatible format. To reduce data entry and analysis errors, you should fill in empty holes in your data by adding "Empty" or "N/A" where no data exists.

■ Each Microsoft data analysis software application has its strengths: Excel contains a wide array of data analysis tools; Access is designed to analyze relational data; the Office Web Components are good for analyzing data over the Web; SQL Server is designed to store very large sets of data; the SQL Server Desktop Engine brings many SQL Server features to the desktop; SQL Server 2000 Analysis Services is designed to store hierarchical data; and Data Analyzer is uniquely designed to analyze hierarchical data.

In Chapter 2, "Basic Data Analysis Techniques," you will learn

■ Fundamental data analysis features that can be used to filter, sort, format, import, export, query, chart, and pivot data.

■ Simple skills to work with data lists, multidimensional and hierarchical data, and Extensible Markup Language (XML) data.

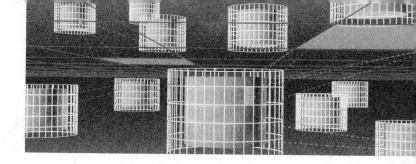

2

Basic Data Analysis Techniques

Before you begin analyzing data with applications such as Microsoft Excel, Microsoft Access, the Microsoft Office Web Components, and Microsoft Data Analyzer, you should understand basic data analysis techniques—for example, sorting, summarizing, trending, filtering, and formatting. In this chapter, I'll provide an overview of these techniques. I'll describe how to use these and more advanced data analysis techniques in specific applications in later chapters.

Objectives

By the end of this chapter, you should be able to

- Understand the basic data analysis concepts of sorting, filtering, formatting, querying, charting, and pivoting data.

- Understand the basics of importing and exporting data.

- Perform basic tasks with data lists, relational and hierarchical data, and XML data.

Sorting Data

Sorting is the easiest data analysis technique to understand because we frequently sort objects. For example, when my wife balances our checkbook every month, she uses a collection of canceled checks along with the bank statement. She usually starts reconciling the bank statement by sorting the checks by check number, from the lowest to the highest. As another example, before I read my e-mail messages, I often sort my unread messages by the date that they were received. I start by reading the message I received first and work through to the message I received most recently. There are, of course, many other examples of sorting: telephone directories that sort by personal or organizational names, grocery stores that sort products by category, hardware stores that sort bolts by size, and so on.

From a business perspective, sorting data allows you to

- Find one or more records more quickly.

- In relatively small groups of records, recognize groups of similar records.

Although sorting data can be quick and easy, by itself, sorting data does not allow you to perform data analysis tasks such as

- Provide overall record counts, overall field totals, minimum and maximum data values for specific fields, and so on. (The data analysis technique used to obtain these results is known as *summarization*.)

- Display numeric increases or decreases over time for specific fields in groups of records. (This data analysis technique is known as *trending*.)

- Display only those records that answer a specific business question. (This data analysis technique is known as *filtering*.)

- Highlight specific data values. (This data analysis technique is known as *formatting*.)

All the Microsoft data analysis software applications covered in this book allow you to sort data, in some cases with just one or two mouse clicks or keystrokes.

Your Turn

This exercise demonstrates how sorting helps you find data values more quickly.

1. Start Excel, and open the CustServ.xls file in the Chap02 folder.

2. On the worksheet named Original Data, shown in Figure 2-1, locate the smallest number in the column labeled Wait Time (column C).

3. Now click the tab for the worksheet named Sorted by Wait Time, shown in Figure 2-2, and locate the smallest number in the Wait Time column.

	A	B	C	D	E	F	G
1	**Month**	**Year**	**Wait Time**	**Cleanliness**	**Host**	**Server**	**Cashier**
2	April	1999	2.44	1.08	3.68	4.42	4.36
3	April	2000	1.84	1.32	4.15	3.16	4.75
4	April	2001	1.67	4.77	3.16	3.56	2.79
5	August	1999	1.52	4.45	3.71	4.79	2.64
6	August	2000	2.47	4.15	2.84	4.8	2.91
7	August	2001	1.11	4.82	2.41	4.51	2.02
8	December	1999	2.28	3.01	3.49	4.53	4.52
9	December	2000	1.3	4.69	3.33	4.97	3.66
10	December	2001	1.39	3.17	4.45	3.22	3.03
11	February	1999	2.66	3.07	3.24	3.54	3.27
12	February	2000	1.01	4.15	2.72	3.81	4.16
13	February	2001	1.69	1.27	4.67	3.66	3.97

Figure 2-1   The original unsorted data.

	A	B	C	D	E	F	G
1	**Month**	**Year**	**Wait Time**	**Cleanliness**	**Host**	**Server**	**Cashier**
2	February	2000	1.01	4.15	2.72	3.81	4.16
3	November	2001	1.04	1.71	4.33	4.29	4.06
4	September	2000	1.07	3.35	4.05	4.27	2.11
5	August	2001	1.11	4.82	2.41	4.51	2.02
6	December	2000	1.3	4.69	3.33	4.97	3.66
7	May	1999	1.35	1.78	4.03	3.15	4.01
8	December	2001	1.39	3.17	4.45	3.22	3.03
9	June	1999	1.46	4.64	2.32	3.91	4.74
10	November	2000	1.48	1.51	2.06	4.94	3.8
11	October	1999	1.49	2.45	3.87	4.72	4.12
12	August	1999	1.52	4.45	3.71	4.79	2.64
13	July	2001	1.53	1.91	4.78	3.83	4.51

Figure 2-2   Data sorted by the Wait Time field.

Finding data values is much faster when the values are sorted.

Summarizing Data

It seems that as often as we sort data, we summarize data. For example, my monthly mobile phone bill lists the total number of phone calls that I made and the total number of airtime minutes that I used. These data values are also sub-totaled by daytime, nighttime, and weekend airtime minutes. As another example, the daily stock report usually provides the opening, closing, highest, and lowest price of various financial markets, among other summary values.

From a business point of view, summarizing data reduces the amount of detailed data you need to review. This allows you to

- Make comparisons to other data over time more easily. For instance, if you are comparing sales profits over two years' time, reviewing a group of monthly or quarterly data values is probably easier than looking at daily or weekly data values.

- Make data trending tasks easier. Using the previous example, stating sales profits by quarter or month is less time-consuming than stating sales profits by week or day.

The data analysis tools described in this book support summarization, but this technique is not a part of all the features in the applications. For example, Access supports summarization in data forms, queries, and reports, but it does not support summarization in data tables.

Your Turn

This exercise demonstrates how you can use summarized data to make quick observations about a set of data.

1. In the CustServ.xls file (located in the Chap02 folder), examine the data on the Original Data worksheet. This data describes a restaurant's average monthly customer service ratings in several measurement areas, from 1 (poor) to 5 (excellent).

2. Now examine the summarizations on the Summarized by Year worksheet, shown in Figure 2-3.

1 2 3		A	B	C	D	E	F	G
	1	Month	Year	Wait Time	Cleanliness	Host	Server	Cashier
+	14		1999 Average	2.1016667	3.28333333	3.68	4.0683	3.7375
+	27		2000 Average	2.0466667	3.24083333	3.14	4.1975	3.69417
+	40		2001 Average	1.8266667	2.67	3.56	3.9308	3.60083
-	41		Grand Average	1.9916667	3.06472222	3.46	4.0656	3.6775

Figure 2-3 Data summarized by year.

After just a few seconds, you can make a couple of observations about the three years' worth of customer service scores:

- Wait times received the lowest scores, while servers received the highest scores.

- Hosts and cashiers received about the same scores.

Summarizations enable you to make observations about large sets of data faster.

Trending Data

A news report might start with a paragraph similar to the following: "The Small-ville County overall crime rate fell by 3% compared to last year. This continues a downward trend for the last 5 years, as the crime rate has fallen an average of 1% per year." This is a simple trend example. In analyzing business data, trending helps to

- Measure the effectiveness of decisions over time. For example, if a car rental company decides to hire more sales agents at the beginning of a year, and the time required to service customers decreases over the course of that year, the company could use the trend to state that their hiring decision may have led to tangible customer benefits. (Of course, there might be other reasons that customer wait times decreased, which would require further data analysis.)

- Alert you to potential business problems. If you notice that a particular data value is worsening over time, you would want to find out why and decide what you could do to reverse the trend. To measure your proposed solution to the problem, you could keep looking at the trend over a longer period of time.

Determining trends in data can involve recognizing simple differences or performing complex "what if" scenarios. All the data analysis software covered in this book can perform simple trending tasks, but Excel also has built-in support for the most difficult data trending scenarios.

Your Turn

This exercise demonstrates how you can quickly tell whether data facts are improving or worsening over a given time period.

1. In the CustServ.xls file (located in the Chap02 folder), examine the data on the Summarized by Year worksheet, which summarizes a restaurant's average monthly customer service ratings in several measurement areas, from 1 (poor) to 5 (excellent), over three years.

2. Next examine the summarizations on the Trended by Year worksheet, shown in Figure 2-4.

1 2 3		A	B	C	D	E	F	G
	1	Month	Year	Wait Time	Cleanliness	Host	Server	Cashier
+	41		Grand Average	1.9916667	3.06472222	3.46	4.0656	3.6775
	42		Trend (1999-2001)	-15%	-23%	-3%	-3%	-4%

Figure 2-4 Data trends for three years' worth of customer service scores.

After a quick review, you can observe a couple of trends in the three years' worth of customer service scores:

■ All measurement areas worsened over the last three years.

■ Cleanliness scores worsened the most.

■ Hosts, servers, and cashiers worsened the least, but all three measurement areas worsened at roughly the same rate.

Trends allow you to assess whether data is improving or worsening over time.

Filtering Data

Along with summarizing and trending, filtering can be an extremely effective analysis technique. For example, looking over a page or two of stock reports in the newspaper can be time-consuming, if not downright frustrating. If you own 20 or 50 stocks, for example, you can't gather results for just the stocks you own (at least without a highlighter pen or scissors!). As another example of filtering, most e-mail programs allow you to automatically delete or move unwanted e-mail messages that meet specific conditions.

The benefits of summarizing data apply to filtering data as well, but filtering differs from summarization in that filtering displays only individual records or fields that match specific conditions. A summary does not necessarily indicate how many records or fields contributed to the final summarized value.

While many filters involve only one condition, most filters applied to business data involve several fields at once. All the data analysis software applications described in this book handle a variety of data filtering tasks.

Your Turn

This exercise demonstrates how you can display data records that match specific conditions.

1. In the CustServ.xls file (located in the Chap02 folder), on the Original Data worksheet, determine how many rows contain a value less than 4 in columns C through G.

2. Next examine the Filtered By <4 Scores worksheet, shown in Figure 2-5, and compare the number of rows you came up with in the previous step.

	A	B	C	D	E	F	G
1	Month ▾	Year ▾	Wait Time ▾	Cleanliness ▾	Host ▾	Server ▾	Cashier ▾
11	February	1999	2.66	3.07	3.24	3.54	3.27
22	June	2001	2.71	3.67	3.33	3.77	3.31
25	March	2001	1.88	2.98	2.52	3.5	3.69
28	May	2001	2.23	1.23	2.1	3.96	3.43

Figure 2-5   Records with all average customer service scores less than 4.

Filtering allows you to select records that match specific conditions.

Formatting Data

If you have ever used a highlighting pen, you understand the value of formatting data. You can highlight data in a variety of ways besides adding color: underlining, bolding, strikethrough, superscripting, subscripting, outlining, capitalization, changing the font type or font size, and so on. For the purposes of analyzing business data, formatting allows you to

- Draw your eyes to significant data values. If the color red means something bad and a red data value appears somewhere in your data, you might need to make a decision based on that value.

- Perform simple data grouping or trending tasks. For instance, if you notice three data values colored green and two data values colored red—and the color green means something good—you can obviously conclude that you have one more good data value than bad.

Because all the Microsoft data analysis software described in this book is highly graphical, you can take advantage of lots of formatting options to help make sense of your data.

Your Turn

This exercise demonstrates how you can use formatting to quickly spot data values, even if the data isn't sorted, summarized, or filtered.

1. In the CustServ.xls file (located in the Chap02 folder), on the Original Data worksheet, determine how many data values are less than the number 2.

2. Next examine the Formatted By <2 Scores worksheet and compare the number of data values you came up with in the previous step. (See Figure 2-6.)

	A	B	C	D	E	F	G
1	Month	Year	Wait Time	Cleanliness	Host	Server	Cashier
2	April	1999	2.44	1.08	3.68	4.42	4.36
3	April	2000	1.84	1.32	4.15	3.16	4.75
4	April	2001	1.67	4.77	3.16	3.56	2.79
5	August	1999	1.52	4.45	3.71	4.79	2.64
6	August	2000	2.47	4.15	2.84	4.8	2.91
7	August	2001	1.11	4.82	2.41	4.51	2.02
8	December	1999	2.28	3.01	3.49	4.53	4.52
9	December	2000	1.3	4.69	3.33	4.97	3.66
10	December	2001	1.39	3.17	4.45	3.22	3.03
11	February	1999	2.66	3.07	3.24	3.54	3.27
12	February	2000	1.01	4.15	2.72	3.81	4.16
13	February	2001	1.60	1.27	4.67	3.66	3.07

Figure 2-6   Formatting highlights customer service scores less than 2.

Formatting can quickly draw your attention to specific data values.

Importing, Exporting, and Querying Data

To store or analyze electronic data, the data must be in a format that a software application recognizes. In many cases, you can import data from an external format that your application recognizes, or you can export data to a format that is compatible with a different software application, provided that your specific software application supports these features.

Importing Data

A data import task always originates from the software application that will end up storing or analyzing the data. Before you import data, you must establish a connection to the data source. After you connect to the data source and have imported the data, you can perform data analysis tasks such as formatting and querying.

> **Note**   Although most of the Microsoft data analysis software applications covered in this book support importing data, the applications cannot connect to every type of data source. You should check with a specific application's documentation to see which data sources the application supports. If a particular data source is not supported, check the documentation for the data source to see whether that application can export the data to a format that is supported.

Exporting Data

With exporting data, instead of making data available in a format your software application understands, you use the application to make data available in a format a different application can work with.

> **Note**   Although all the Microsoft data analysis software applications covered in this book support exporting data, the applications cannot export data to every type of data source.

Querying Data

Similar to filtering data, querying data allows you to select data records that match specific conditions. But querying can do much more than filtering. You can use queries to sort, group, summarize, and trend data. Provided that the information is available, you can also use queries to find out *metadata*, or the overall properties, of your group of data records. Metadata frequently includes the names of the data fields, who typed the data records, when the data records were created, and so on.

All the data analysis applications described in this book support querying data, but some of the applications, Access for example, allow for more advanced types of queries.

Charting Data

Although a list of data facts can yield interesting business conclusions, there is something about the way data is displayed in a chart that can foster faster and easier data analysis. If the old saying "a picture is worth a thousand words" is true, perhaps we can state with equal conviction that "a chart is worth a thousand data records." Stock charts, weather maps, pie charts, bell curves, and growth charts are just a few of the many examples of charts that we use in our everyday lives. You can use several types of charts in Microsoft data analysis software applications:

Column charts, *bar charts*, and *line charts* usually display one column, bar, or line per data field or category. Columns, bars, and lines can also be stacked on top of, in front of, or behind each other instead of side by side. Columns and bars are commonly represented as rectangles, but they can also be represented as cylinders, cones, or pyramids.

Pie charts, *doughnut charts*, and *area charts* usually display one slice of the pie, doughnut, or portion of the total chart area per data field or category. The pie and doughnut pieces or portions can touch each other, or the pieces or portions can be separated (a technique known as *explosion*) for visual clarity.

Scatter charts and *bubble charts* usually display groups of dots or other symbols, usually with one dot or symbol representing each data fact. Bubbles differ from dots or other symbols in that bubbles can be larger or smaller depending on the data values being measured.

Radar charts and *surface charts* can display data relative to a specific center point or axis.

Finally, *stock charts* can display multiple series of data values, such as highs, lows, opens, closes, and volume, in a single column.

Your Turn

This exercise demonstrates how charts can help make sense of large amounts of data.

1. In the CustServ.xls file (located in the Chap02 folder), on the Summarized by Year worksheet, examine the values in the Grand Average row.

2. Next examine the chart on the PivotChart Report tab. Although you can see the grand averages on both worksheets, you should be able to spot and compare the averages more quickly in the chart, shown in Figure 2-7.

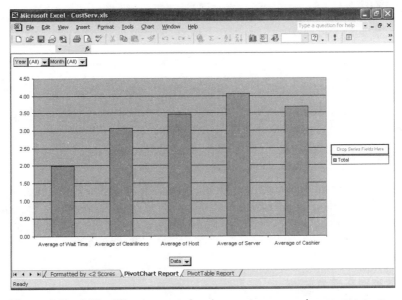

Figure 2-7   A PivotChart report showing customer service scores summarized by year.

Charts can be easier to understand than lots of text-based data values. You will learn more about charting in the next four chapters.

Pivoting Data

Pivoting data is a relatively straightforward concept to grasp, but drawing real-world analogies to the concept is somewhat difficult. When you think of the word *pivot*, you might think of a door pivoting on its hinges, using your pivot foot during a basketball game to avoid a traveling penalty, a wheel pivoting on an axle, and so on. In all of these cases, something is moving around a fixed object. In data analysis, when you pivot data, a particular data field is fixed and other data facts move around the fixed field. Although you will practice several exercises in Chapter 4 and Chapter 6 to understand pivoting data, here is an exercise to introduce you to this very powerful data analysis technique.

Your Turn

This exercise demonstrates the use of PivotTable reports.

1.   In the CustServ.xls file (located in the Chap02 folder), display the PivotTable Report worksheet. Notice that the Average Of Cashier data value for all years is 3.68.

2.   In cell B1, click the arrow, select 1999 from the list, and then click OK. The data values now reflect only the values for 1999. The Average Of Cashier data value changes to 3.74.

3.   Click cell A1, hold the mouse button down, and drag the pointer to between cells A4 and B4. When the pointer is displayed as an I-beam, as shown in Figure 2-8, release the mouse button. As Figure 2-9 illustrates, you can now see the average data values by year and by measurement category.

	A	B
1	Year	1999 ▾
2	Month	(All) ▾
3		
4	Data ▾	Total
5	Average of Wait Time	2.10
6	Average of Cleanliness	3.28
7	Average of Host	3.68
8	Average of Server	4.07
9	Average of Cashier	3.74

Figure 2-8   Dragging the Year data field to another location in the PivotTable report.

	A	B	C
1			
2	Month	(All) ▼	
3			
4	Data ▼	Year ▼	Total
5	Average of Wait Time	1999	2.10
6		2000	2.05
7		2001	1.83
8	Average of Cleanliness	1999	3.28
9		2000	3.24
10		2001	2.67
11	Average of Host	1999	3.68
12		2000	3.14
13		2001	3.56
14	Average of Server	1999	4.07
15		2000	4.20
16		2001	3.93
17	Average of Cashier	1999	3.74
18		2000	3.69
19		2001	3.60
20	Total Average of Wait Time		1.99
21	Total Average of Cleanliness		3.06
22	Total Average of Host		3.46
23	Total Average of Server		4.07
24	Total Average of Cashier		3.68

Figure 2-9   The results of dragging the Year data field to another location in the PivotTable report.

You can summarize and filter data values by using PivotTable reports.

Working with Data Lists

It is important to understand what data lists are and how you should create them. All too often, the structure and field names used in a data list are not given much thought. Not until hundreds or thousands of data records are created do problems arise. These problems might cause the data to become invalid, force the lists to be restructured, and require that someone enter the data records again from the beginning.

Although lists come in all shapes and sizes, data lists are unique because they are highly structured, sharing common field names and data values. For instance, a simple grocery list contains a number of items, but these items amount to little more than notes about product names and quantities. For some items, you might write down a product category rather than a specific product name—you know in your mind what you want to buy—but of course you don't use the grocery list for hard-core data analysis.

When you create data lists, be sure of the following:

- All the records in the data list share the same field names. For instance, in one record, if you have the fields First Name, Middle Name, and Last Name, don't use one Complete Name field for the next record to store the same type of data.

- All the data values for each field are consistent. For example, if the Total Sales field for one record has two decimal places, another record should not have four decimal places for the data in this field.

- All the data values have some type of data in each field, even if the real data value is unknown. For instance, if the data value for a particular field in a record is zero, use the number 0 in the field. If the data value is unknown, use the word *Unknown* for that data value. If a data value is left blank, it can sometimes be difficult to determine whether the value is zero or the data value was forgotten somehow.

- Only one list should appear on each worksheet. Techniques such as sorting, grouping, and filtering work best when they are restricted to single lists on single worksheets.

- Field names are descriptive but not verbose. For example, a field named First Name is more descriptive than a field named Field A. Likewise, a field named Sales Total might be just as easy to understand as a field named Sales Total That Appears At The Bottom Of The Sales Receipt.

- Fields are separated into their most basic parts. For instance, instead of a Complete Address field, create separate fields that are named Street Address, City, State (or Province or Region), and Zip (or Postal) Code. This makes data analysis tasks such as sorting and filtering much easier.

Working with Relational and Multidimensional Data

Data appears not only in data lists, but also in tables, groups of records separated by characters (such as a comma), and so on. When a group of data records (for example a single data list, a data table, or a file of character-separated data values) exists on its own without relying on another group of data records, the data is said to be *nonrelational*. When a group of records relies on other groups of records for complete, detailed business facts, the data is known as *relational*. Relationships are usually defined on a one-record-to-one-record basis or on a one-record-to-many-records basis. (These relationships are also known as *one-to-one relationships* and *one-to-many relationships*.)

In the terms of data analysis, *multidimensional* data is different from relational data. The concepts used in working with relational data are vastly different from those used to work with multidimensional data. While relational data is usually stored in a file-based or server-based database management system, multidimensional data usually resides in an online storage location such as a *data warehouse*, a central repository for capturing large amounts of data records.

Working with Relational Data

You work with relational data when you bring together business facts that are spread out over multiple, related data tables in order to analyze sets of values, fields, or records. Relational data lends itself well to data analysis techniques such as sorting, filtering, and querying. You can also summarize relational data, but because of the time it takes to create summarizations, if you are working with thousands or millions of data records, you should consider moving the data to a multidimensional format, which I'll discuss in more detail in the next section.

Your Turn

In this exercise, you will explore the difference between relational and nonrelational data.

1.   Start Microsoft Access.

2.   Open the Relation.mdb file in the Chap02 folder.

3.   On the View menu, point to Database Objects and then click Tables.

4.   In the Database window, double-click the Nonrelational Data icon. Notice in Figure 2-10, which shows the Nonrelational Data table, that many addresses are repeated.

Receipt Num	Customer Numb	Address	Phone	City	State	Zip Code	Total Purchased	Date Purchased
1	100	123 Main St.	(425) 555-1212	Anytown	WA	91885	$25.50	8/1/2002
2	101	456 - 3rd St.	(206) 555-1212	Smallville	CA	30999	$13.95	8/1/2002
3	100	123 Main St.	(425) 555-1212	Anytown	WA	91885	$17.04	8/2/2002
4	101	456 - 3rd St.	(206) 555-1212	Smallville	CA	30999	$29.71	8/2/2002
5	102	567 Butterfly Ct	(312) 555-1212	Anywhere	OR	55111	$19.90	8/3/2002
6	102	567 Butterfly Ct	(312) 555-1212	Anywhere	OR	55111	$18.42	8/4/2002
7	101	123 Main St.	(425) 555-1212	Smallville	CA	30999	$16.67	8/5/2002
8	100	123 Main St.	(425) 555-1212	Anytown	WA	91885	$20.01	8/6/2002
9	100	123 Main St.	(425) 555-1212	Anytown	WA	91885	$29.98	8/7/2002

Figure 2-10   The Nonrelational Data table.

5. Close the Nonrelational Data table.

6. In the Database window, double-click the Relational Data–Customer Info icon. Notice in Figure 2-11 that in this table each address appears only once. This illustrates good relational database design: if you need to change a particular customer's information, you need to change it in only one place and for only one record in the Relational Data–Customer Info table.

Customer Number	Address	Phone	City	State	Zip Code
100	123 Main St.	(425) 555-1212	Anytown	WA	91885
101	456 - 3rd St.	(206) 555-1212	Smallville	CA	30999
102	567 Butterfly Ct.	(312) 555-1212	Anywhere	OR	55111

Figure 2-11   The Relational Data–Customer Info table.

7. Close the Relational Data–Customer Info table.

8. In the Database window, double-click the Relational Data–Receipts icon. Notice here that the addresses are not displayed; you see only the receipt information, shown in Figure 2-12. Customer information is related to receipts by customer number.

Receipt Number	Customer Number	Amount Purchased	Date Purchased
1	100	$25.50	8/1/2002
3	100	$17.04	8/2/2002
8	100	$20.01	8/6/2002
9	100	$29.98	8/7/2002
2	101	$13.95	8/1/2002
4	101	$29.71	8/2/2002
7	101	$16.67	8/5/2002
5	102	$19.90	8/3/2002
6	102	$18.42	8/4/2002

Figure 2-12   The Relational Data–Receipts table.

9. Close the Relational Data–Receipts table.

10. On the Tools menu, click Relationships. In the Relationships window, notice that the Relational Data–Customer Info table is related to the Relational Data–Receipts table by customer number. (See Figure 2-13.) What this means is that for each receipt in the Relational Data—Receipts table, there must be a customer number in the Relational Data–Customer Info table. This also means that if you remove a customer's information from the Relational Data–Customer Info table, Access might prevent you from doing so if removing the information would result in *orphaned* records (records with no matching records in another table) in the Relational Data–Receipts table.

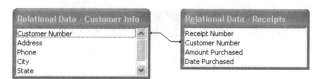

Figure 2-13   Two tables related by Customer Number.

Relational data reduces duplicate data values. You will learn more about relational data in Chapter 5.

Working with Multidimensional Data

In contrast to relational data, you should use a multidimensional data format when you want to look at overall data summarizations or trends, especially when you need to analyze thousands or even millions of data records. The more time an organization invests in planning its specific multidimensional data formats, the more data summarizations the organization should be able to produce.

Your Turn

In this exercise, you will explore data in a multidimensional format.

> **Note**   These steps do not work in Excel 2000.

1. Start Excel.

2. On the File menu, click Open.

3. In the Files Of Type list, select All Files.

4. Locate and open the Sales.cub file in the Chap02 folder. A PivotTable report appears.

5. From the PivotTable Field List window, drag the Product icon to the Drop Page Fields Here area of the PivotTable report.

6. From the PivotTable field list, drag the Customers icon to the Drop Row Fields Here area of the PivotTable report.

7. Drag the Profit icon to the Drop Data Items Here area of the PivotTable report. Your report layout should look similar to the report layout shown in Figure 2-14.

	A	B
1	Product	All Products ▼
2		
3	Profit	
4	Country ▼	Total
5	USA	339610.8964
6	Grand Total	339610.8964

Figure 2-14   PivotTable report layout.

8. In cell A4, click the arrow, click the plus symbol (+) next to the USA check box, select the check boxes for CA, OR, and WA, and then click OK. Profits are displayed for all three states. Check your progress against Figure 2-15.

	A	B	C
1	Product	All Products ▼	
2			
3	Profit		
4	Country ▼	State Province	Total
5	USA	CA	95637.4149
6		OR	85504.5694
7		WA	158468.9121
8	USA Total		339610.8964
9	Grand Total		339610.8964

Figure 2-15   PivotTable report showing profits for all three states.

9. In cell B1, click the arrow, click the plus symbol next to All Products, click Drink, and then click OK. Profits are displayed for just drink products, as you can see in Figure 2-16.

	A	B	C
1	Product	Drink ▼	
2			
3	Profit		
4	Country ▼	State Province	Total
5	USA	CA	8540.9664
6		OR	7300.9358
7		WA	13517.0732
8	USA Total		29358.9754
9	Grand Total		29358.9754

Figure 2-16   PivotTable report showing profits for drink products.

Multidimensional data allows you to perform faster data summarizations. You will learn more about multidimensional data in Chapters 7 through 9.

Working with XML Data

Most data analysis software applications are designed to work best with a specific data format. As data proliferates inside organizations, and organizations that use different software applications need to share data with each other, the need to present and share data without regard to proprietary data formats has become more urgent.

Extensible Markup Language (XML) is a data format that's independent of any particular software application or software manufacturer. Because no single company owns the XML data format, and because the XML data format is so flexible, more software manufacturers are supporting XML in their applications and extending existing application features to work with XML data.

The growing support for XML and its flexibility does not necessarily mean that you should switch all your business data to the XML format. Before you make the move to XML, you should consider whether the data you have already needs to be restructured. You should also determine whether your data analysis software applications can handle data in XML format. The applications covered in this book can handle XML formatted data in some way.

A full treatment of XML is beyond the scope of this book. However, you need to know a few simple XML concepts before you can analyze XML data:

Elements and Attributes

Elements are the building blocks of XML data. Elements have names, may contain data values, and may be related to other elements. Elements can also carry descriptive information called *attributes*. Elements and attributes are described by using a special series of symbols. These symbols specify where the information within an element or attribute starts and ends. For example, the *firstname* element in the example below has a data value of *Paul*. The *address* element contains no data value, but it does have an attribute, *city*.

```
<firstname>Paul</firstname>
<address city="Redmond"/>
```

Attributes are the properties of an element. Just as the properties of an automobile include the type of transmission (automatic or manual), its body paint (red, for example), and the number of wheels (4), an element can have attributes such as a unique identifier. For instance, the following *receipt* element has an attribute named *id*, and the *id* attribute's value is F0123:

```
<receipt id="F0123"/>
```

Namespaces

Namespaces in XML differentiate elements with the same names. For example, the following two elements are different (even though each is named *month*) because they are prefaced with a different namespace. The first element is *my:month*, and the second element is *your:month*.

```
<my:month xmlns:my="http://www.microsoft.com/myNamespace/">January</month>
<your:month xmlns:your="http://www.microsoft.com/yourNamespace/">January
</month>
```

> **Note**   Although these attribute values look like Internet addresses, these addresses do not refer to actual Web sites. Although namespaces can be just about any series of characters, as a rule of thumb an organization should use their main Web site address followed by some unique series of characters that the organization decides on or assigns among its members.

Your Turn

In this exercise, you will practice interpreting XML data in a file.

1. Start Microsoft Internet Explorer.

2. On the File menu, click Open.

3. In the Open dialog box, click the Browse button.

4. In the Files Of Type list, select All Files.

5. Locate and click the Sale2001.xml file in the Chap02 folder, and then click Open. When the Open dialog box reappears, click Open.

6. Locate the month with the highest sales total. The correct answer is November, as you can see in Figure 2-17.

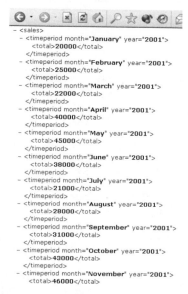

Figure 2-17   An XML data file.

Although data in XML files can look more dense than data in electronic spreadsheets, once you know how to interpret XML files, they are not too difficult to use. You will learn more about how to work with XML data in Chapter 10.

Summary

In this chapter, you learned

- Sorting helps you find the highest or lowest values in a list of data records.

- Summarizations help you find sums and averages of a list of data values.

- Trending helps you understand how data changes, typically over time.

- Filtering helps you find one or more data values or data records that match specified criteria.

- Formatting data can help draw your eye to potential business anomalies.

- Charting data provides a visual alternative to long lists of data values, as well as a way to graphically represent summarizations and trends.

- Pivoting data provides a means to conveniently look at data summarizations from different perspectives without changing the underlying data values.

- XML data is a set of technologies with which to create, store, and share data regardless of the types of software applications you use. Microsoft is providing more and more XML data support in its software applications and data analysis tools.

In the next chapter, "Analyzing Data with Microsoft Excel," you will learn how to

- Use basic Excel features for sorting, filtering, formatting, and importing data.

- Work with spreadsheet functions.

- Work with charts.

- Work with Web-based data.

- Use the features of the Analysis ToolPak and the Solver Add-In.

3

Analyzing Data with Microsoft Excel

Microsoft Excel provides several features and tools that you can use to analyze data in various formats. Understanding how these features work can significantly expand the types of data analysis tasks that you can complete.

Many data analysis tasks in Excel consist of sorting, filtering, formatting, and summarizing data. More sophisticated data analysis tasks can be performed with the built-in and add-in functions that Excel supplies. In this chapter, you'll learn basic sorting, filtering, and querying skills as well as learn about the tools you use for more sophisticated statistical analysis and "what-if" scenarios. You will not only learn how to work with data stored in Excel worksheets, but also how to bring external data into Excel—data from a server-based database or data from the Web, for example—and use Excel's data analysis features and tools on the imported data.

As the basis for the examples in this chapter, you'll analyze data in a spreadsheet that records occupancy rates and purchasing habits for a fictional hotel chain's preferred guests. You should imagine yourself to be the hotel's marketing specialist, trying to figure out how to increase business from these preferred guests by using the data analysis features of Excel. The spreadsheet you'll use, named Hotel.xls, is included in the Chap03 folder at the location where you copied the sample files for this book.

Objectives

In this chapter, you will learn how to analyze data in Excel by

- Using basic features for sorting, filtering, formatting, and importing data.

- Using worksheet functions.

- Creating and interpreting charts.

- Importing and analyzing data from external data sources and the Web.

- Using the basic features of the Analysis ToolPak and the Solver Add-In.

Sorting and Filtering Data

Sorting and filtering data are among the most basic data analysis tasks that you can perform. But even though these tasks are usually quick and simple, they can still yield meaningful business facts. The following sections show you how to sort and filter data records.

Sorting Data

Sorting data is a great technique when you need to

- Find the absolute highest or lowest data value in a list of data records.

- Find a group of values that are the top or bottom values in a list of data records.

- Rank data values in highest-to-lowest or lowest-to-highest order.

- Group repeating data values together.

For instance, you might want to quickly know the absolute highest sale order amount or the top three months of sales figures. You might need to figure out how a particular customer purchased items as compared to similar customers or how many times a particular product was ordered. Sorting can help you answer these types of questions. Sorting data is easy; select the cells you want to sort, click Sort on the Data menu, and then complete the information in the Sort dialog box.

> **Tip**   To select all the data in the active worksheet, press CTRL+A.

Your Turn

In this exercise, you want to discover who is the preferred customer with the highest total room service charges in any single month so that you can reward the customer with a $100.00 gift certificate. This type of data analysis task is best suited for a simple sort.

1.   Start Excel, and open the Hotel.xls file in the Chap03 folder.
2.   Press CTRL+A to select all the records.
3.   On the Data menu, click Sort.
4.   In the My List Has area, click Header Row.
5.   In the Sort By list, select Total Room Service.
6.   Select the Descending sort order option.
7.   Compare your results to Figure 3-1, and then click OK.

Figure 3-1   The Sort dialog box.

(continued)

8. Compare your results to Figure 3-2. Edgar has the highest total room service charges, $1,835.40 in August.

	A	B	C	D
1	**Gold Customer Name**	**Month**	**Nights Booked**	**Total Room Service**
2	Edgar	August	20	$1,835.40
3	Ventura	March	19	$1,794.55
4	Xavier	January	20	$1,758.40
5	Xavier	August	18	$1,680.48
6	Finch	January	20	$1,620.00
7	Davis	February	19	$1,590.49
8	Cornell	September	17	$1,574.37
9	Oaktree	April	18	$1,567.44
10	Jensen	June	19	$1,516.20
11	Zimmerman	January	19	$1,504.23
12	Garfield	June	19	$1,482.19
13	Johstad	May	19	$1,479.15

Figure 3-2 Customers sorted by highest room service charges in descending order.

Note Although you can sort cells by selecting the cells you want to sort and clicking the Sort Ascending button or Sort Descending button on the Standard toolbar, you might not get the sorting results that you expect.

Filtering Data

Filtering data is an ideal data analysis technique when you want to display a group of records that match specific conditions and hide records that don't match. (Data is not deleted from hidden rows.) For instance, you may want to find out how many customers purchased a particular product or service or how many products or services came from a particular supplier.

Filtering data is similar to sorting, but filtering displays only the data that matches the filter conditions. You should use filtering when you want to focus your attention on specific records that match your filter conditions.

Filter conditions (also known as *filter criteria*) can be simple (values in your worksheet) or advanced (criteria that you enter separate from the data values in your worksheet). To filter records in the active worksheet by using simple filter criteria, click any cell in the list of records. Then, on the Data menu, point to Filter, click AutoFilter, and select one of the choices in the AutoFilter lists. The arrow in a cell turns blue to confirm that data is being filtered by criteria selected in that column. You can apply another filter to the data that remains if you want to select even more specific records. If none of the list's choices meet your needs, you can select Custom from the AutoFilter list to display the Custom AutoFilter dialog box, in which you can specify your own filter criteria. You can use the *?* and *** characters to represent single and multiple "wildcard" characters, respectively, in custom filter criteria expressions. You can also click the And or Or options to specify whether matching records must meet two criteria or either of the custom filter criteria you enter.

Your Turn

In this exercise, you want to find records for all of the room service charges in August for your preferred customers. Because this group of records is related by containing an identical data value in a specific field, this task is a good candidate for a filtering operation.

1.   Open Hotel.xls. If the file is open already, close it without saving the file and open it again.

2.   On the Data menu, point to Filter and then click AutoFilter.

3.   In cell B1, the Month column, click the arrow and then click August. Only the records for August are displayed. Your results should look similar to Figure 3-3.

	A	B	C	D
1	Gold Customer Name	Month	Nights Booked	Total Room Service
2	Abercrombie	August	17	$1,185.58
5	Bell	August	7	$517.72
30	Cornell	August	3	$197.88
41	Davis	August	9	$758.43
59	Edgar	August	20	$1,835.40
61	Finch	August	10	$828.50
66	Garfield	August	12	$496.08
93	Harrison	August	14	$55.02
99	Ichabod	August	12	$4.80
115	Jensen	August	7	$627.13
116	Kelly	August	2	$149.56
129	Lombard	August	9	$795.33
149	Montgomery	August	2	$96.46
163	Nelson	August	11	$343.42
206	Oaktree	August	2	$10.48
214	Phillips	August	2	$109.78
216	Queensland	August	12	$130.44
217	Roberts	August	1	$70.77
222	Simpson	August	8	$165.68
227	Trevor	August	13	$161.07
234	Underhill	August	18	$407.34
240	Ventura	August	6	$158.16
257	Williams	August	18	$599.04
269	Xavier	August	18	$1,680.48
302	Young	August	12	$1,015.80
305	Zimmerman	August	7	$453.53

Figure 3-3   The August data records.

Note   The row numbers in your spreadsheet might not match the row numbers in Figure 3-3. The data should be the same, however.

Tip   To remove filters from the active worksheet, on the Data menu, point to Filter and then click Show All. To remove all filters from the active worksheet and remove the arrows next to each of the row's cells, point to Filter on the Data menu and then click AutoFilter.

As you experiment with filtering, you might discover some cases in which you aren't able to use either the AutoFilter list or the Custom AutoFilter dialog box to set up the exact combination of filter criteria that you need. In these cases, you should specify advanced filter criteria. To filter a list of records by using advanced filter criteria, you first need to insert at least three blank rows above the list to which you want to apply the filter.

Tip   A list to which you apply advanced filter criteria must contain a header row. Also, leave at least one blank row between the group of cells making up the advanced filter criteria and the header row of the list to which you want to apply the filter. Otherwise, Excel might not be able to determine where your filter criteria ends and the list of records begins.

After you have inserted the blank rows, in separate cells in the first blank row, type the name of each column by which you want to filter. Then, in the second and subsequent rows, type the advanced filter criteria. Click any cell in the list to which you want to apply the filter criteria, point to Filter on the Data menu, and then click Advanced Filter. Finally, provide the filter criteria in the Advanced Filter dialog box and click OK to apply the filter.

Your Turn

In this exercise, you want to move some of your Gold customers to Platinum status by finding out which customers booked more than 15 nights and spent more than $1,500.00 on room service in any single month during the first quarter of the year. Because these filter criteria involve ranges of potential data values, this is a typical task for an advanced filter.

1. Open the Hotel.xls file. If the file is open already, close it (do not save the file) and then open the file again.

2. Insert five blank rows above the data list. To do so, select cells A1 through A5 and then click Rows on the Insert menu.

3. Type the information shown in Figure 3-4 into cells A1 through C4.

	A	B	C
1	Month	Nights Booked	Total Room Service
2	January	>15	>1500
3	February	>15	>1500
4	March	>15	>1500

Figure 3-4   Advanced filter criteria.

4. Click cell A6, and then, on the Data menu, point to Filter and click Advanced Filter.

5. In the List Range box, leave the default value of $A$6:$D$318.

6. Click in the Criteria Range box, and then select cells A1 through C4, inclusive. Compare your results to Figure 3-5.

Figure 3-5   The Advanced Filter dialog box.

(continued)

7.   Click OK. The customers that booked more than 15 nights and spent more than $1,500.00 in any single month during the first quarter of the year include Davis, Finch, Ventura, Xavier, and Zimmerman, as shown in Figure 3-6.

	A	B	C	D
1	**Month**	**Nights Booked**	**Total Room Service**	
2	January	>15	>1500	
3	February	>15	>1500	
4	March	>15	>1500	
5				
6	**Gold Customer Name**	**Month**	**Nights Booked**	**Total Room Service**
44	Davis	February	19	$1,590.49
67	Finch	January	20	$1,620.00
261	Ventura	March	19	$1,794.55
283	Xavier	January	20	$1,758.40
307	Zimmerman	January	19	$1,504.23

Figure 3-6   Results of running the advanced filter.

Here are additional advanced filters that you can try:

- Customers that booked less than 5 nights or more than 15 nights in any given month. (See Figure 3-7.)

	A
1	**Nights Booked**
2	<5
3	>15

Figure 3-7   Advanced criteria for customers that booked less than 5 or more than 15 nights in any given month.

- Customers that booked less than 5 nights or more than 15 nights and spent less than $100.00 or more than $1,500.00 on room service in any given month. (See Figure 3-8.)

	A	B
1	**Nights Booked**	**Total Room Service**
2	<5	<100
3	>15	>1500

Figure 3-8   Advanced criteria for customers that booked less than 5 or more than 15 nights and spent less than $100.00 or more than $1,500.00 on room service in any given month.

Putting It Together

You can use a combination of filtering and sorting to quickly reduce the amount of visual clutter while at the same time organizing the data you want to analyze. In the last three exercises, you practiced sorting and filtering data as separate data analysis tasks. In this exercise, you'll combine sorting and filtering to find out which customer had the highest total room service charge in February. You want to display only the February room service totals and rank the totals in descending order.

1. Open the Hotel.xls file. If the file is open already, close it (do not save the file) and open the file again.

2. On the Data menu, point to Filter and then click AutoFilter.

3. Click the arrow in cell B1, the Month column, and then click February.

4. Select all of the records by pressing CTRL+A.

5. On the Data menu, click Sort.

6. Click the Header Row option.

7. In the Sort By list, select Total Room Service and then click OK.

   Customer Davis had the highest February total room service charge ($1,590.49).

Using Worksheet Functions

Worksheet functions are built-in Excel formulas that perform calculations. An example of a simple function is the *SUM* formula which, as you might know, adds together the values in two or more cells. The result of the function =*SUM(3, 2)* is, of course, 5. In this case, the numbers 3 and 2 are called the function's *arguments*, and the number 5 is called the function's *result*. In technical terms, a function *returns* a result. The result a formula returns is displayed in the cell that contains the formula.

Very few meaningful data analysis tasks can be accomplished without calculations. Understanding how spreadsheet functions work is important; functions not only yield important business facts, but they also allow you to increase the range of data analysis tasks that you can perform. For example, by using spreadsheet functions you can

- Display the average insurance claim amount for a given year.

- Return the highest or lowest sales order without needing to also sort data values.

- Display values such as In Stock, Out of Stock, Back Ordered, or Must Reorder to highlight specific product stock levels.

Here's a list of some popular business data analysis functions, the results they return, and a description of how you will likely use them in your daily data analysis tasks.

Function	Result
AND	Returns TRUE if all the arguments are true or FALSE if one or more of the arguments is false. This function is helpful for evaluating whether several data values, when taken as a group, meet specific business criteria. For instance, *=AND(2+2=4, 1+3=3)* returns FALSE.
AVERAGE	Returns the average (or mean) value of the arguments. For example, *=AVERAGE(3, 2, 5, 7)* returns 4.25.
CEILING	Returns a number rounded up to the nearest multiple that you specify. For instance, *=CEILING(15.25, 0.50)* returns 15.5, while *=CEILING(15.25, 1)* returns 16. This function, along with the *FLOOR* function described later, are ideal for rounding to specific financial increments, like eighths or quarters of points or dollars.
COUNT	From a group of cells, returns the number of cells that contain numbers. This function is helpful for ignoring cells that contain text values such as N/A or None. Contrast this function to the *ISBLANK* function described later.
COUNTIF	From a group of cells, returns the number of cells that match specific conditions. This function is helpful when you need a quick sum of matching data records but you don't want to apply a filter, which could hide some of the data records.
FLOOR	In contrast to the *CEILING* function described earlier, returns a number rounded down to the nearest multiple that you specify. For instance, *=FLOOR(15.25, 0.50)* and *=FLOOR(15.25, 1)* both return 15.

Function	Result
FREQUENCY	Returns a vertical list of numbers, grouped into "bins" or "buckets," that describes how often specific data values occur within a given list. This function is useful for grouping data values without sorting the original list of data records, which could disrupt the original list's sort order.
IF	Based on a condition that you specify, returns one value if the condition is TRUE or returns another value if the condition is FALSE. This function is ideal for displaying word pair results such as In Stock/Out Of Stock, Yes/No, and so on. For example, *=IF(1+1=3, "Correct", "Incorrect")* returns Incorrect.
INT	Strips off the fractional part of a number. For instance, *=INT(123.456)* returns 123. This function is helpful in financial analyses where you want to remove portions of dollars from the result without rounding.
ISBLANK	Returns TRUE if the cell referred to is blank. This function is helpful for accounting for data-entry errors in which specific cells don't contain data.
LARGE	Based on the values in a group of data values, returns the *n*th largest value using the position you specify. For example, *=LARGE({2100, 3300, 1000, 5000, 4575}, 3)* returns 3300, the third largest value in the group of numbers.
MAX	Returns the largest number in a group of data values, regardless of the number's position. For instance, *=MAX(5, 4, 3, 2, 1)* returns 5.
MEDIAN	Returns the middle value in a group of data values. For example, *=MEDIAN(99, 42, 50, 1, 3)* returns 42. Note that the median is not the same as the mean (or average).
MIN	The opposite of the *MAX* function; returns the smallest number in a group of data values, regardless of the number's position. For instance, *=MIN (5, 4, 3, 2, 1)* returns 1.
MODE	Returns the most frequently occurring number in a group of data values. For example, *=MODE(5, 4, 3, 3, 2)* returns 3. This function is helpful when you want to determine information such as the most frequently ordered product ID or product number.
OR	Similar to the *AND* worksheet function, returns TRUE if one or more of the arguments are true, or FALSE if all of the arguments are false. For instance, *=OR(2+2=4, 1+3=3)* returns TRUE.
PERCENTILE	Based on the percentile that you specify, returns the percentile value of a group of data values. For example, *=PERCENTILE({1, 2, 3, 4, 5}, 0.9)* returns 4.6. This function is helpful in determining which data values are above a certain cutoff point, such as a sales quota.

(continued)

Function	Result
PERCENTRANK	Similar to the *PERCENTILE* function; returns where a specific data value ranks percentage-wise in a group of data values. For example, =*PERCENTRANK({1, 2, 3, 4, 5}, 4)* returns 0.75, or 75%. This function is very helpful for ranking data values next to each other for comparisons.
ROUND	Rounds a data value to a specified number of digits. For instance, =*ROUND(15.755, 1)* returns 15.8. This function is helpful for rounding when you don't want to drop fractional portions of numbers but you want some degree of accuracy.
SMALL	The opposite of the *LARGE* function; based on the values in a group of data values, returns the *n*th smallest number using the position you specify. For example, =*SMALL({3300,1000,2100,5000,4575}, 2)* returns 2100, the second smallest number in the group.
SUMIF	Similar to the *SUM* function, but adds only values that match specific conditions. This function is helpful, for instance, if you need to sum data values for multiple sales promotion figures occurring in the same list.

Tip   Although the examples in the preceding table used actual data values, you can substitute cell addresses, and Excel will substitute the value of the cell when the function performs the calculation. For example, if you have the value 2 in cell A1 and the value 3 in cell A2, =SUM(A1, A2) would return 5.

Tip   For a group of cells that touch each other, you can specify the first cell's address in the group, followed by a colon (:), followed by the last cell's address in the group. For instance, A1:B3 refers to the group of cells A1, A2, A3, B1, B2, and B3.

Inserting a function into a worksheet cell is simple. First click the spreadsheet cell in which you want the function's result to appear. Then, on the Insert menu, click Function. Select the function name and click OK. Fill in any empty boxes with data values, cell addresses, or other arguments, and then click OK to insert the function. Press Enter to run the function.

Functions are organized by category. If you know the function's category, you can select the category in the Insert Function dialog box and then select the function's name. (Excel 2000 presents only a list of function categories and function names. It doesn't give you the ability to search for functions.) If you know the name of the function, you can type it in the Insert Function dialog box's Search For A Function box, click Go, and then select the function's name in the Select A Function list.

Tip   You can also display the Insert Function dialog box by clicking the Insert Function button next to the Formula Bar. If the Formula Bar is not visible, on the View menu, click Formula Bar to display it.

Your Turn

In this exercise, you will run various functions on several groups of cells to yield additional facts about your preferred customers. You can use the information to see whether you notice any trends or anomalies in your data.

1. Open Hotel.xls. If the file is already open, close it (do not save it) and open the file again.

2. In cell F2, type *=SUM(D2:D313)* and then press Enter. This returns the total amount of room service charges for the year ($147,683.80).

3. In cell F3, type *=MAX(D2:D313)* and then press Enter. This returns the highest monthly room service charge ($1,835.40).

4. In cell F4, type *=MIN(D2:D313)* and then press Enter. This returns the lowest monthly room service charge ($0.00).

5. In cell F5, type *=AVERAGE(D2:D313)* and then press Enter. This returns the average monthly room service charge ($473.35).

(continued)

6. In cell F6, type =*LARGE(D2:D313, 2)* and then press Enter. This returns the second highest monthly room service charge ($1,794.55).

7. In cell F7, type =*MEDIAN(D2:D313)* and then press Enter. This returns the monthly room service charge midpoint ($384.10).

8. Add descriptions for each of these results in column E. For example, in cell E2 type *Sum of All Room Service Charges*. Compare your results to Figure 3-9.

E	F
Sum of All Room Service Charges	$147,683.80
Maximum Room Service Charge	$1,835.40
Minimum Room Service Charge	$0.00
Average Room Service Charge	$473.35
Second Largest Room Service Charge	$1,794.55
Room Service Charge Midpoint	$384.10

Figure 3-9 Summary of room service charges.

What anomalies or trends do you notice based on this exercise? For example:

■ Some preferred customers had no room service charges in some months.

■ The average monthly room service charge was about 23 percent higher than midpoint.

What would you do, if anything, as the hotel chain's marketing specialist, to influence these findings in the future? To answer this question, of course, you would need to know in a more in-depth manner than this sample scenario how the hotel deals with aspects of room service and how it treats its customers.

Applying Conditional Formatting

Formatting involves changing the size, font, color, bolding, underlining, and other characteristics of text. Conditional formatting involves changing text properties if specific conditions are met.

To understand conditional formatting, imagine an electronic digital kitchen timer. When the time reaches zero, usually an audible beep sounds, a bell rings, the number flashes, or something similar occurs. You can apply this same kind of behavior to the formats of one or more worksheet cells. If a cell value were less than the number 100, for instance, you could display the value in red. Similarly, if a cell value were greater than 1000, you could change the cell's background color to green.

Applying conditional formatting is most helpful when you want to scan a list of values and note anomalies such as numbers that are above or below certain thresholds that can be harmful to your business. For example, if an insurance policy holder makes a claim for more than $5,000.00, you might want to display the claim amount in red.

In Excel, you can easily change the following cell properties:

- The font type
- Whether the font is bold, italic, or both
- The font's size
- Whether the font has a single or double underline
- Whether the font has strikethrough, superscripted, or subscripted formatting
- The font color
- To which edges of a border special line thickness will be applied
- The border thickness
- The border color
- The cell's background shading color
- The cell's background pattern type, such as dashes, dots, or lines

To apply conditional formatting to one or more worksheet cells, select the cells to which you want to apply the formatting. Then, on the Format menu, click Conditional Formatting. Provide the conditional formatting properties in the Condition 1 area. If you want to add more cell formatting options, click the Add button and provide the conditional formatting properties in the Condition 2 area. (You can create up to three conditional formats per cell.) Finally, click the OK button to apply the conditional formatting.

Your Turn

In this exercise, you will color red all the cells in the Nights Booked column whose value is 5 or less, apply yellow to a cell if its value is 6 to 14, and apply green if the value is 15 or more.

(continued)

1. Open Hotel.xls. If the file is already open, close it (do not save it) and open it again.

2. Select cells C2 through C313 in column C, the Nights Booked column.

3. On the Format menu, click Conditional Formatting.

4. In the Condition 1 area's Between list, select Less Than Or Equal To.

5. In the box to the right, type 5.

6. Click Format, and then click the Patterns tab.

7. Click a red-colored box, and then click OK.

8. Click Add.

9. In the boxes next to the Condition 2 area's Between list, type 6 in the first box and 14 in the second box.

10. Click Format, click a yellow-colored box on the Patterns tab, and then click OK.

11. Click Add. In the Condition 3 area's Between list, select Greater Than Or Equal To, and then type 15 in the box to the right. Click Format, and then click a green-colored box on the Patterns tab.

12. Click OK, and compare your results to Figure 3-10.

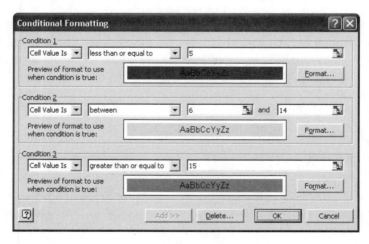

Figure 3-10   The Conditional Formatting dialog box set up to highlight values in the number of nights booked.

13. Click OK, and compare your results to Figure 3-11.

	A	B	C	D
1	**Gold Customer Name**	**Month**	**Nights Booked**	**Total Room Service**
2	Abercrombie	January	14	$1,357.72
3	Abercrombie	February	1	$66.31
4	Abercrombie	March	3	$248.70
5	Abercrombie	April	9	$426.15
6	Abercrombie	May	5	$293.85
7	Abercrombie	June	1	$33.16
8	Abercrombie	July	8	$722.40
9	Abercrombie	August	17	$1,185.58
10	Abercrombie	September	19	$1,423.48
11	Abercrombie	October	13	$297.44
12	Abercrombie	November	18	$1,110.96
13	Abercrombie	December	19	$396.53

Figure 3-11   Nights booked with conditional formatting.

Conditional formatting can really help you spot individual data values more quickly.

Working with Charts

Charts are a great way to organize, simplify, categorize, and present data. Most of us can comprehend facts better if they are presented visually or in a graphical way. You might scratch your head when you try to analyze a worksheet full of numbers, but looking at a well-designed chart makes you say "A-ha" because the data is logically grouped or summarized. Although you might have worked with charts of all types, it's helpful to understand the terminology that Excel uses to identify the items that a chart comprises. Figure 3-12 shows a sample Excel chart. An explanation of the different parts of the chart follows.

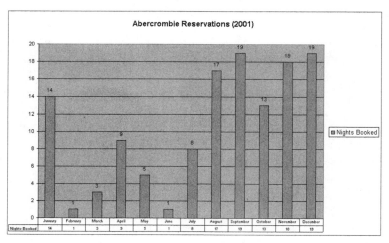

Figure 3-12   The Abercrombie Reservations (2001) chart.

■ The *chart title* is Abercrombie Reservations (2001).

■ The *category axis* contains the months January through December. A chart can have multiple category axes.

■ The *value axis* contains the numbers 0 through 20. Having multiple value axes in a chart is also possible.

■ The *gridlines* are the lines touching the numbers 0, 2, 4, and so on, extending across the chart. These are also known as *major gridlines* because they touch values on the axis. A chart can also have *minor gridlines* drawn between major gridlines for clarity. It is possible to have category axis gridlines as well as value axis gridlines.

■ The *data labels* are the numbers 14, 1, 3, 9, and so on directly above each column. To show multiple data labels in a single column, a chart can use *legend keys* to differentiate which data label matches which portion of the column.

■ The *data table* consists of the numbers 14, 1, 3, 9, and so on that appear at the very bottom of the chart.

■ The *legend* is the box containing the words Nights Booked.

The following table provides some suggestions about what types of charts you should use when you work with data that is presented in various formats.

Chart Type	Type of Data to Analyze
Column or bar	Ideal for charting a relatively small number of data fields that you want to display as columns or bars.
Line	Also ideal for charting a relatively small number of data fields, but a line chart is used in cases in which you want to connect the values in an unbroken line.
Pie	Similar to a column or bar chart, but the chart displays the data as a pie instead of a column or a bar.
Scatter	Ideal for charting two fields' worth of data values when the values do not necessarily follow a trend that can be connected in a reasonably unbroken line.
Area	Similar to line charts; use an Area chart when you want to fill in areas of the chart on one or both sides of the line.
Doughnut	Ideal for charting a relatively greater number of fields. Values are displayed in concentric rings, and the results look somewhat similar to a pie chart.

Chart Type	Type of Data to Analyze
Radar	Ideal for displaying a relatively small number of fields; corresponding data values are displayed relative to a fixed data value.
Surface	Ideal for displaying more than two fields in cases in which you want to represent values along a multidimensional surface.
Bubble	Ideal for charting three fields of data; a bubble chart is similar to a scatter chart, but the size of the scatter point can vary.
Stock	Ideal for fields that follow an open-high-low-close-volume pattern or a similar stock valuation pattern.

> **Note**   A pie chart and a doughnut chart can have a chart title, a legend, data labels, and legend keys, but the rest of the chart components do not apply. Pie charts can also contain leader lines that extend from data labels to pie pieces for visual clarity. Radar charts, surface charts, and bubble charts do not have options for data tables. Surface charts do not have options for data labels.

Here are some examples of when you should use specific chart types:

- If your fields consist of a customer name and a purchase amount, column, bar, line, pie, area, and radar charts are good choices.

- If your fields consist of a customer name, cost of goods, and purchase amount, column, bar, line, area, doughnut, surface, and bubble charts are reasonable choices.

The more fields you add, the more you should lean toward doughnut and surface charts or use PivotChart reports with page fields. PivotChart reports are covered in detail in Chapter 4 and Chapter 6.

Inserting a chart into a spreadsheet is a relatively straightforward process. However, customizing and working with the various chart types may take a little getting used to. To insert a chart into a spreadsheet, select the cells containing the data values that you want to include in your chart, click the Chart Wizard button on the Standard toolbar, and then provide the chart settings as requested by the Chart Wizard.

Your Turn

In this exercise, you want to see whether your data shows any month-to-month correlation between the number of nights that customer Abercrombie books and how much room service charges are for those nights. A chart is a good choice for visualizing this type of potential correlation.

1. Open Hotel.xls. If the file is open already, close it (do not save it) and open it again.

2. Select cells B1 through D13, inclusive.

3. On the Insert menu, click Chart.

4. Click the Custom Types tab.

5. In the Chart Type list, select Line–Column On 2 Axes.

6. Click the Next button three times.

7. Click the As New Sheet option, and then click Finish. Compare your results to Figure 3-13.

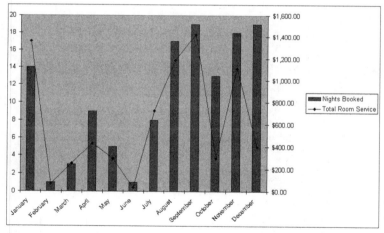

Figure 3-13 Comparing number of nights booked to room service charges.

Is there a strong month-to-month correlation between the number of nights that customer Abercrombie books and how much room service charges are for those nights? Do a simple analysis:

❑ Number of months in which the diamond is within one notch of the top of the bar: 7.

❑   Number of months in which the diamond is more than one notch from the top of the bar: 5.

On the face of it, there may be a correlation. Is it a very strong one? Answering this question successfully depends on how well you understand your business.

Importing External Data

To analyze data with Excel, you must first provide the data in a format that Excel recognizes. You can do this in two ways: you can open a data source in a format that Excel knows how to work with, or you can import the data into an Excel worksheet.

> **Tip**   When you import data into Excel, you generally are creating a copy of the data, separate from the original data source. As a rule of thumb, if you want to see updates to the original data, you should open the data in Excel instead of importing the data into Excel.

The types of data that you can open in Excel (other than Excel files) include

- Web pages
- XML files (Excel 2002 only)
- Text files
- Microsoft Access database files
- Lotus 1-2-3 files
- Quattro Pro/DOS files
- Microsoft Works 2.0 files
- dBase files
- Any other ODBC or OLE DB source for which you have a corresponding driver (data source connection software), including Microsoft SQL Server 2000 databases and Microsoft SQL Server 2000 Analysis Server databases.

> **Note** The following procedure does not work in Excel 2000. You can open a file or import data from a text file in Excel 2000, but you cannot import data from formats other than text files.

To import external data into a spreadsheet:

1. Click the cell in which you want the first item of the external data to appear.

2. On the Data menu, point to Import External Data and then click Import Data. The Select Data Source dialog box appears.

3. If you know that the data file or data source connection file already exists, locate and click the file, click Open, and then follow the directions Excel provides to finish importing the data. For example, if your data source is an Access database, you are asked to select a specific data table or data view.

   To create a new data source connection file, click the New Source button. The Data Connection Wizard appears and displays the Welcome To The Data Connection Wizard page.

4. On the wizard's first screen, select a data source and then click Next.

5. Depending on the type of data source you want to connect to, follow the steps to specify connection properties. For example, if you are connecting to a Microsoft SQL Server 2000 database, you are asked to provide a database logon name and password, a database name, and a data table or data view name.

6. After you have specified the connection properties, click Finish. The Select Data Source dialog box reappears.

7. Click the data source connection file, click Open, and then follow the on-screen directions to finish importing the data.

Filtering Imported Data

Excel allows some types of data sources to be filtered. To filter imported data after you import the data, point to Import External Data on the Data menu and then click Edit Query. One of the Query Wizard screens appears; which one depends on your specific data source. Figure 3-14 shows an example of the Choose Columns page.

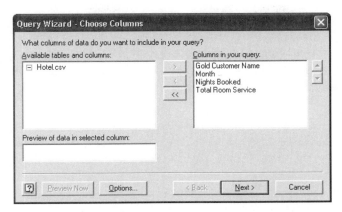

Figure 3-14   The Query Wizard - Choose Columns page.

After you import data into Excel, you can begin analyzing this data as you would analyze data on any other Excel worksheet. Note that this data is a copy of the external data, and therefore changes cannot be made to the external data source from the Excel worksheet.

Querying External Data

You can use a program called Microsoft Query, included with Microsoft Excel, to query certain types of external data and bring the query results into an Excel worksheet for further data analysis. If the external data changes, you can see the updated data in the Excel worksheet. In short, importing extracts a copy of the data, while querying links directly to the data.

> **Note**   As with external data you import, when you query external data, you cannot save changes that you make to the data in Excel to the original data source. To make changes to the external data, you need to use the application in which the external data originated.

To query external data and place the query results into a worksheet:

1.   On the Data menu, point to Import External Data and then click New Database Query. The Choose Data Source dialog box appears.

2.   If your data source is visible on the Databases tab, double-click the data source and go to step 9 below. Otherwise, click New Data Source on the Databases tab and then click OK.

> **Note**   If your data is in an OLAP cube stored on a Microsoft
> SQL Server 2000 Analysis Server computer, see Chapter 8 for
> details on how to use Microsoft Query to query data in an
> OLAP cube.

3. In the What Name Do You Want To Give Your Data Source box, type a name for the data source that's descriptive yet easy for you to remember.

4. In the Select A Driver For The Type Of Database You Want To Access list, select the type of data source from which you want to query data.

5. Click the Connect button. The ODBC Setup dialog box appears.

6. Provide the information in the ODBC Setup dialog box to connect to the data source (the information varies depending on the type of database you want to query), and then click OK to return to the Create New Data Source dialog box.

7. In the Select A Default Table For Your Data Source list, click a table to use as the basis for your database query and then click OK.

8. Click OK in the Choose Data Source dialog box to start the Query Wizard. The Choose Columns page appears.

9. In the Available Tables And Columns list, double-click each column that you want to include in your database query to move the column to the Columns In Your Query list.

> **Tip**   Click the Preview Now button to see which data values
> will be included in the query. Click the Options button to show
> or hide tables and other database objects, show the objects in
> alphabetical order, and set other options.

10. Click Next. The Filter Data page appears.

11. You can filter the data to be displayed by clicking a column in the Column To Filter list and specifying filter conditions in the Only Include Rows Where area.

12.   Click Next. The Sort Order page appears.

13.   Click an entry in the Sort By list to specify a column by which to sort. Click the Ascending or Descending option to specify the sort order.

> **Tip**   You can specify additional sorting options by repeating the previous step with the Then By list on the Sort Order page.

14.   Click Next. The Finish page appears.

15.   Click one of the options: to return the data to an Excel worksheet, view or edit the data in Microsoft Query, or create an OLAP cube from the data that the query returns. Click Finish.

> **Note**   When you click the Create An OLAP Cube From This Query option, the OLAP Cube Wizard dialog box appears. For details about how to use the OLAP Cube Wizard dialog box, see Chapter 8.

> **Tip**   Click the Save Query button on the Finish page to save the selections that you made in the Query Wizard dialog box to a query file. This query file can then be shared with other users.

Your Turn

In this exercise, let's assume that you're receiving data from your hotel chain's corporate headquarters, where data is stored on a mainframe computer. The data has been exported from the mainframe to a comma-separated value (CSV) format. The CSV file is named Hotel.csv and is located in the Chap03 folder. You want to see only those records in which customers spent more than $1,500.00 on room service in any one month.

(continued)

1. Start Excel. If Excel is already running, create a new worksheet.

2. On the Data menu, point to Import External Data and then click New Database Query.

3. On the Databases tab, click New Data Source and then click OK.

4. Name your data source *Hotel CSV 2*.

5. In the Select A Driver For The Type Of Database You Want To Access list, click Microsoft Text Driver.

6. Click Connect.

7. Clear the Use Current Directory box, and then click Select Directory.

8. Select the Chap03 folder, and then click OK. Note that you cannot select the Hotel.csv file in this step. You will select it in the next step.

9. Click OK in the ODBC Text Setup dialog box, and then click Hotel.csv in the Select A Default Table For Your Data Source list.

10. Click OK to return to the Choose Data Source dialog box.

11. On the Databases tab, click Hotel CSV 2 and then click OK.

12. Double-click the available columns to move them to the Columns In Your Query list.

13. Continue clicking Next on the rest of the wizard's pages, specifying any filtering and sorting options that you want, until you get to the Finish page.

14. Click the View Data Or Edit Query In Microsoft Query option, and then click Finish.

15. On the Criteria menu, click Add Criteria.

16. In the Field list, select Total Room Service.

17. In the Operator list, select Is Greater Than.

18. In the Value box, type *1500*.

19. Click Add, and then click Close. Your results should look similar (although perhaps not exactly the same as) Figure 3-15.

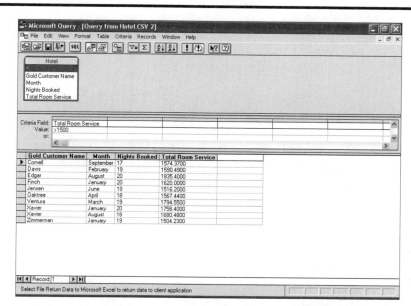

Figure 3-15 The Microsoft Query user interface, where filter criteria can be added.

20. Click the Return Data button, and then click OK to place the data into the existing worksheet. Your results should look similar to Figure 3-16.

	A	B	C	D
1	Gold Customer Name	Month	Nights Booked	Total Room Service
2	Cornell	September	17	1574.37
3	Davis	February	19	1590.49
4	Edgar	August	20	1835.4
5	Finch	January	20	1620
6	Jensen	June	19	1516.2
7	Oaktree	April	18	1567.44
8	Ventura	March	19	1794.55
9	Xavier	January	20	1758.4
10	Xavier	August	18	1680.48
11	Zimmerman	January	19	1504.23

Figure 3-16 Microsoft Query data returned to Excel.

Querying Data on the Web

You can query data imported from a Web site just like you can other types of external data. For example, you may want to query sales data on your organization's intranet site and do further data analysis on the sales data in Excel. For the best query results, the Web-based data should be displayed in a row-and-column format similar to an Excel spreadsheet.

> **Note** The appearance of the New Web Query dialog box and the steps to configure the dialog box are different in Excel 2000 and Excel 2002, but the end result is the same.

> **Tip** As with other types of external data, when you query data imported from a Web site, you cannot save changes that you make to the Web-based data in Excel to the original data source. To make changes to the original data, talk to the Webmaster or Web site administrator to see which application to use and to obtain any necessary permissions.

To query Web-based data, click the cell in the spreadsheet where you want to insert the first item of data. On the Data menu, point to Import External Data and then click New Web Query. In the Address box, type the address for the data and then click Go. The Web page containing the data appears. Click the arrows next to the data tables that you want to query, click the Import button, and then click OK.

Your Turn

In this exercise, you will import a list of preferred customer information from your hotel chain's Web site. For simplicity's sake, you will use the Hotel.htm file, located in the Chap03 folder, as the Web page containing the information.

1. Start Excel. If Excel is already running, create a new worksheet.

2. On the Data menu, point to Import External Data and then click New Web Query.

3. In the Address box, type *c:\Microsoft Press\Excel Data Analysis\Sample Files\Chap03\Hotel.htm* (or the path for the location where you copied the book's sample files) and click Go. Compare your results to Figure 3-17.

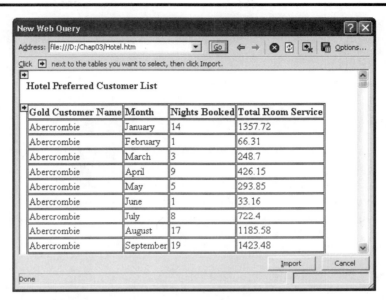

Figure 3-17   The New Web Query dialog box.

4.   Click the arrow next to the Gold Customer Name field. Compare your results to Figure 3-18, and then click Import.

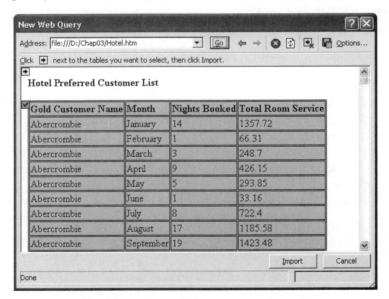

Figure 3-18   Selecting the preferred customer data table.

> **5.** Click OK to display the data in the existing worksheet. You can now begin analyzing this data as you would analyze data on any other Excel worksheet.

Analyzing Data in Lists

As you learned in Chapter 2, data lists are highly structured, and they share common field names and data values. Because of this, many of Excel's features, although they are not considered true data analysis tools, can still provide quick facts about data lists. This section provides some additional, miscellaneous tasks that you can perform with lists.

To reiterate, for the best results when using these data list features, be sure of the following:

- The data values in a data list share the same field names.

- The data values for each field are presented consistently.

- The data values have some type of data in each field, even if the data value is 0, N/A, or Unknown.

- Only one list appears on each worksheet.

- Field names are descriptive but not verbose.

- Fields are separated into their most basic parts.

One helpful data analysis task for lists of values is to add subtotals to the list. Adding subtotals is much simpler and faster than inserting numerous *SUM* or *SUMIF* worksheet functions. To add subtotals, select the data you want to summarize, click Subtotals on the Data menu, and then provide the subtotal settings in the Subtotal dialog box.

Subtotals work best when the data contains a header row. You should also perform any required sorting or filtering of the data before adding subtotals. Use the outline buttons and the plus and minus buttons to show or hide data and subtotals. These buttons are located to the left of the row number indicators, as shown in Figure 3-19.

1 2 3		A	B	C	D
	1	Gold Customer Name	Month	Nights Booked	Total Room Service
+	14	Abercrombie Total		127	$7,562.28
·	15	Bell	January	4	$123.00
·	16	Bell	February	19	$1,298.65
·	17	Bell	March	5	$262.90
·	18	Bell	April	18	$1,340.28
·	19	Bell	May	9	$444.96
·	20	Bell	June	11	$61.49
·	21	Bell	July	6	$46.08
·	22	Bell	August	7	$517.72
·	23	Bell	September	12	$1,049.04
·	24	Bell	October	3	$129.96
·	25	Bell	November	11	$863.94
·	26	Bell	December	1	$52.39
−	27	Bell Total		106	$6,190.41
+	40	Cornell Total		122	$6,426.99

Figure 3-19   Use the outline buttons and the plus and minus buttons to the left of the row number indicators to work with subtotals.

Tip   To remove subtotals, click Subtotals on the Data menu and then click Remove All in the Subtotal dialog box.

Your Turn

To determine any visible trends, you want to quickly subtotal the number of nights booked and the room service charges for each preferred customer for the entire year.

1. Open Hotel.xls. If the file is already open, close it (do not save it) and open the file again.

2. Click cell A1, the column heading for Gold Customer Name.

3. On the Data menu, click Subtotals.

4. In the At Each Change In list, select Gold Customer Name.

5. In the Add Subtotal To list, select the Nights Booked and Total Room Service options.

6. Click OK.

(continued)

7. Click outline button 2 to display subtotals by nights booked and total room service. Compare your results with Figure 3-20.

1 2 3		A	B	C	D
	1	Gold Customer Name	Month	Nights Booked	Total Room Service
	14	Abercrombie Total		127	$7,562.28
	27	Bell Total		106	$6,190.41
	40	Cornell Total		122	$6,426.99
	53	Davis Total		116	$6,054.95
	66	Edgar Total		148	$8,311.96
	79	Finch Total		128	$4,952.38
	92	Garfield Total		161	$8,113.41
	105	Harrison Total		110	$6,642.05
	118	Ichabod Total		115	$4,882.59
	131	Jensen Total		146	$4,923.31
	144	Kelly Total		93	$4,936.56

Figure 3-20 Subtotals displayed by nights booked and total room service.

Another helpful data analysis task to perform with lists is to quickly display simple function results in the Excel status bar for selected cell groups. To do so, select a group of cells (the cells should all be in the same column), and then right-click anywhere in the status bar to display a list of common data analysis functions. (See Figure 3-21.)

Figure 3-21 A list of simple status bar functions.

If you click a function, such as *Sum*, the status bar shows the simple function's result, as you can see in Figure 3-22.

Tip To display the status bar if it is not visible, click Options on the Tools menu. On the View tab, select the Status Bar check box and then click OK.

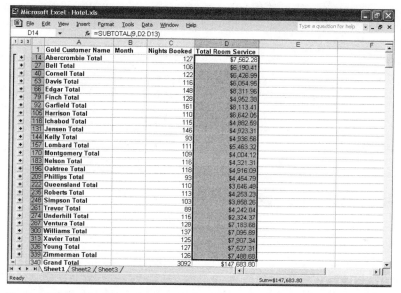

Figure 3-22   The sum of the subtotals for total room service is displayed in the status bar.

Your Turn

You want to display simple function results for customer Abercrombie.

1.   Open the Hotel.xls file. If the file is already open, close it (do not save it) and open it again.

2.   Select cells D2 through D13 in column D.

3.   Right-click anywhere in the status bar, and then click Average. The average month's room service charge was $630.19.

Experiment with other summary functions such as *Count*, *Max*, *Min*, and *Sum*.

Using the Analysis ToolPak

Excel includes a set of data analysis tools, called the Analysis ToolPak, that you can use to develop complex statistical or engineering analyses. Although this book is not geared toward statisticians, engineers, mathematicians, or academic researchers, this section will describe some of the functions in the Analysis ToolPak that are very helpful for analyzing business data. Because the Analysis ToolPak is not very widely understood, this section details the components of common Analysis ToolPak dialog boxes and demonstrates how to use these dialog boxes in common data analysis scenarios. To use the Analysis ToolPak, simply click Data Analysis on the Tools menu. (See the following if the command is not on the menu.) Click a tool in the list, and then complete the information in the resulting dialog box to perform the analysis.

Installing the Analysis ToolPak

If the Data Analysis command doesn't appear on the Tools menu, click Add-Ins on the Tools menu, select the Analysis ToolPak check box, and then click OK. If the Analysis ToolPak check box is not visible, be sure you have your original Microsoft Office or Excel installation media handy, double-click the Add/Remove Programs icon in Control Panel, and do one of the following:

For Microsoft Windows 2000, Windows Millennium Edition, and Windows XP:

■ If you installed Excel as part of Microsoft Office, click Microsoft Office in the Currently Installed Programs box and then click the Change button.

■ If you installed Excel individually, click the Excel program entry in the Currently Installed Programs box and then click the Change button.

For Microsoft Windows 98 and Windows NT 4.0:

■ If you installed Excel as part of Microsoft Office, click Microsoft Office on the Install/Uninstall tab and then click the Add/Remove button.

■ If you installed Excel individually, click the Excel program entry on the Install/Uninstall tab and then click the Add/Remove button.

Follow the instructions on the screen. The Analysis ToolPak can be found by expanding the Microsoft Excel for Windows node and then expanding the Add-Ins node.

Some of the useful Analysis ToolPak tools for business analysis include the following:

■ Descriptive Statistics, which provides a quick list of summarizations such as minimum, maximum, median, mode, and other results.

■ Histogram, which provides a categorization of data values into similar groupings, or *bins*.

■ Moving Average, which provides a series of data values averaged over time, for use in forecasting or trending.

■ Rank and Percentile, which provides a list of how data values compare or rank against each other.

■ Sampling, which selects a random number of representative data values. Sampling is especially helpful when you want to quickly analyze a smaller number of data values that you believe are representative of a much larger group of data values.

The rest of this section describes how to use these tools. In any of the dialog boxes for these individual Analysis ToolPak functions, you'll need to provide the following information:

■ **Input Range**   In this box, type the cell address for the group of data values that you want to analyze.

■ **Grouped By**   (part of the Descriptive Statistics and Rank and Percentile dialog boxes). Select the Columns option if your data is grouped by columns; select the Rows option if your data is grouped by rows.

■ **Labels In First Row**   (simply the Labels option in the Histogram and Sampling dialog boxes). Select this option if the first row or column of your input range contains field names.

■ **Chart Output**   (part of the Histogram and Moving Average dialog boxes). Select this option to display a chart along with the resulting data table.

■ **Output Range**   Select this option to place the results in the active worksheet. In the corresponding text box, enter the cell address of the cell where you want the results to start. Excel will display a message before it tries to place results in any cell that already contains a data value.

■ **New Worksheet Ply**   Use this option to place the results in a new worksheet in the active workbook. Type the name of the worksheet in the corresponding box.

■ **New Workbook**   Use this option to place the results in a new workbook.

The Descriptive Statistics Tool

To use the Descriptive Statistics tool, on the Tools menu, click Data Analysis. Click Descriptive Statistics, and then click OK. The Descriptive Statistics dialog box is shown in Figure 3-23.

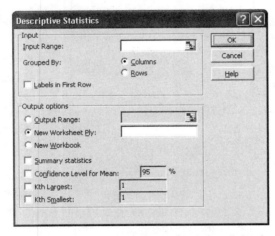

Figure 3-23   The Descriptive Statistics dialog box.

In addition to the input range and other standard options, use the following options in the dialog box depending on the information you're analyzing:

■ **Summary Statistics**   Select this option if you want Excel to produce the mean, standard error, median, mode, standard deviation, variance, kurtosis (a measure of how data is distributed), skewness (the degree of data distribution), and other related statistics for the selected group of cells.

- **Confidence Level For Mean**   Select this option if you want to measure the confidence level for the mean summarization. For example, if the mean for a cell group of 10 values is 50, the standard deviation is 38.7, and you want a 95 percent confidence level, the result is 24. This means that 95 percent of the time, any single data value in the cell group should fall between the range of data values 26 and 74.

- **Kth Largest**   Use this option to include the kth largest value in the cell group in the result. In the corresponding box, type the number to use for k. If you type 3, for example, the result is the third largest value in the cell group.

- **Kth Smallest**   Select this option to include the kth smallest value in the cell group. If you type 5 for example, the results will show the fifth smallest value in the group of cells.

Your Turn

In this exercise, you will run the Descriptive Statistics tool on the total nights booked for all customers for all months.

1. Open Hotel.xls. If it is already open, close it (do not save it) and open it again.

2. On the Tools menu, click Data Analysis, click Descriptive Statistics, and then click OK.

3. Click the Input Range box, and then select cells C2 through C313.

4. In the Grouped By area, click Columns.

5. Click the New Worksheet Ply option.

6. Select the Summary Statistics and Confidence Level For Mean check boxes.

7. Check the Kth Largest option, and then type 5 in the adjacent box.

(continued)

8. Check the Kth Smallest option, and then type 7 in the adjacent box. Compare your results to Figure 3-24.

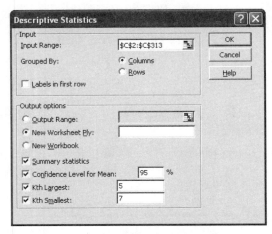

Figure 3-24   Completing the Descriptive Statistics dialog box.

9. Click OK, and then compare your results to Figure 3-25.

Column1	
Mean	9.91025641
Standard Error	0.32850856
Median	10
Mode	11
Standard Deviation	5.802618097
Sample Variance	33.67037678
Kurtosis	-1.173925895
Skewness	0.058362163
Range	20
Minimum	0
Maximum	20
Sum	3092
Count	312
Largest(5)	20
Smallest(7)	1
Confidence Level(95.0%)	0.646379694

Figure 3-25   Results of running the Descriptive Statistics tool.

The Histogram Tool

To use the Histogram tool, click Data Analysis on the Tools menu. Click Histogram, and then click OK. The Histogram dialog box is shown in Figure 3-26.

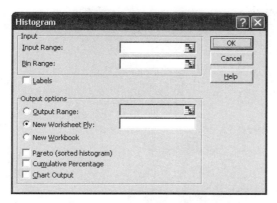

Figure 3-26   The Histogram dialog box.

In addition to the input range and other standard options, use the following options in the dialog box depending on the information you're analyzing:

- **Bin Range**   In the Bin Range box, type the cell address for the group of data values (preferably in ascending order) that you want to use for the histogram grouping bins. If you leave this box blank, Excel will create a set of evenly distributed bins using the data's minimum and maximum values.

- **Pareto (Sorted Histogram)**   Select this option to present the histogram grouping bins in descending order of frequency.

- **Cumulative Percentage**   Select this option to display a histogram column for cumulative percentages and to include a cumulative percentage line in the histogram.

Your Turn

You want to generate a histogram to display the frequency of nights booked per month for all of the preferred customers.

1.   Open Hotel.xls. If the file is already open, close it (do not save it) and open it again.

2.   In cell F1, type the number *1*. In cell F2, type *2*, and so on through the number 20 in cell F20. The values you enter will be used as the bins in the histogram.

3.   On the Tools menu, click Data Analysis.

(continued)

4. Click Histogram, and then click OK.

5. Click the Input Range box, and then select cells C2 through C313.

6. Click the Bin Range box, and then select cells F1 through F20.

7. Click the Output Range option, click the Output Range box, and then click cell H1.

8. Select the Pareto (Sorted Histogram) check box.

9. Select the Chart Output check box, and then compare your results to Figure 3-27.

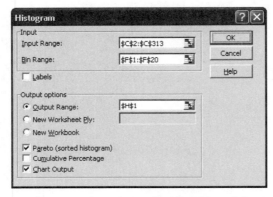

Figure 3-27   Completing the Histogram dialog box.

10. Click OK and compare your results to Figure 3-28.

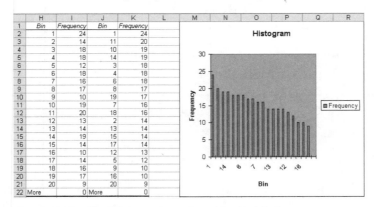

Figure 3-28   The histogram produced for Hotel.xls.

The number of nights stayed per month that recur most often are 1, 11, 10, and 14.

The Moving Average Tool

To use the Moving Average tool, click Data Analysis on the Tools menu. Click Moving Average, and then click OK. The Moving Average dialog box appears, as shown in Figure 3-29.

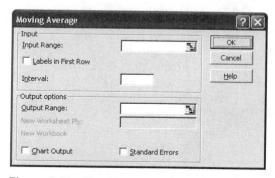

Figure 3-29   The Moving Average dialog box.

For a moving average, the output range must be on the same worksheet as the input range. For this reason, the New Worksheet Ply and New Workbook options are not available. In addition to the input range and other standard options, the Moving Average dialog box includes two items that you set to perform your analysis:

■   **Interval**   For this option, enter the number of values that you want to include in the moving average. The default interval is 3.

■   **Standard Errors**   Use this check box to have Excel generate a two-column table, showing standard error values in the right column.

Your Turn

You want to forecast what room service charges might be for the next year by using a three-month moving average of preferred customer Abercrombie's room service charges during the past year.

1.   Open Hotel.xls. If it is already open, close it (do not save it) and open it again.

2.   On the Tools menu, click Data Analysis.

(continued)

3. Click Moving Average, and then click OK.

4. Click the Input Range box, and then select cells D2 through D13 in the Total Room Service column.

5. In the Interval box, type *3*.

6. Click the Output Range box, and then click cell F1.

7. Select the Chart Output check box, compare your results to Figure 3-30, and then click OK. Compare the chart output to Figure 3-31.

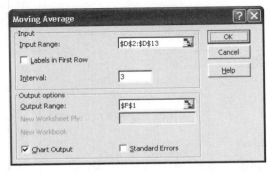

Figure 3-30 Completing the Moving Average dialog box.

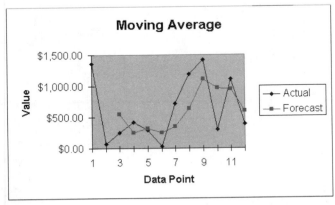

Figure 3-31 The chart showing actual and forecasted room service charges.

The numbers starting in cell F1 next to the chart are a result of running the moving average for each month, using the interval you entered. For example, for March, an average of the room service charges for January, February, and March is calculated. For April, an average of the room service charges for February, March, and April is calculated. You don't see any moving average calculations for January or February because the data for the previous months (November and December of the preceding year) is not available.

It's hard to say with certainty what preferred customer Abercrombie's monthly room charges will be next year. However, overall the trend is downward in the last quarter, which could carry over into the next year. Hopefully, you will take some sort of action with this customer to turn things around.

The Rank and Percentile Tool

To use the Rank and Percentile tool, click Data Analysis on the Tools menu, click Rank And Percentile, and then click OK. Figure 3-32 shows the Rank And Percentile dialog box.

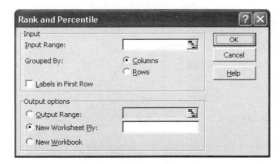

Figure 3-32   The Rank And Percentile dialog box.

Your Turn

You want to give all preferred customers who spent monthly room service charges in the 90th percentile or higher a special thank-you gift.

1.   Open Hotel.xls. If the file is already open, close it (do not save it) and open it again.

(continued)

2.   On the Tools menu, click Data Analysis, click Rank And Percentile, and then click OK.

3.   Click the Input Range box, and then select cells D2 through D313 in the Total Room Service column.

4.   Click the Output Range option, click in the Output Range box, click cell F1, and compare your results to Figure 3-33.

5.   Click OK, and compare the output to Figure 3-34. The 90th percentile cut-off point is $1,153.40 in any one month. (The numbers in the Point column refer to an item's order in the list.)

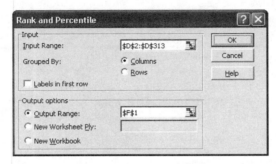

Figure 3-33   Completing the Rank And Percentile dialog box.

F	G	H	I
Point	Column1	Rank	Percent
298	$1,153.40	32	90.00%
81	$1,113.72	33	89.70%
11	$1,110.96	34	89.30%
266	$1,094.55	35	89.00%

Figure 3-34   All the values above this point are in the 90th percentile.

The Sampling Tool

To use the Sampling tool, click Data Analysis on the Tools menu, click Sampling, and then click OK. The Sampling dialog box appears, as shown in Figure 3-35.

The sampling method options include the following:

■   **Periodic**   Use this option if you want to sample the kth value in the group of cells you select for input. Enter the value of k in the Period box.

■   **Random**   Use this option if you want to sample values randomly. Type the number of sample values in the Number Of Samples box.

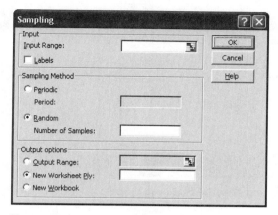

Figure 3-35   The Sampling dialog box.

Your Turn

In this exercise, you'll determine the average amount of monthly room charges made by each of your preferred customers. You'll start by averaging about 10 percent of the data values to see whether they are representative of the 310 data values in the list.

1.   Open Hotel.xls. If it is already open, close it (do not save the file) and open the file again.

2.   On the Tools menu, click Data Analysis, click Sampling, and then click OK.

3.   Click the Input Range box, and then select cells D2 through D313 in the Total Room Service column.

4.   Click the Random option, and in the Number Of Samples box, type 31.

5.   Click the Output Range option, and then click cell F1. Compare your results to Figure 3-36.

6.   Click OK and compare your output to Figure 3-37. Because you've used random samples, your results will vary.

(continued)

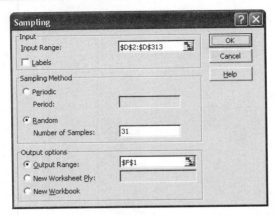

Figure 3-36   Completing the Sampling dialog box for a random number of samples.

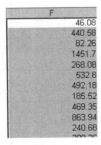

Figure 3-37   Running the Sampling tool for a random number of samples.

7.   With the randomly picked values selected, right-click anywhere in the status bar, and click Average.

What is the average monthly room service charge? Compare this amount to the average monthly room service charge of $473.35 for all preferred customers. Were the values picked representative? Now try a fixed number of data values.

8.   On the Tools menu, click Data Analysis, click Sampling, and then click OK.

9.   Click the Periodic option, and in the Period box, type *12*.

10.   Click the Output Range box, and click cell G1.

11.   Click OK, and compare the output to Figure 3-38.

Figure 3-38   Running the Sampling tool for a periodic number of samples.

12. With the new sample values selected, right-click in the status bar and click Average.

   The average monthly room service charge based on these records is $522.37. Again, compare this to the average monthly room service charge of $473.35 for all of the preferred customers. Perhaps every 12th value that was sampled was not representative either. Experiment with higher values for both the number of random samples and the number of periodic values to see whether you can get closer to $473.35.

Putting It Together

You can use a number of Analysis ToolPak tools together to perform several analyses at once and spot trends. In the following exercise, you will compare the average of monthly room service charges to their rank and percentile.

1. Open Hotel.xls. If the file is open already, close it (do not save the file) and reopen the file again.

2. On the Tools menu, click Data Analysis.

(continued)

3. Click Descriptive Statistics, and then click OK.

4. Click the Input Range box, and then select cells D2 through D313 in the Total Room Service column.

5. Click the Columns and New Worksheet Ply options.

6. Select the Summary Statistics check box, and then click OK.

7. Click the worksheet labeled Sheet1.

8. On the Tools menu, click Data Analysis.

9. Click Rank And Percentile, and then click OK.

10. Click the Input Range box, and then select cells D2 through D313 in the Total Room Service column.

11. Click the Columns and New Worksheet Ply options, and then click OK.

12. Compare the Descriptive Statistics worksheet's Mean value (473.3455, or $473.35) to the values in the Rank And Percentile worksheet's Column1 and Percent columns.

    You should notice that the mean (average) of $473.35 falls between the 60.1 and 60.4 percentiles. This is more than 10 percentage points higher than the median (midpoint), which is between $380.36 and $387.84 in the Rank And Percentile worksheet's Column1 column, or $384.10 in the Descriptive Statistics worksheet's Median row value.

Is this percentage difference good or bad for business? Although you have some big spenders among your customers, this could actually be bad for business in the long run. Here's why: if the average was closer to the midpoint, this would most likely mean that most customers were making steady, predictable, evenly distributed room service orders. However, because the average is somewhat higher than the midpoint, this means that many of the preferred customers are making either large or small, less predictable room service orders, which could be difficult to plan for in the long run, especially if those big spenders stop purchasing. How do you correct this? The answer comes in knowing how the hotel chain goes about influencing its preferred customers' purchasing habits and what it can do to keep the big spenders coming back or making the small spenders purchase more room service.

Using the Solver Add-In

The Solver Add-In is part of a suite of commands sometimes called *what-if analysis tools*. With Solver, you can find an optimal value for a formula in one cell—called the *target cell*—on a worksheet. Solver works with a group of cells that are related, either directly or indirectly, to the formula in the target cell. Solver adjusts values in cells you specify—called the *adjustable cells*—to produce the result you specify from the target cell formula. You can apply constraints to restrict the values Solver can use in the model, and the constraints can refer to other cells that affect the target cell formula.

You can use Solver to determine the maximum or minimum value of one cell by changing other cells—for example, you can change the amount of your projected advertising budget and see the effect on your projected profit.

To use the Solver add-in:

1. On the Tools menu, click Solver. The Solver Parameters dialog box appears, shown in Figure 3-39.

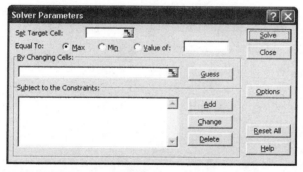

Figure 3-39   The Solver Parameters dialog box.

If the Solver command does not appear on the Tools menu, click Add-Ins on the Tools menu, select the Solver Add-in check box, and then click OK. If the Solver check box is not visible, you can follow the directions for installing the Analysis TookPak provided earlier in the chapter. Substitute Solver for the Analysis TookPak, of course.

2. In the Set Target Cell box, type the address for the cell that you want to set to a certain data value or that you want to maximize or minimize. The cell must contain a worksheet formula.

3. Click the Max option if you want to maximize the value; click the Min option if you want to minimize the value. Click the Value Of option if you want a specific value. If you click the Value Of option, type the value in the adjacent box.

4. In the By Changing Cells box, type the address for the cells that can be adjusted until the problem's conditions are reached and the cell specified in the Set Target Cell box reaches its target. The cells referred to in the By Changing Cells box must be related directly or indirectly to the cell referred to in the Set Target Cell box.

> **Tip** You can click the Guess button to have Excel try to figure out the nonformula cells referred to by the cell in the Set Target Cell box and place their cell addresses in the By Changing Cells box.

5. To add conditions, also known as constraints, click Add for each constraint. To change or delete an existing constraint, click the Change or Delete buttons, respectively.

6. If you add a constraint, the Add Constraint dialog box appears. (See Figure 3-40.) In the Cell Reference box, type the cell address; in the operator list, select an operator (such as <=); and in the Constraint box, type another cell address. Click Add to add another constraint, or click OK to return to the Solver Parameters dialog box.

Figure 3-40   The Add Constraint dialog box.

7. Click the Options button to display the Solver Options dialog box, which allows you to specify how the Solver add-in solves your problems.

8. Click the Solve button to solve the problem.

Tip   You can click the Reset All button to clear the current problem and reset all of the Solver add-in's settings to their original values.

Your Turn

You want to find out how much extra revenue your hotel would have generated during the past year if your preferred customers had spent an average of $65.00 on room service per night, without increasing the number of nights they booked during the year. You will use the Solver add-in to help make this analysis.

1.   Open Hotel.xls. If it is already open, close it (do not save it) and open it again.

2.   Calculate the total number of nights booked. To do this, type =SUM(C2:C313) in cell C314 and then press Enter. The total number of nights booked is 3,092.

3.   Calculate the amount that all customers spent on room service. In cell D314, type =SUM(D2:D313) and then press Enter. The amount is $147,683.80.

4.   Calculate the average room service charge per customer per night booked. To do this, type =D314/C314 in cell E314 and then press Enter. The average spent on room service per customer per night is $47.46.

5.   Provide a baseline difference between the current room service charges and the results that the Solver add-in will calculate. To do this, type =D314-147683.80 in cell D315 and then press Enter. The result should be zero for now, as you can see in Figure 3-41.

(continued)

	A	B	C	D	E
300	Young	November	18	$947.52	
301	Young	December	14	$894.74	
302	Zimmerman	January	19	$1,504.23	
303	Zimmerman	February	11	$1,056.22	
304	Zimmerman	March	7	$439.60	
305	Zimmerman	April	15	$308.85	
306	Zimmerman	May	6	$223.80	
307	Zimmerman	June	4	$231.08	
308	Zimmerman	July	17	$417.35	
309	Zimmerman	August	7	$453.53	
310	Zimmerman	September	11	$1,024.54	
311	Zimmerman	October	10	$415.60	
312	Zimmerman	November	3	$128.76	
313	Zimmerman	December	16	$1,285.12	
314			3092	$147,683.80	$47.76
315				$0.00	
316					
317					

Figure 3-41 The Hotel.xls workbook set up with the information required to run the Solver add-in calculation

Now let's see what happens when the average amount spent on room service per customer per night is raised to $65.00.

1.   On the Tools menu, click Solver.

2.   Click the Set Target Cell box, and then click cell E314. The Set Target Cell box should display $E$314.

3.   Click Value Of, and then type *65.00* in the adjacent box.

4.   Click the By Changing Cells box, and then click cell D314. The By Changing Cells box should display $D$314.

5.   Because you don't want the Solver add-in to change the number of nights that were booked, click Add to add a constraint.

6.   Click the Cell Reference box, and then click cell C314. The Cell Reference box should display $C$314.

7.   In the adjacent list, select the equals symbol (=).

8.   Click the Constraint box, type *3092*, and then click OK. The Subject To The Constraints box should display $C$314 = 3092. Compare your result to Figure 3-42.

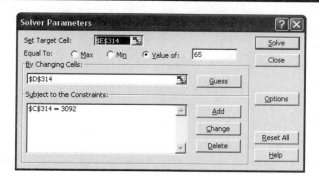

Figure 3-42   The Solver Parameters dialog box with the problem's cell references and a constraint.

9.   Click Solve. Cell D315 changes from zero to $53,296.20. If customers had spent an average of $65.00 per night booked during the last year (instead of the amount they actually spent on average—$47.46), the hotel would have collected an additional $53,296.20 in room service revenue.

10.   In the Solver Results dialog box, click OK.

Summary

In this chapter, you learned how to use Excel to

■   Find the absolute highest or lowest data value in a list by sorting.

■   Filter records to show only the data you're interested in.

■   Highlight data trends and anomalies through conditional cell formatting.

■ Import external data, including Web-based data, to use Excel's analysis tools on the data.

■ Extend data analysis tasks with worksheet functions.

■ Create charts to spot data details and trends more quickly.

■ Use the Analysis ToolPak to display a list of descriptive statistics, a histogram, a moving average, relative data value rank and percentile, and representative data sampling.

■ Use the Solver Add-In to run best-case or worst-case scenarios or "what if" scenarios.

In the next chapter, "Analyzing Data with PivotTable and PivotChart Reports," you will learn what PivotTable reports and PivotChart reports are used for, as well as how to analyze data with PivotTable reports and PivotChart reports.

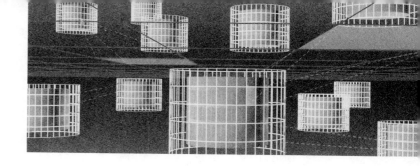

4

Analyzing Data with PivotTable and PivotChart Reports

After working through the exercises in the previous chapter to sort, filter, format, chart, and subtotal data, you have a good foundation on which to build when you want to analyze data in Microsoft Excel. In this chapter you will enhance and extend these skills through a data analysis technique called *pivoting*.

Suppose you have a large list of data; for example, figures for 2,000 sales receipt line items. You need to analyze this data to answer the following business questions:

■ Which are my best selling products by volume?

■ Which products generate the most revenue?

■ Which sales receipts are discounted the most?

Simple sorting, filtering, or subtotaling are not good choices for answering these business questions. Sorting and filtering help you see the bottom, top, or selected sales figures, but these techniques don't summarize the sales figures. Subtotals summarize the data, but to view a different set of subtotals for comparison, you need to repeat a lot of steps to reset the subtotals and create new subtotals. To answer these business questions, you can create PivotTable reports and PivotChart reports, interactive tables and charts that organize and summarize your data. You can use these reports to make comparisons, detect patterns, and analyze trends in a highly graphical manner. To make these analyses, you can easily move (or *pivot*) entire fields and records to view different data summarizations. You can look at data summarizations from one business perspective to answer a certain set of business questions, and then you can quickly change the perspective so that you're viewing another set of data summarizations that help answer a different set of business questions.

PivotTable reports and PivotChart reports are so rich and flexible that this entire chapter is devoted to understanding how to use them for business data analysis.

Objectives

In this chapter, you will

- Understand how PivotTable reports and PivotChart reports make summarizing and analyzing large amounts of data easier.

- Learn how to create, customize, and link PivotTable reports and PivotChart reports.

- Learn how to use the PivotTable report and PivotChart report toolbars and shortcut menus.

- Learn how to filter, sort, and display the top items in a PivotTable report.

- Learn how to enhance PivotTable report and PivotChart report data analysis by creating calculated fields and calculated items.

Understanding PivotTable and PivotChart Reports

As you saw in the previous chapter, analyzing lists with a few hundred records is fairly manageable. But data sources that consist of only a few hundred records are rare. Data sources usually contain from tens of thousands to millions of data records. To make sense of the information in large data sources, you can use PivotTable reports and PivotChart reports to extract and summarize these sources of data.

PivotTable reports organize data in a list format: each column contains similar data, the columns have headings in the first row, and the list isn't interrupted by any blank rows or columns (although having blank cells within the data source is perfectly acceptable). For even greater organization, you can separate a PivotTable report or PivotChart report into *pages* so that you can view a manageable subset of the data. With pages, you can display data as you would with a stack of index cards: one page might have data for the first quarter's sales, the next page data for the second quarter's sales, and so on.

To understand the rest of the concepts and procedures in this chapter you need to understand some terminology that applies to PivotTable reports and PivotChart reports. Figure 4-1 shows the framework from which you start building a PivotTable report. In the list that follows, I'll explain each item.

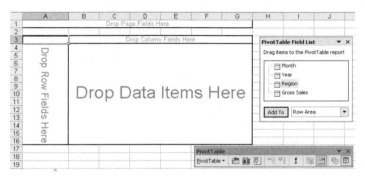

Figure 4-1   An empty PivotTable report.

■   The PivotTable Field List window contains an entry for each field in the data source. In Figure 4-1, the data source is a list of records, and the fields in the list are Month, Year, Region, and Gross Sales.

> **Note**   The PivotTable Field List window does not exist in Excel 2000. Instead, the available fields are included as part of the PivotTable toolbar. If you are using Excel 2000, in the procedures and exercises in this chapter, drag fields to PivotTable reports or PivotChart reports from the PivotTable toolbar instead of the PivotTable field list.

■   *Areas* are locations on the PivotTable report where you place and organize data. As you can see in Figure 4-1, the areas are labeled Drop Page Fields Here, Drop Column Fields Here, Drop Row Fields Here, and Drop Data Items Here. These areas are also referred to as *drop zones* because you can drag fields from the PivotTable field list and drop them in one of the report areas. Notice that the areas in which you can place data are outlined with a thick blue border. If you click outside these borders, the thick blue borders disappear, the PivotTable Field List window disappears, and the PivotTable toolbar options are disabled. When the borders are visible, the PivotTable report is said to be *active*.

■ A *row field* is a field in the data source that you assign to the row area in a PivotTable report. In Figure 4-2, the Month field (with the values 1, 2, 3, and so on) is a row field. Row fields are one of the basic building blocks of PivotTable reports. Row fields can contain child fields. For example, you might have a Month field with a child Week field and so on, which allows you to see different levels of summarization.

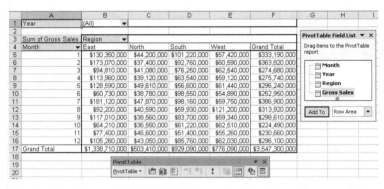

Figure 4-2   A completed PivotTable report. Month has been assigned as a row field, and Region as the column field. The data is the sum of gross sales.

■ A *column field* is a field from the data source that you assign to the column area in a PivotTable report. In Figure 4-2, the Region field (with the values East, North, South, and West) is a column field. Column fields are ideal for visual data comparisons. For example, you can quickly spot the differences among the monthly figures for the East, North, South, and West regions. With the Month and Region fields, you can compare data across both time and geography. Without the Region column field, you could compare figures only across time.

■ A *page field* is a field from the data source that you assign to the page (or filter) area in a PivotTable report. In Figure 4-2, the Year field (with the value All) is a page field. Page fields are typically used to organize data into manageable screens of data. In this example, you could use the Year field to display data for all years or filter the data to display information for only a specific year.

- An *item* is a subcategory of a row, column, or page field. For instance, you could subcategorize a department store by clothes, housewares, toys, and so on. In Figure 4-2, the Region column field contains the items East, North, South, and West.

- A *data field* is a field from the data source that contains the values to be summarized. In Figure 4-2, the Sum Of Gross Sales field (displaying the dollar figures) is a data field. For most types of data, you can choose how to summarize data (for example, by sum, average, or count). A data field usually summarizes numbers, but it can also summarize text values. For example, you can count the number of times a specific word (such as North or South) appears in a field.

PivotChart reports are a more graphical version of PivotTable reports. In Excel, a PivotChart report is associated with a specific PivotTable report. When you pivot data in a PivotTable report, any PivotChart report associated with that PivotTable report changes its display to synchronize with the PivotTable report's view of the data. The process works the other way as well: changing a PivotChart report's layout changes the data displayed in any PivotTable report to which the PivotChart report is associated.

The concepts used in a PivotChart report are much the same as with a PivotTable. The basic layout of a PivotChart report is shown in Figure 4-3. Figure 4-4 shows a completed PivotChart.

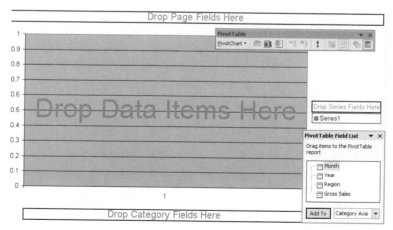

Figure 4-3   An empty PivotChart report.

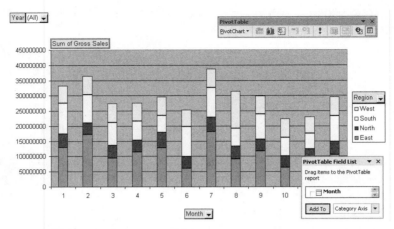

Figure 4-4   A completed PivotChart report.

■ Similar to the PivotTable report, the PivotTable field list contains one field for each field in the data source.

■ Areas or drop zones on a PivotChart, as you can see in Figure 4-3, include Drop Page Fields Here, Drop Data Items Here, Drop Series Fields Here, and Drop Category Fields Here. The names of the areas reflect that charts use series and categories instead of columns and rows. Notice also that before you place data in a PivotChart report, the areas in which you can place data are outlined with a thick blue border (except for the Drop Data Items Here area). Unlike a Pivot-Table report, however, after you drop a field into a PivotChart report area, any thick blue border associated with the area disappears.

■ A *category field* is a field from the data source that you assign to the category axis in a PivotChart report. In Figure 4-4, the Month field (with the values 1, 2, 3, and so on) is a category field.

■ A *series field* is a field from the data source that you associate with the series axis in a PivotChart report. In Figure 4-4, the Region field (with the values East, North, South, and West) is a series field.

> **Note**   For information about category fields and series fields, see the descriptions of category axes and series axes in Chapter 3, "Analyzing Data with Microsoft Excel."

■ A *page field* is a field from the data source that you assign to a page (or filter) area in a PivotChart report. In Figure 4-4, the Year field (with the value All) is a page field. Similar to the way you use a page field in a PivotTable report, you can use a page field in a PivotChart to display all data or filter data for a particular view.

■ An *item* is a subcategory of a series or category field. In Figure 4-4, the Month category field contains the items 1 through 12. Similarly, the Region series field contains the items West, South, North, and East.

■ A *data field* is a field from the data source that contains the values to be summarized. In Figure 4-4, the Sum of Gross Sales field (displaying the dollar figures on the left side of the PivotChart report) is the data field.

Now that you have a sense of the terminology used to define a PivotTable report and PivotChart report, try out the following exercise to become more familiar with these data analysis tools.

Putting It Together

In this exercise, you will discover why PivotTable reports and PivotChart reports are such valuable tools. Let's say that you're a sales analyst, and you want to draw some conclusions about last month's sales activity, such as the highest overall order price, the product with the most sales, and the orders with the highest discount.

1.   Start Excel, and open the SaleOrd.xls file in the Chap04 folder. Using the techniques you learned in the previous chapter, can you determine which order had the highest overall price? You might try inserting subtotals in the list.

2.   Click cell A1.

3.   On the Data menu, click Subtotals and then click OK.

4.   Click the button labeled "2" in the subtotals area at the left of the worksheet.

      The list includes a large number of subtotals. Can you spot the highest one? You might consider sorting the list by the Extended Price field and then creating subtotals. However, with

(continued)

the list sorted in this manner, the items are no longer in order by Order ID. If you add subtotals for each order ID at this point, the subtotals apply to each item in an order, not to the entire order. Also, if you want to ask questions such as which product sold the most or which order had the highest discount, you would have to go through these steps again. You can see that even if you sort or filter a list of this size, it is difficult to see the trends and results. You have too many records to analyze at a glance. The solution is to create a PivotTable report. Let's tackle the first problem: creating a report to display and sort the order subtotals. You must remove subtotals first, so click Subtotals on the Data menu and then click Remove All.

5. On the Data menu, click PivotTable And PivotChart Report.

6. Click Finish.

7. On the worksheet labeled Sheet1, drag the Order ID icon from the PivotTable field list to the Drop Row Fields Here area.

8. Next drag the Extended Price icon to the Drop Data Items Here area.

9. Click cell A4.

10. On the PivotTable toolbar, click the PivotTable menu and then click Sort And Top 10.

11. Click the Descending option.

12. In the Using Field list, click Sum Of Extended Price. Compare your results to Figure 4-5, and then click OK. As you can see in Figure 4-6, order ID 10865 has the highest total price ($16,387.50).

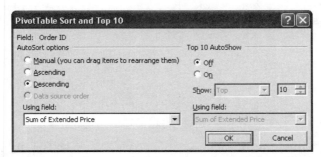

Figure 4-5   The PivotTable Sort And Top 10 dialog box for order IDs sorted by Sum Of Extended Price.

	A	B
1	Drop Page Fields Here	
2		
3	Sum of Extended Price	
4	Order ID ▼	Total
5	10865	16387.5
6	10981	15810
7	11030	12615.05
8	10889	11380
9	10417	11188.4
10	10817	10952.84
11	10897	10835.24
12	10479	10495.6
13	10540	10191.7
14	10691	10164.8
15	10515	9921.3

Figure 4-6   Order IDs sorted by highest overall total price.

13. Now let's figure out which product had the most sales. To do so, right-click cell A4 and then click Hide.

14. From the PivotTable field list, drag the Product icon to cell A4 (labeled "Total").

15. On the PivotTable toolbar, click the PivotTable menu and then click Sort And Top 10.

16. Click the Descending option.

17. In the Using Field list, click Sum Of Extended Price and then click OK. Côte de Blaye has the highest overall total sales of $141,396.73, as shown in Figure 4-7.

	A	B
1	Drop Page Fields Here	
2		
3	Sum of Extended Price	
4	Product ▼	Total
5	Côte de Blaye	141396.73
6	Thüringer Rostbratwurst	80368.69
7	Raclette Courdavault	71155.7
8	Tarte au sucre	47234.96
9	Camembert Pierrot	46825.48
10	Gnocchi di nonna Alice	42593.06
11	Manjimup Dried Apples	41819.65
12	Alice Mutton	32698.38
13	Carnarvon Tigers	29171.88
14	Rössle Sauerkraut	25696.64
15	Mozzarella di Giovanni	24900.13

Figure 4-7   Products sorted by highest overall total sales.

18. Finally, let's figure out which orders had the highest discount. Start by right-clicking cell A4 and then clicking Hide.

19. Right-click cell A3, and then click Hide.

20. From the PivotTable field list, drag the Order ID icon to the Drop Row Fields Here area. Drag the Discount icon to the Drop Data Items Here area.

(continued)

21. Right-click cell A3, and then click Field Settings.

22. In the Summarize By list, click Max and then click OK.

23. Click cell A4, click the PivotTable menu, and then click Sort And Top 10.

24. In the Top 10 AutoShow area, click the On option.

25. In the Using Field list below the On option, click Max Of Discount. Compare your results to Figure 4-8, and then click OK. Notice in Figure 4-9 that the highest discount for an order was 25 percent. That discount was the same for 72 orders. (To get the order count, select cells B5 through B76, right-click anywhere on the status bar, and click Count).

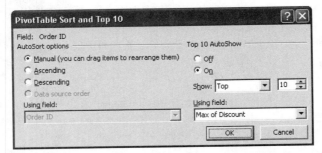

Figure 4-8   The PivotTable Sort And Top 10 dialog box with options for showing the 10 order IDs with the highest discount.

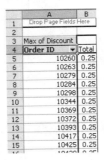

Figure 4-9   Order IDs with the highest discount.

Analyzing Data with PivotTable Reports

Understanding the terminology and basic layout is only one third of mastering PivotTable report skills. The next third is creating a PivotTable report, and the final third includes using features such as the PivotTable field list, the PivotTable toolbar, the PivotTable report shortcut menu, and filtering PivotTable report data.

To get started, a convenient way to create PivotTable reports and Pivot-Chart reports in Excel is by using the PivotTable And PivotChart Report wizard. To start the wizard, click PivotTable And PivotChart Report on the Data menu. On the wizard's first screen, shown in Figure 4-10, you need to identify the source or location of the data you want to analyze and select the option for which type of report to create. Select PivotChart Report (With PivotTable Report) if you want to create a PivotTable report with a PivotChart report that uses the PivotTable report as its data source.

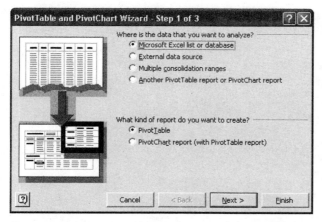

Figure 4-10   The PivotTable And PivotChart Wizard - Step 1 Of 3.

The options for data sources include the following:

■   **Microsoft Excel List Or Database**   You can use this option for data that's stored in the active workbook or in another Excel file. If you select this option, you'll see the dialog box shown in Figure 4-11. Use the Range box to identify the group of cells you want to include in the PivotTable report.

If the data is stored in another Excel file, you should have that file open at the same time you run the PivotTable And PivotChart Wizard. Switch to the other Excel file and select the cells you want to use as the basis of the pivot report. Then click Next. (You can also click the Browse button, select an Excel worksheet, and then specify the cell range at the end of the file name in the Range box. Having the external worksheet open is the easier operation.)

Figure 4-11   The PivotTable And PivotChart Wizard - Step 2 Of 3 page for an Excel list or database.

- **External Data Source**   If you select External Data Source, you'll see the dialog box shown in Figure 4-12. The Get Data button opens the Choose Data Source dialog box. Click the appropriate tab and select your data source, or double-click New Data Source to specify a new data source.

Figure 4-12   The PivotTable And PivotChart Wizard - Step 2 Of 3 page for an external data source.

- **Multiple Consolidation Ranges**   Use this option if the data is in more than one group of cells in one or more Excel files. If you select Multiple Consolidation Ranges, you'll see a series of dialog boxes. In step 2a of the wizard, shown in Figure 4-13, select the number of page fields to create. The wizard creates a single page field for you, or you can create the page fields yourself before the PivotTable is displayed. For example, you might want to group pages not only by time but also by, say, geographic regions. So, one page could show only West region sales figures for the year 2000, another page could show only East region sales figures for the year 2001, a third page could show only North region sales for the year 2002, and so on.

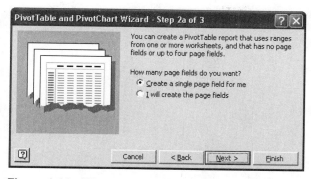

Figure 4-13   When basing a PivotTable or PivotChart on more than one cell range, you can designate one or more page fields.

If you select the Create A Single Page For Me option, you'll see the dialog box shown in Figure 4-14. Click the Range box, and then select a group of cells that you want to include in your PivotTable report. Click Add to add the group of cells, and then designate the other groups of cells that you want to include in your PivotTable report.

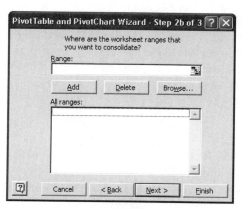

Figure 4-14   This PivotTable And PivotChart Wizard - Step 2b Of 3 page is displayed if you choose to have the wizard create a single page field.

If you choose to create your own page fields, you'll see the dialog box shown in Figure 4-15. Click the Range box, select a group of cells that you want to include in your PivotTable report, and then click Add. Follow this step for each group of cells that you want to include in your PivotTable report. Click the number of page fields that you want, and give each item a label.

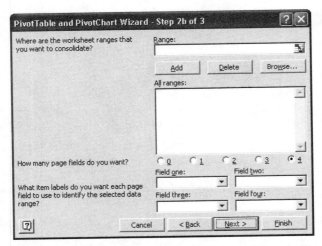

Figure 4-15   This PivotTable And PivotChart Wizard - Step 2b Of 3 page lets you create your own page fields.

Note   If the data is stored in other Excel files, you should have those files open at the same time you run the PivotTable And PivotChart Wizard. Switch over to the other open Excel files, and, file by file, select the cell groups that you want to use as the basis of the pivot reports. After you select each individual cell group, click Add. (You can also use the Browse button and add the cell reference to the sheet selected in the Range box.)

■ **Another PivotTable Report Or PivotChart Report**   Select this option if the data source is an existing PivotTable report or Pivot-Chart report in the same workbook. In the dialog box shown in Figure 4-16, click a PivotTable report name.

Figure 4-16   The PivotTable And PivotChart Wizard - Step 2 Of 3 page, which you use to select another PivotTable report or PivotChart report as a data source.

Step 3 of the PivotTable And PivotChart Wizard appears in Figure 4-17. In this step you have the option to have Excel create a new worksheet and place the PivotTable report on it, or have Excel place the PivotTable report on an existing worksheet. If you click the Existing Worksheet option, click the accompanying box and then click the cell on the worksheet where you want the PivotTable report to start.

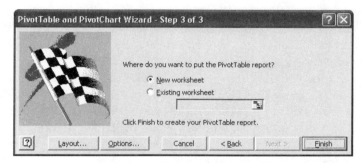

Figure 4-17   The PivotTable And PivotChart Wizard - Step 3 Of 3 page.

> **Tip**   Click the Layout button to construct the PivotTable report within the wizard instead of constructing the PivotTable report on the worksheet itself. This option is especially helpful if your source data is from a large external database, in which case the worksheet layout may be too time-consuming.

> **Tip**   Click the Options button to set additional PivotTable report options; for example, whether grand totals are automatically displayed for columns and rows, what to display for empty rows (such as "N/A"), and how often to automatically refresh the report's data.

After you have created a PivotTable report, there are several additional options and features available to you, including the PivotTable field list, the PivotTable toolbar, and the PivotTable report shortcut menu. You can use these options and features to refine the ways in which pivot reports present and analyze your data.

Using the PivotTable Field List

The PivotTable Field List window, included in Excel 2002, is shown in Figure 4-18. The window has two main areas. The field list itself contains the fields in the data source. As you saw in the exercise earlier in this chapter, to include a field in a PivotTable report, you drag the field from the list to the area where it's required on the PivotTable report.

At the bottom of the PivotTable field list is the drop zone list, which provides an alternative way of including fields in a PivotTable report, especially for users who have difficulty dragging fields to precise areas in a PivotTable report. You can use the drop zone list to add fields to a PivotTable more quickly than by dragging fields. To use the drop zone list, click a field in the field list, click an entry in the drop zone list below the field list, and then click the Add To button.

To remove a field from a PivotTable report, drag a field off the PivotTable report to an unused portion of the Excel worksheet. You don't have to drag the field back to the PivotTable field list, and you don't have to worry about the field disappearing from the PivotTable field list either.

> **Tip**   To make the best use of screen real estate, when you begin adding fields to a PivotTable report, add the field with the fewest number of items to the page area, the field with the next fewest number of items to the column area, and then other fields to either the page or row areas.

Figure 4-18   The PivotTable field list.

Putting It Together

Imagine you are a real estate sales manager and you want to quickly create and analyze a PivotTable report from last year's sales figures for the United States. In this exercise, you will create a PivotTable report, dragging items from the PivotTable field list to the PivotTable report and using the drop zone list to include items in the PivotTable report. You will switch perspectives in the PivotTable report to analyze the data and create a second PivotTable report based on the first PivotTable report while leaving the first PivotTable report's layout unchanged.

1. Start Excel, and open the HomeSale.xls file in the Chap04 folder.

2. On the United States worksheet, click cell A1.

3. On the Data menu, click PivotTable And PivotChart Report and then click Finish in step 1 of the wizard.

4. From the PivotTable field list, drag the Month icon to the Drop Row Fields Here area.

5. In the PivotTable field list, click the Gross Sales icon, click Data Area in the drop zone list, and click Add To.

6. In the PivotTable field list, click the Region icon, click Column Area in the drop zone list, and click Add To. Compare your results to Figure 4-19.

	A	B	C	D	E	F
1			Drop Page Fields Here			
2						
3	Sum of Gross Sales	Region				
4	Month	East	North	South	West	Grand Total
5	1	130350000	44200000	101220000	57420000	333190000
6	2	173070000	37400000	92760000	60590000	363820000
7	3	94810000	41080000	76250000	62540000	274680000
8	4	113960000	39120000	63540000	59120000	275740000
9	5	128590000	49610000	56600000	61440000	296240000
10	6	60730000	38780000	98550000	54890000	252950000
11	7	181120000	47870000	98160000	59750000	386900000
12	8	92200000	40590000	59930000	121200000	313920000
13	9	117010000	38560000	83700000	59340000	298610000
14	10	64210000	36550000	61220000	62510000	224490000
15	11	77400000	46600000	51400000	55260000	230660000
16	12	105260000	43050000	85760000	62030000	296100000
17	Grand Total	1338710000	503410000	929090000	776090000	3547300000

Figure 4-19   The sum of gross sales across regions by month.

(continued)

7. Experiment with switching perspectives by dragging the Month field to the column area, dragging the Region field to the row area, and dragging either the Month field or the Region field to the page area.

8. Now create a second PivotTable report that gets its data from the first PivotTable report. Click any cell outside the PivotTable report, and then click PivotTable And PivotChart Report on the Data menu.

9. Select the option Another PivotTable Report Or PivotChart Report, and then click Finish.

10. As you experiment with the new PivotTable report, notice that the first PivotTable report's layout doesn't change. Creating a second report is helpful when you want to present two perspectives of the same data for side-by-side analysis.

Using the PivotTable Toolbar and Shortcut Menu

The PivotTable toolbar, shown in Figure 4-20, provides commands that you use to format the data in your report and to organize the data for analysis.

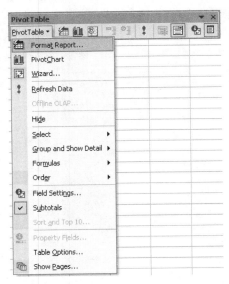

Figure 4-20   The PivotTable toolbar and PivotTable menu.

From left to right across the toolbar, the commands include

■ The PivotTable menu. I'll cover these menu commands in the next section.

■ The Format Report button, which displays the AutoFormat dialog box. The AutoFormat dialog box provides options with which you can format a PivotTable report's text and colors.

■ The Chart Wizard button, which automatically creates a PivotChart report based on the PivotTable report's data.

■ The MapPoint button, which, if you have Microsoft MapPoint installed, creates a map based on the PivotTable report's data. (Not included in Microsoft Excel 2000.)

■ The Hide Detail button, which reduces the amount of detail displayed in the PivotTable report.

■ The Show Detail button, which increases the amount of detail displayed in the PivotTable report.

   To see the effects of using the Hide Detail and Show Detail buttons, click a field label in a PivotTable report's row area or column area, click Show Detail, click a field containing the detail you want to see, and then click OK. The PivotTable report's layout changes to show detailed data for just that item. Click Hide Detail to remove the detailed data. To return to the original report layout, click Undo on the Edit menu until you return to the layout you want.

■ The Refresh Data button, which retrieves the latest data from the PivotTable report's data source.

■ The Include Hidden Items In Totals button, which contributes items that are hidden to visible totals in a PivotTable report. (Not included in Microsoft Excel 2000.)

■ The Always Display Items button, which, when selected, makes customizing PivotTable report layouts faster by hiding individual items until you add a data field.. (Not included in Microsoft Excel 2000.)

■ The Field Settings button, which allows you to view different data field summarizations (such as Sum, Average, and Max) and set data display formats (such as currency and dates) and visual layout options (such as indented, grouped, or subtotaled). I'll cover field settings in more detail in the next section.

■ The Hide Field List button, which hides the PivotTable field list (or, if you are using Excel 2000, hides the available fields in the Pivot-Table toolbar). If the PivotTable field list is hidden, clicking the Hide Field List button will display the list of available fields. (If you're using Excel 2000, the available fields are displayed on the PivotTable toolbar.)

The PivotTable menu, also shown in Figure 4-20, contains the following commands:

■ The Format Report, PivotChart, Refresh Data, and Field Settings commands are identical to the corresponding buttons on the PivotTable toolbar.

■ The Wizard command displays the PivotTable and PivotChart Wizard.

■ The Offline OLAP command creates an OLAP cube from the Pivot-Table report and makes it available offline. (Not included in Microsoft Excel 2000.) Using OLAP cubes with PivotTable reports is covered in Chapter 8.

■ The Hide command hides the selected data in the PivotTable report. (Not included in Excel 2000.)

■ The Select command allows you to quickly select different parts of the PivotTable report.

■ The Group And Show Detail command groups or ungroups selected data, or increases or decreases data details, in the PivotTable report. (In Excel 2000, this command is named Group And Outline and is available only on the PivotTable shortcut menu.)

■ The Formulas command allows you to create your own additional data fields and data summarizations, called *calculated fields* and *calculated items*. You will learn how to create calculated fields and calculated items later in this chapter.

■ The Order command allows you to reorder PivotTable report items. (In Excel 2000, this command is available only on the PivotTable shortcut menu.)

■ The Subtotals command allows you to display subtotals in the Pivot-Table report. (Not included in Excel 2000.)

■ The Sort And Top 10 command displays the PivotTable Sort And Top 10 dialog box, which allows you to sort PivotTable report items as well as display only the top number of items in a PivotTable report. (Not included in Excel 2000.)

■   The Property Fields command displays property fields associated with an OLAP cube. (Not included in Excel 2000.)

■   The Table Options command displays the PivotTable Options dialog box, which allows you to specify options such as what to display for error values in cells, empty cell values, and more.

■   The Show Pages command displays one worksheet per page field item in the PivotTable report.

Additionally, when you right-click in any PivotTable report area, a short-cut menu appears. Many of the shortcut menu commands are identical to their PivotTable toolbar counterparts. The following commands are available only on the PivotTable report shortcut menu:

■   The Format Cells command displays the Format Cells dialog box, which allows you to specify cell properties for text, alignment, color, borders, patterns, and protection.

■   The Hide PivotTable Toolbar command hides the PivotTable toolbar. (Not included in Excel 2000.) If the PivotTable toolbar is hidden, the command reads Show PivotTable Toolbar.

Your Turn

In this exercise, you will use some of the commands on the PivotTable toolbar to format and display a PivotTable report.

1.   Start Excel, and open the HomeSale.xls file in the Chap04 folder. If it is already open, close the file (do not save it) and open the file again.

2.   Click cell A1.

3.   On the Data menu, click PivotTable And PivotChart Report and then click Finish in the wizard.

4.   From the PivotTable field list, drag the Month icon to the Drop Row Fields Here area. Drag the Region icon to the Drop Column Fields Here area, and drag the Gross Sales icon to the Drop Data Items Here area.

(continued)

5. On the PivotTable toolbar, click the Format Report button.

6. Click the Report 2 picture, and then click OK.

7. Click the Chart Wizard button. A linked PivotChart is created.

8. On the worksheet labeled Sheet1, click cell C5.

9. On the PivotTable toolbar, click Field Settings.

10. Click the Number button, and then click Currency in the Format Cells dialog box.

11. In the Decimal Places box, type *0*.

12. Click OK, and then click OK again. The sales figures are formatted as currency.

13. From the PivotTable field list, drag the Region icon to the Drop Page Fields Here area.

14. On the PivotTable toolbar, click the PivotTable menu and then click Show Pages.

15. Click OK. Excel creates worksheets labeled East, North, South, and West, showing views of the different regions.

Field Settings

The Field Settings button on the PivotTable toolbar opens the PivotTable Field dialog box. This dialog box provides a variety of options; the options displayed in the dialog box depend on the sort of field or item you select in the Pivot-Table. The options provide the means for changing the way data is displayed in a PivotTable, including summarization options and a set of custom calculations that you can use to compare the items in your data.

Clicking any PivotTable report field and then clicking the Field Settings button always displays the following two options:

■ The Name box, which allows you to change the field's display name in the PivotTable report (but not in the field list).

■ The Number button, which allows you change the display format for a field's value, provided the display format makes sense for the specified values (for example, displaying text as currency has no effect).

Clicking a page, row, or column field and then clicking the Field Settings button gives you the following options:

■   The Subtotals options and list, which allow you to display, where applicable, function subtotals for a field's items, such as Sum, Max, Min, and so on.

■   The Advanced button, which allows you to display a field's items in ascending, descending, or a custom order, as well as display the top or bottom values in a field.

If your PivotTable report includes more than one row field, clicking an outer row field (any row that isn't the one closest to the data) and then clicking the Field Settings button adds the Layout button. The PivotTable Field Layout dialog box provides options for you to display the field's items in tabular or outline form and to insert page breaks between items for printing purposes.

Clicking a data field and then clicking the Field Settings button provides the following options:

■   The Summarize By list, which allows you to display data items' function results as Sum, Count, Min, Max, and so on.

■   The Show Data As list (viewed by clicking the Options button), which allows you to show custom calculations—values based on other items in the data area. For example, you can display values in the Sum of Sales data field as a percentage of June's sales or as a running total of the items in a Month field. To produce these calculations, you pick from the list of calculations and then pick a base field and a base item that serve as starting points for the calculations and comparisons. These custom calculations include the following:

❑   **Difference From**   Displays data as the difference from the value you select in the Base Item list for the base field.

❑   **% Of**   Displays data as a percentage of the value of the item you select in the Base Item list for the base field.

❑   **% Difference From**   Displays data as the percentage difference from the value of the item you select in the Base Item list for the base field.

❑   **Running Total In**   Displays the data as a running total for the field you select in the Base Field list.

❑   **% Of Row**   Displays the data in each column in a row or category as a percentage of the total for the row or category.

❑   **% Of Column**   Displays the data in each row in a column or series as a percentage of the total for the column or series.

❑   **% Of Total**   Displays data as a percentage of the grand total of all the data or data points in the report.

❑   **Index**   Calculates data using the following formula: ((value in cell) x (Grand Total of Grand Totals)) / ((Grand Row Total) x (Grand Column Total))

Filtering PivotTable Report Fields

So far, you have learned how to create, format, and rearrange fields in a PivotTable report. You can also filter PivotTable report fields to match specific criteria.

To filter PivotTable report data, with the PivotTable report active, click an arrow in the PivotTable report associated with a row field, column field, or data field, or the list next to a page field. You'll see a menu such as the one shown in Figure 4-21.

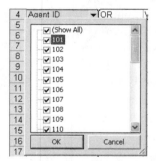

Figure 4-21   List of items for the Agent ID field; you can filter the data to show records for all agents, one agent, or a particular combination.

For row fields, column fields, and data fields, select or clear check boxes to display or hide fields. For page fields, click the item in the list associated with the page of data that you want to display.

Putting It Together

In this exercise, you will find the top five sales months for the East region's home sales, sorted in order with the highest sales month at the top of the list. You will accomplish this by filtering a PivotTable report to show only East region sales figures and then use the Sort And Top 10 dialog box to show only the top five sales months, sorted in descending order.

1. Start Excel, and open the HomeSale.xls file in the Chap04 folder. If the file is already open, close it (do not save the file) and reopen the file.

2. On the worksheet labeled United States, click cell A1.

3. On the Data menu, click PivotTable And PivotChart Report and then click Finish in the wizard.

4. From the PivotTable field list, drag the Month icon to the Drop Row Fields Here area. Drag the Region icon to the Drop Page Fields Here area, and drag the Gross Sales icon to the Drop Data Items Here area.

5. In cell B1, click the arrow, click East, and then click OK. Compare your results to Figure 4-22. Only figures for the East region are displayed.

	A	B
1	Region	East
2		
3	Sum of Gross Sales	
4	Month	Total
5	1	130350000
6	2	173070000
7	3	94810000
8	4	113960000
9	5	128590000
10	6	60730000
11	7	181120000
12	8	92200000
13	9	117010000
14	10	64210000
15	11	77400000
16	12	105260000
17	Grand Total	1338710000

Figure 4-22   Filtering data for the East region in the Region field.

(continued)

6. Click cell A4. Open the PivotTable menu, and then click Sort And Top 10.

7. Click the Descending option. In the Using Field list directly below, select Sum of Gross Sales.

8. Click the On option. In the box next to the Top box, replace the number *10* with the number *5*. In the Using Field list directly below, select Sum of Gross Sales.

9. Click OK, and compare your results to Figure 4-23. July (month number 7) had the highest sales month for the East region.

	A	B
1	Region	East
2		
3	Sum of Gross Sales	
4	**Month**	Total
5	7	181120000
6	2	173070000
7	1	130350000
8	5	128590000
9	9	117010000
10	Grand Total	730140000

Figure 4-23   Top five sales months, sorted in descending order, for the East region.

Creating and Using Calculated Fields and Calculated Items

The fields and items that you've analyzed so far correspond to specific values in a group of data records. You can also create fields and items, known as *calculated fields* and *calculated items*, that are calculated on the basis of specific values. The calculated values can then be used as if they were fields and items that already exist in the group of data records. For example, you might want to calculate sales ratios or merge geographical locations to enhance the level of your PivotTable report's summarizations.

Note   You cannot create calculated fields or calculated items in reports based on online analytical processing (OLAP) data. For more information about OLAP, see Chapter 7.

To create a calculated field, first click a field in an active PivotTable report. Click the PivotTable menu, point to Formulas, and then click Calculated Field. The Insert Calculated Field dialog box appears, as shown in Figure 4-24. Type a name and formula to use for the field, click Add to place the field in the PivotTable field list, and then click OK.

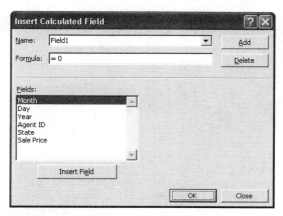

Figure 4-24   The Insert Calculated Field dialog box.

> **Note**   Calculated fields always use only the *SUM* summary function.

To create a calculated item, you first click an item in an active PivotTable report. On the PivotTable toolbar, click the PivotTable menu, point to Formulas, and click Calculated Item. The Insert Calculated Item dialog box appears, as shown in Figure 4-25. Type a name and formula to use for the item, click the Add button to add the item to the PivotTable report, and then click OK.

> **Tip**   Click a field in the Fields list if you do not want to type field names manually into the Formula box. For calculated items, click an item in the Items list if you do not want to type item names into the Formula box. Click the Add button to add more calculated items or calculated fields without closing the Insert Calculated Item or Insert Calculated Field dialog box.

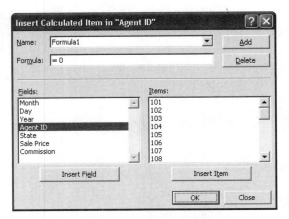

Figure 4-25   The Insert Calculated Item dialog box.

Your Turn

In this exercise, you will create a field that calculates a sales agent's commission and create a calculated item that represents a sales agent's overhead proceeds for sales in Washington state.

1. Start Excel, and open the HomeSale.xls file in the Chap04 folder. If the file is already open, close it (do not save the file) and then reopen the file.

2. On the worksheet labeled West Region, click cell A1.

3. On the Data menu, click PivotTable And PivotChart Report and then click Finish in the wizard.

4. Build the PivotTable report by dragging the Month icon from the PivotTable field list to the Drop Page Fields Here area, the Agent ID icon to the Drop Row Fields Here area, the State icon to the Drop Column Fields Here area, and the Sale Price icon to the Drop Data Items Here area.

5. Click cell A5.

6. On the PivotTable toolbar, click the PivotTable menu, point to Formulas, and then click Calculated Field.

7. In the Name list, type *Commission*.

8. In the Formula box, type = *'Sale Price' * .0035*.

9. Click Add. Compare your results to Figure 4-26, and then click OK. The Commission field is added to the PivotTable field list and the PivotTable report.

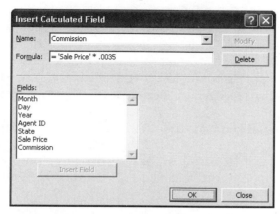

Figure 4-26   The insert calculated field dialog box for the Commission field.

10. Click cell C4. On the PivotTable toolbar, click the PivotTable menu, point to Formulas, and click Calculated Item.

11. In the Name list, type *WA Overhead Proceeds*.

12. In the Formula box, type *= WA * 0.00175*.

13. Click Add. Compare your results to Figure 4-27, and then click OK. The calculated item is added to the PivotTable report.

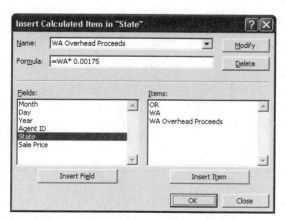

Figure 4-27   The Insert Calculated Item dialog box for the WA Overhead Proceeds field.

Analyzing Data with PivotChart Reports

As PivotTable reports help make sense of large quantities of data, PivotChart reports help bring PivotTables to life by adding visual context and meaning to the data. In Excel, PivotChart reports are always linked to PivotTable reports.

To create a PivotChart report, you follow the same steps to create a Pivot-Table report (described earlier in the chapter), but in step 1 of the wizard, you select PivotChart Report (With PivotTable Report). When you create a Pivot-Chart report, the report is bound to a PivotTable report. Any changes that you make in the PivotChart report are reflected in the PivotTable report's layout and vice versa.

The field list and shortcut menu for a PivotChart report behave the same way as they do for a PivotTable. The PivotTable toolbar contains fewer commands for a PivotChart report than for a PivotTable report. For a PivotChart report, the PivotTable menu is renamed *PivotChart*.

Your Turn

In this exercise, you will use the PivotTable And PivotChart Wizard to create a PivotTable report and a linked PivotChart report.

1. Start Excel, and open the HomeSale.xls file in the Chap04 folder. If the file is already open, close it (do not save the file) and reopen the file.

2. On the worksheet labeled West Region, click cell A1.

3. On the Data menu, click PivotTable And PivotChart Report.

4. Click the PivotChart Report (With PivotTable Report) option, and then click Finish.

5. On the worksheet labeled Chart1, from the PivotTable field list, drag the Month icon to the Drop Category Fields Here area of the PivotChart report.

6.   From the PivotTable Field List, drag the Year icon to the Drop Page Fields Here area, drag the State icon to the Drop Series Fields Here area, and drag the Sale Price icon to the Drop Data Items Here area. Compare your results to Figure 4-28.

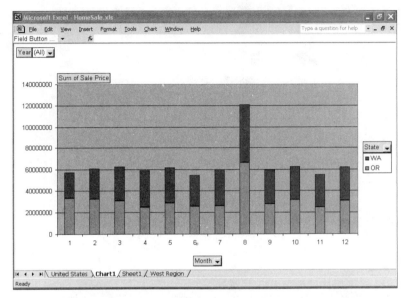

Figure 4-28   PivotChart report for yearly West region home sales.

On the worksheet labeled Sheet1, notice the layout of the PivotTable report. Now let's change the PivotChart report layout and see what happens to the PivotTable report layout.

1.   On the worksheet labeled Chart1, from the PivotTable field list, drag the State icon next to the Month field in the category drop zone. Compare your results to Figure 4-29.

On the worksheet labeled Sheet1, notice that the data in the PivotTable report has changed to reflect the layout of the PivotChart report. Now let's change the PivotTable report layout and see what happens to the PivotChart report layout.

(continued)

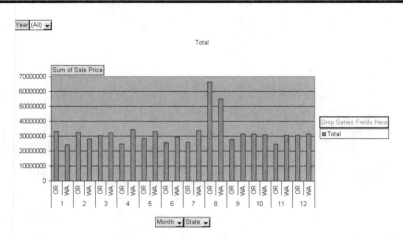

Figure 4-29 PivotChart report displaying columns for both state and month.

2. On the worksheet labeled Sheet1, click the arrow in cell B4 and clear the Show All check box.

3. Select the OR box, and then click OK. Compare your results to Figure 4-30.

	A	B	C
1	Year	(All) ▼	
2			
3	Sum of Sale Price		
4	Month ▼	State ▼	Total
5	1	OR	33260000
6	1 Total		33260000
7	2	OR	32520000
8	2 Total		32520000
9	3	OR	30390000
10	3 Total		30390000
11	4	OR	24620000
12	4 Total		24620000
13	5	OR	28320000
14	5 Total		28320000
15	6	OR	25540000
16	6 Total		25540000
17	7	OR	25900000
18	7 Total		25900000
19	8	OR	66290000
20	8 Total		66290000

Figure 4-30 PivotTable report displaying sales figures for Oregon state.

On the worksheet labeled Chart1, notice the layout of the PivotChart report has changed to reflect the data shown in the PivotTable report.

Experiment with dragging fields from the PivotTable field list to the various areas of the PivotChart report and the PivotTable report. As you make changes to the reports, go back and forth between the reports to see how the data is synchronized.

Summary

In this chapter, you learned:

- PivotTable reports and PivotChart reports are helpful in analyzing data that consists of thousands of data records or more. These reports can quickly summarize your data for faster business decision making.

- The PivotTable And PivotChart Report Wizard step you through the process of creating PivotTable reports and PivotChart reports. Once the reports are created, you can use the PivotTable field list, the PivotTable toolbar, and the PivotTable shortcut menu to graphically modify the reports.

- You can also filter PivotTable report fields, as well as create calculated fields and calculated items in a PivotTable report for more advanced data analysis.

In the next chapter, "Analyzing Data with Microsoft Access," you will learn

- The differences between relational and nonrelational data.

- How to import and link Access databases to external data sources.

- How to filter, sort, and query data in Access.

- How to create Access reports.

- How to analyze data by using Access PivotTable and PivotChart views.

5

Analyzing Data with Microsoft Access

As you've discovered over the last couple of chapters, Microsoft Excel is a great software application for analyzing data, especially lists of nonrelational data that comprise a few data rows or up to tens of thousands of data rows. Microsoft Access, however, is better able to handle the creation, storage, and analysis of relational data and is better suited to situations in which data is entered by multiple users at the same time and for large data sources that are several hundred megabytes or larger in size.

Access includes tools and features for sorting, filtering, and querying data. Access also includes a report writer that you can use to present visually compelling reports that group data and calculate totals and trends. In Access 2002, PivotTable views and PivotChart views allow you to bring the powerful data analysis features of PivotTable reports and PivotChart reports to the work you do in Access. Also, Access easily integrates with data stored in Microsoft SQL Server 2000 and provides tools for accessing data over the Web.

Objectives

In this chapter, you will learn

- The main differences between relational and nonrelational data.

- How to import data into an Access database and how to link tables in an Access database to tables in an external data source.

- ■ How to retrieve the data you need to analyze (to filter, sort, and query data) from Access tables and forms.

- ■ How to create Access reports organized with data grouping and subtotals.

- ■ How to analyze data by using Access PivotTable views and PivotChart views.

- ■ How to use Access to work directly with SQL Server 2000 databases.

- ■ How to create Access data pages to view data over the Web.

Understanding Relational and Nonrelational Data

Before you start analyzing data with Access, you need to understand the differences between *nonrelational data* and *relational data*.

Nonrelational data is often a list of row-and-column data records. The data is self-contained and does not rely on other data sources or data tables to convey all the facts about itself. An example of nonrelational data is the information in the rows in an Excel worksheet. Usually most, if not all, of the facts about the data in an Excel worksheet are included on the worksheet itself. See Figure 5-1 for an example of nonrelational data.

Customer Number	Address	Phone	City	State	Zip Code	Receipt Number	Amount Purchased	Date Purchased
100	123 Main St.	(425) 555-1212	Anytown	WA	91885	1	$25.50	8/1/2002
101	456 - 3rd St.	(206) 555-1212	Smallville	CA	30999	2	$13.95	8/1/2002
100	123 Main St.	(425) 555-1212	Anytown	WA	91885	3	$17.04	8/2/2002
101	456 - 3rd St.	(206) 555-1212	Smallville	CA	30999	4	$29.71	8/2/2002
102	567 Butterfly Ct.	(312) 555-1212	Anywhere	OR	55111	5	$19.90	8/3/2002
102	567 Butterfly Ct.	(312) 555-1212	Anywhere	OR	55111	6	$18.42	8/4/2002
101	456 - 3rd St.	(206) 555-1212	Smallville	CA	30999	7	$16.67	8/5/2002
100	123 Main St.	(425) 555-1212	Anytown	WA	91885	8	$20.01	8/6/2002
100	123 Main St.	(425) 555-1212	Anytown	WA	91885	9	$29.98	8/7/2002

Figure 5-1   Sample nonrelational data.

In this simple group of records, all you need to know is contained within the records themselves. However, the customer data is repeated, which results in a larger file size, an increased risk of data entry errors, and time wasted updating identical field values if customers change their address information.

Relational data, on the other hand, relies on other data sources or data tables to convey all the facts about itself. When you're working with relational data, you usually consult more than one related table to assemble a complete set of facts. Figure 5-2 shows an example of a single data table that would draw on other data tables to provide the set of facts shown in Figure 5-1.

Receipt Number	Customer Number	Amount Purchased	Date Purchased
1	100	$25.50	8/1/2002
3	100	$17.04	8/2/2002
8	100	$20.01	8/6/2002
9	100	$29.98	8/7/2002
2	101	$13.95	8/1/2002
4	101	$29.71	8/2/2002
7	101	$16.67	8/5/2002
5	102	$19.90	8/3/2002
6	102	$18.42	8/4/2002

Figure 5-2   Single data table that relies on other relational data tables.

In this example, you see the data records for customer purchases, but you don't see the customer's name, address, and so on. To do so, you would refer to a data table (or tables) that provides this information. The benefits of relational data can include a smaller file size (in this example, no customer address information is repeated), and if a customer changes its address information, the data needs to be updated in only one record in one data table, reducing data entry errors and data input time.

To relate data tables to one another, you use *primary keys* and *foreign keys*. A primary key is a unique value that identifies one and only one data record in a table. For example, you can use personal identification numbers, United States social security numbers, credit card numbers, telephone numbers with country or region codes and area codes, or any other unique series of characters for a primary key. A foreign key is a field in a data table in which each value in that field matches a primary key value in another data table. For instance, if you use the characters *ALF001* in a primary key field to identify a customer in a table of customer billing addresses, you could use *ALF001* in the foreign key field in a table of sales orders to refer to customer ALF001, thereby relating the customer billing address to the customer's orders. Because customer ALF001's address is stored only once, if you need to update ALF001's billing address, you need to update it only in the billing address table and not for every record for customer ALF001 in the sales order table.

Understanding how relational data is stored is important because to gather a complete set of facts in relational data sources, you often need to cross-reference two or more data tables. Returning a complete set of facts requires referencing multiple primary and foreign keys to get at the correct records in multiple data tables.

For more information about building relational databases in Access, you can read one or more of the books listed on the next page.

- *Designing Relational Database Systems* by Rebecca Riordan (Microsoft Press, 1999).

- *Microsoft Access Version 2002 Inside Out* by Helen Feddema (Microsoft Press, 2002).

- *Microsoft Access Version 2002 Step by Step* by Online Training Solutions, Inc. (Microsoft Press, 2001).

- *Database Design for Mere Mortals: A Hands-On Guide to Relational Database Design* by Michael J. Hernandez (Addison-Wesley, 1996).

Connecting to External Data

Some of the data analysis you'll conduct in Access might require you to bring external data into Access first. Access provides two ways to retrieve external data: *importing* and *linking*. Data that you import is copied from the original data source, and changes you make to the imported data in Access are not reflected in the original data source. Linked data remains in the original data source, and changes you make to the linked data in Access are carried through to the original data.

You should import data when

- You want to store and manage the data within Access.

- Network connectivity is limited or does not exist. (Linked data requires a live data connection, usually to a data source on another computer.)

- You do not often change the original data.

- You want to take "snapshots" of the original data for data analysis purposes only.

You should link to data when

- You want to use the Access data analysis features and tools, but you do not want to store or cannot store the original data in Access (for example, the original data is several gigabytes in size).

- You need more robust database management features, such as greater disaster recovery of your data, which typically means your data is stored on a server.

- You have dedicated and abundant network connectivity; for example a desktop computer connected directly to a high-bandwidth corporate intranet.

- Dozens or perhaps hundreds of users are constantly changing the data at the same time.

- You want to see everyone's changes to the original data frequently or in real time.

Importing Data

To import external data into the active database, point to Get External Data on the File menu and then click Import. In the Files Of Type list, select a file type. Acceptable file types include the following:

- Another Access database

- dBase

- Excel

- Microsoft Exchange or Microsoft Outlook folder or address book

- Hypertext Markup Language (HTML)

- Lotus 1-2-3

- Paradox

- Text

- Extensible Markup Language (XML); not available in Access 2000

- Any other data source for which you have an Open Database Connectivity (ODBC) driver.

Choose a file of the file type you selected, and then click Import, or follow the directions Access displays on your screen to import the data from the data source. For example, if you import an Excel workbook, Access asks you to select the worksheet in the workbook that contains the data you want to import.

Importing Data from Excel

Because of the similarity of the row-and-column structure between Excel worksheets and Access data tables, Access is well equipped to import Excel data into a new Access data table or append Excel data to an existing Access data table.

When you import Excel data, the Access Import Spreadsheet Wizard can detect column headings and use those column headings as field names. It also allows you to select named cell groups or cell groups on different worksheets in a workbook.

If the structure of the Excel data is not the same as the Access data table into which you're importing data, you might run into import errors. To minimize these errors, do the following:

■   Excel data should be available as lists of data records, and lists should start in cell A1 of an Excel worksheet. Also, only one data list should be in the worksheet.

■   Each column of the Excel data must have the same data type (for example, text, a date, or currency) as the corresponding field in the destination table, and the fields must be in the same order (unless you're using the first row of the data list as field names, in which case the field names must match).

■   Ensure that data records you're importing do not contain duplicate values for any corresponding primary key defined in the destination table.

■   Make sure that each worksheet has the same number of columns as fields in the destination data table.

Your Turn

In this exercise, you will import data from an Excel workbook and then use Access to create a data entry form and a report based on the imported data.

1.   Start Access, and open the Northwind.mdb file in the Chap05 folder. (If the Welcome screen appears, click OK to close it. Also, if the Main Switchboard form appears, click the Display Database Window button to display the Database window.)

2.   On the File menu, point to Get External Data and then click Import.

3.   In the Files Of Type list, select Microsoft Excel.

4.   Locate and select the CustServ.xls file in the Chap02 folder, and then click Import.

5.   Click Next, select the First Row Contains Column Headings check box, and then click Next.

6. Click Next two more times, and then click the No Primary Key option.

7. Click Finish, click OK, and compare your results to Figure 5-3. Notice that the data from the CustServ.xls file's Original Data worksheet is imported and becomes a data table in Access.

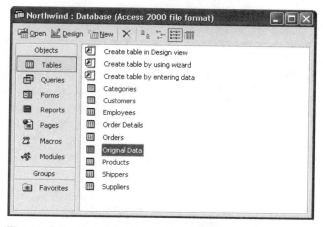

Figure 5-3 Results of importing the CustServ.xls file's Original Data worksheet.

Now create a data entry form for entering new data into the data table.

1. On the Insert menu, click Form.

2. Click Form Wizard, and then click OK.

3. Move all of the items in the Available Fields list to the Selected Fields list, and then click Finish. A data entry form is created and displayed.

Finally, create a report that summarizes some of the data in the data table.

1. Close the form, and then click Report on the Insert menu.

2. Select Report Wizard. In the Choose The Table Or Query Where the Object's Data Comes From list, select Original Data, and then click OK.

3. Move the Year, Month, and Cleanliness items from the Available Fields list to the Selected Fields list, and then click Next.

(continued)

4.   In the Do You Want To Add Any Grouping Levels List, click Year, click the right arrow (>), and then click Next.

5.   Click the Summary Options button, select the Avg check box, click the Detail And Summary Only option, click OK, and then click Finish.

You can see the yearly summarizations and averages in the report.

Linking to External Data

To create a table in the active database that's linked to a table in an external database, point to Get External Data on the File menu and then click Link Tables. The Link dialog box appears. In the Files Of Type list, select a file type. Acceptable file types include the following:

- ■   Another Access database
- ■   dBase
- ■   Excel
- ■   Microsoft Exchange or Microsoft Outlook folder or address book
- ■   Hypertext Markup Language (HTML)
- ■   Paradox
- ■   Text
- ■   Any other data source that supports linked tables and for which you have an Open Database Connectivity (ODBC) driver.

Choose a file of the file type you selected, and then click Link, or follow the directions Access provides to link to the data source. These directions will be similar to those for linking to an Excel workbook.

Your Turn

In this exercise, you will link to a table in another Access database file. To show that the data is linked, you will make changes to the data in the external data table and see the changes reflected in the linked data table.

1. If the Northwind.mdb file is not already open, start Access and open the Northwind.mdb file in the Chap05 folder. (Close the Welcome screen if it appears; if the Main Switchboard form appears, click the Display Database Window button to display the Database window.)

2. On the File menu, point to Get External Data and then click Link Tables.

3. Locate and select the Relation.mdb file in the Chap02 folder, and then click Link.

4. On the Tables tab, select Nonrelational Data in the list of tables and then click OK. Compare your results to Figure 5-4. The Nonrelational Data table appears in the list of tables in the Northwind database and is marked with an arrow icon to indicate that the table is linked.

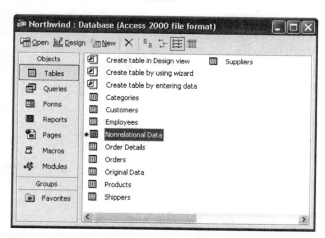

Figure 5-4   Results of linking to the Relation.mdb file's Nonrelational Data table.

5. Open the linked Nonrelational Data table and notice the address for receipt number 1 (123 Main St.)

6. Open the Relation.mdb database in the Chap02 folder, and then open the Nonrelational Data table.

7. Change the address for receipt number 1 to 789 Central Court.

8. Open the Northwind.mdb database in the Chap05 folder, open the linked Nonrelatonal Data table, and notice that the address for receipt number 1 has changed to 789 Central Court.

Sorting and Filtering Data

Once you have entered data in Access or have imported or linked to external data from your Access database file, you can use Access features and tools to analyze that data. Like Excel, Access provides tools for basic sorting and filtering so that you can quickly find one or more data records and data values.

Depending on how you view your data in Access, the sorting and filtering tools may not be available. Sorting tools are available in all views except Design view; filtering tools are available only in Datasheet view and Form view. Access data forms allow all view types, while Access data tables allow all view types except Form view. If you aren't sure which view you are using for a table or form, look at the View button on the main toolbar or click the View menu and see which view is active. To change the view, click the arrow next to the View button or select a different view from the View menu.

> **Note** Access provides other views of your data. Design view is used to design Access database objects such as tables, forms, queries, and so on. PivotTable views and PivotChart views (not available in Access 2000) are used with tables, queries, and forms. The pivot views are described later in this chapter.

Simple Sorting

There are two types of Access data-sorting tasks: simple and complex. Simple sorts are similar to the operations you perform with the Excel sorting feature, but you can sort by only one data field at a time in an Access table or form. To perform a simple sort in Datasheet view or Form view, click a field name. On the Records menu, point to Sort, and then click Sort Ascending or Sort Descending. Complex sorts are accomplished by using a special Access user interface, which I'll describe later in this section.

Your Turn

In this exercise, you will locate the sales order with the highest freight charge. Once you find the highest freight charge, you will drill into information about the sales order's related line items using a subdatasheet.

1. If the Northwind.mdb file is not already open, start Access and open the Northwind.mdb file in the Chap05 folder.

2. In the list of tables in the Database window, double-click the Orders table to open it.

3. Click the Freight field to select the entire Freight column.

4. On the Records menu, point to Sort and then click Sort Descending. Compare your results to Figure 5-5. Order 10540 had the highest freight charge, $1,007.64.

Order ID	Freight	Ship Name
10540	$1,007.64	QUICK-Stop
10372	$890.78	Queen Cozinha
11030	$830.75	Save-a-lot Markets
10691	$810.05	QUICK-Stop
10514	$789.95	Ernst Handel
11017	$754.26	Ernst Handel
10816	$719.78	Great Lakes Food Market
10479	$708.95	Rattlesnake Canyon Grocery
10983	$657.54	Save-a-lot Markets
11032	$606.19	White Clover Markets
10897	$603.54	Hungry Owl All-Night Grocers
10912	$580.91	Hungry Owl All-Night Grocers

Figure 5-5   Orders sorted by highest freight charge.

5. On the Format menu, point to Subdatasheet and then click Expand All. The data expands, displaying related records from the Order Details table.

Although the Order Details table data is not actually part of the Orders table, displaying its data in a subdatasheet can be helpful for seeing data details in context. For more information about subdatasheets, see the Access online help or read the books about Access listed earlier in this chapter.

Filtering Data

If you need to find multiple Access data records or data values, you should apply a filter. Access has various filtering features that enable you to select records that match a value in a single field or in multiple fields, as well as custom filter conditions that you can specify.

■   Use Filter By Selection to quickly find records that have a matching value in a single field, such as all records that have the value North-west in the Region field. You can also exclude records that have a certain value. After selecting a value, point to Filter on the Records menu and then click Filter Excluding Selection.

- Use Filter By Form to find records that have multiple matching field values.

- Use Advanced Filter/Sort to apply a wider range of conditions to filter and sort records. This feature also allows you to filter and sort records at the same time.

To filter data by selection in Datasheet view or Form view, click an instance of the value that you want data records to match to be included in the results. Select all or part of the value. On the Records menu, point to Filter and then click Filter By Selection. After the matching records are displayed, you can repeat this process until you have the group of records you want.

Here are some tips for how to filter records by selection:

- To find records that match the entire value in a field, select the entire contents of the value or click inside a cell containing the value. For example, select *Sales Representative* in the Title field to display only records that contain Sales Representative in the Title field.

- To find records in which the value in a field starts with a specific set of characters, select the characters in an instance of that field, starting with the first character. For example, select only *Sales* in the Title field to display records that have a Title field containing the values Sales Representative, Sales Manager, or any other title starting with the word Sales.

- To find records in which all or any part of the value in a field contains a specific set of characters, select the characters, starting after the first character in a field. For example, select only *Manager* in the Title field to display records that have a Title field containing the value Sales Manager, Regional Manager, of any other title containing the word *Manager*.

Your Turn

In this exercise, you will use Filter By Selection to display sales orders that were made by the QUICK-Stop company through employee Janet Leverling and shipped by Federal Shipping.

1. If the Northwind.mdb file is not already open, start Access and open the Northwind.mdb file in the Chap05 folder.

2. In the Database window, double-click the Orders table to open it.

3. Look for the word *QUICK-Stop* anywhere in the Customer column and click it.

4. On the Records menu, point to Filter, click Filter By Selection, and compare your results to Figure 5-6. Only orders made by the QUICK-Stop company are displayed.

Order ID	Customer	Employee	Order Date
10273	QUICK-Stop	Leverling, Janet	05-Aug-1996
10285	QUICK-Stop	Davolio, Nancy	20-Aug-1996
10286	QUICK-Stop	Callahan, Laura	21-Aug-1996
10313	QUICK-Stop	Fuller, Andrew	24-Sep-1996
10345	QUICK-Stop	Fuller, Andrew	04-Nov-1996
10361	QUICK-Stop	Davolio, Nancy	22-Nov-1996
10418	QUICK-Stop	Peacock, Margaret	17-Jan-1997
10451	QUICK-Stop	Peacock, Margaret	19-Feb-1997
10515	QUICK-Stop	Fuller, Andrew	23-Apr-1997
10527	QUICK-Stop	King, Robert	05-May-1997
10540	QUICK-Stop	Leverling, Janet	19-May-1997
10549	QUICK-Stop	Buchanan, Steven	27-May-1997

Figure 5-6   Orders made by the QUICK-Stop company.

5. In the Employee column, look for a cell containing the words *Leverling, Janet* and click it.

6. On the Records menu, point to Filter and then click Filter By Selection.

7. In the Ship Via column, look for a cell with the words *Federal Shipping* and click it.

8. On the Records menu, point to Filter and then click Filter By Selection.

Through the repeated use of a simple filter, you can find quite detailed information.

To filter data by form in Datasheet view or Form view, point to Filter on the Records menu and then click Filter By Form. The records disappear, and a blank record is displayed. Enter the filter conditions in one or more fields. To add multiple sets of filter conditions, you can click the Or tab and add other filter conditions. After you have added your filter conditions, click Apply Filter/ Sort on the Filter menu. To remove the filter, click Remove Filter/Sort.

> **Tip**   If you enter more than one filter condition on the Look For tab, only data records that meet all the filter conditions are displayed when you apply the filter. Using the Or tabs adds flexibility. For a data record to be selected, it must match the filter conditions on the Look For tab or a condition on an Or tab.

> **Tip**   When you save a data table or form, the last set of filter conditions is saved with the table so that you can apply it later. Only the last set of filter conditions is saved. To work with multiple filters on tables or forms, you should create queries. See the section "Querying Data" later in this chapter for details about how to create and work with queries.

Your Turn

In this exercise, you will find all the sales orders booked by employee Margaret Peacock and shipped via Federal Shipping or Speedy Express.

1.   If the Northwind.mdb file is not already open, start Access and open the Northwind.mdb file in the Chap05 folder.

2.   In the Database window, double-click the Orders table to open it.

3.   On the Records menu, point to Filter and then click Filter By Form.

4.   Click the empty cell underneath the Employee field and type "*Peacock, Margaret*".

5.   Click the empty cell underneath the Ship Via field and type "*Federal Shipping*". Compare your results to Figure 5-7.

Figure 5-7   Completing the Filter By Form screen.

6.   On the Filter menu, click Apply Filter/Sort and compare your results to Figure 5-8. Margaret Peacock booked 40 orders that were shipped via Federal Shipping.

Order ID	Customer	Employee	Order Date	Required Date	Shipped Date	Ship Via
10257	HILARIÓN-Abastos	Peacock, Margaret	16-Jul-1996	13-Aug-1996	22-Jul-1996	Federal Shipping
10259	Centro comercial Moct	Peacock, Margaret	18-Jul-1996	15-Aug-1996	25-Jul-1996	Federal Shipping
10328	Furia Bacalhau e Frutc	Peacock, Margaret	14-Oct-1996	11-Nov-1996	17-Oct-1996	Federal Shipping
10337	Frankenversand	Peacock, Margaret	24-Oct-1996	21-Nov-1996	29-Oct-1996	Federal Shipping
10338	Old World Delicatesse	Peacock, Margaret	25-Oct-1996	22-Nov-1996	29-Oct-1996	Federal Shipping
10347	Familia Arquibaldo	Peacock, Margaret	06-Nov-1996	04-Dec-1996	08-Nov-1996	Federal Shipping
10360	Blondel père et fils	Peacock, Margaret	22-Nov-1996	20-Dec-1996	02-Dec-1996	Federal Shipping
10363	Drachenblut Delikatess	Peacock, Margaret	26-Nov-1996	24-Dec-1996	04-Dec-1996	Federal Shipping
10373	Hungry Owl All-Night C	Peacock, Margaret	05-Dec-1996	02-Jan-1997	11-Dec-1996	Federal Shipping
10403	Ernst Handel	Peacock, Margaret	03-Jan-1997	31-Jan-1997	09-Jan-1997	Federal Shipping
10417	Simons bistro	Peacock, Margaret	16-Jan-1997	13-Feb-1997	28-Jan-1997	Federal Shipping
10451	QUICK-Stop	Peacock, Margaret	19-Feb-1997	05-Mar-1997	12-Mar-1997	Federal Shipping

Figure 5-8   Orders placed by Margaret Peacock and shipped by Federal Shipping.

7.   To add the orders that Margaret Peacock booked and that were shipped via Speedy Express, point to Filter on the Records menu and then click Filter By Form.

8.   Click the Or tab.

9.   Click the empty cell underneath the Employee field and type *"Peacock, Margaret"*.

10.   Click the empty cell underneath the Ship Via field and type *"Speedy Express"*.

11.   On the Filter menu, click Apply Filter/Sort. You now see that Margaret Peacock booked 86 orders that were shipped via Federal Shipping or Speedy Express.

Putting It Together

Frequently, you use a combination of filtering and sorting to gather the data you need to review and make decisions about. After you complete the preceding Your Turn exercise, sort the filtered data by clicking any cell in the Shipped Date column, pointing to Sort on the Records menu, and then clicking Sort Descending. The 86 records are sorted by shipped date in descending order. (The most recent shipped date is displayed at the top.)

Advanced Filter/Sort

To perform a complex filter or complex sort by using the Advanced Filter/Sort feature, point to Filter on the Records menu and then click Advanced Filter/Sort. The records disappear, and the Advanced Filter/Sort window appears. Enter the filter conditions in the grid as appropriate. After you have added all of your filter conditions, click Apply Filter/Sort on the Filter menu. To remove the filter, click Remove Filter/Sort. The following table lists some of the filter operators and expressions you can use as filter conditions:

Operator	Example	Meaning
>	> 123	Greater than the number 123
<	< 456	Less than the number 456
<=	<= 789	Less than or equal to the number 789
Between...And	Between #01/01/2002# And #12/31/2002#	On or between the dates 1 January 2002 and 31 December 2002
Not	Not "Maine"	Not the value *Maine*
	Not "M*"	No value starting with *M*
In	In ("Seattle", "Redmond")	The value *Seattle* or *Redmond*
Like	Like "A*"	Any value starting with *A*
Left	Left([Postal Code], 5) = "98052"	Any value in the Postal Code field starting with *98052*
Right	Right([Street Address]), 9) = "Boulevard"	Any value in the Street Address field ending with *Boulevard*

Your Turn

In this exercise, you will find all of the sales orders booked by employee Janet Leverling during 1997. You will then save the filter as a query for use again later.

1. If the Northwind.mdb file is not already open, start Access and open the Northwind.mdb file in the Chap05 folder.

2. In the Database window, double-click the Orders table to open it.

3. On the Records menu, point to Filter and then click Advanced Filter/Sort. Delete any existing information in the grid.

4. In the first grid column, click the Field cell, click the arrow, and then select OrderID from the list.

5. Click the Sort cell, click the arrow, and select Ascending from the list.

6. In the second grid column, click the Field cell, click the arrow, and select EmployeeID from the list.

7. Click the Criteria cell, type *3* (Janet Leverling's employee ID), and then press Enter.

8. In the third grid column, click the Field cell, click the arrow, and select OrderDate from the list.

9. Click the Criteria cell, type *Between #01/01/1997# And #12/31/1997#*, and then press Enter. Compare your results to Figure 5-9.

10. On the Filter menu, click Apply Filter/Sort. Compare your results to Figure 5-10. Janet Leverling booked 71 orders during 1997.

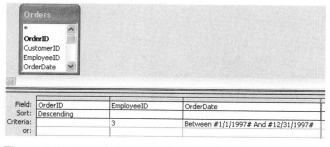

Figure 5-9   Completing the advanced filter/sort.

(continued)

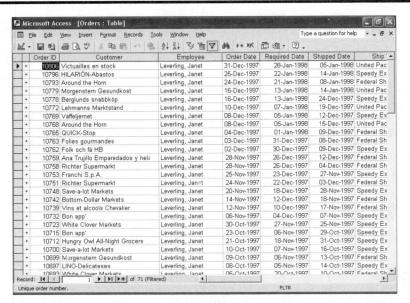

Figure 5-10   Orders booked by Janet Leverling during the month of July, 1997.

11.   To save the filter as a query for later reuse, on the Records menu, point to Filter and then click Advanced Filter/Sort. On the File menu, click Save As Query, type a name for the query, click OK, and then click Close.

12.   To apply the filter again later, point to Objects on the View menu and then click Queries. Double-click the icon matching the name of the filter to apply it.

Querying Data

Queries allow you to enhance data filtering actions. Queries are more powerful than filters because queries not only select data, but they also use more advanced filter criteria and expressions; provide a crosstab view of data (similar to a PivotTable); create new data tables; and update, append, and delete data in existing data tables. You can design and run several different types of queries in Access.

- A *select query*, as its name implies, selects data from one or more data tables. The results of a select query are stored in temporary computer memory only until the query is closed. Select queries can be saved and used as the basis for data-entry forms and reports.

- A *crosstab query* summarizes data from one or more data tables. The results of a crosstab query look similar to a PivotTable report; however, crosstab queries cannot be pivoted. Similar to a select query, the results of a crosstab query are stored in temporary computer memory only until the query is closed. A crosstab query can be saved if you want to review that set of results regularly.

- A *make-table query* creates a new data table and places the results of the query as records in the table. The original data is unaffected and is not linked to the new data table.

- An *update query* modifies data in a data table with the results of the query.

- An *append query* adds the results of the query to a data table as new records.

- A *delete query* deletes data from an existing data table.

For data analysis purposes, you will most frequently use a select or crosstab query. I'll cover these types of queries in more detail in this section. For information about the other query types, see Microsoft Access Help or the book *Microsoft Access Version 2002 Inside Out* (Microsoft Press, 2002).

To create and run a select query, first click Query on the Insert menu. In the list, click Design View and then click OK. Fill in the grid with one or more query conditions. On the Query menu, click Run to see the query results.

Your Turn

In this exercise, you will display all sales orders booked by employee Steven Buchanan in the month of January 1998, and that were shipped via United Package.

1. If the Northwind.mdb file is not already open, start Access and open the Northwind.mdb file in the Chap05 folder.

2. On the Insert menu, click Query.

3. Click OK.

(continued)

4. Above the query grid, right-click any visible table and click Remove Table.

5. On the Query menu, click Show Table.

6. Click Orders, and then click Add.

7. Click Employees, and then click Add again.

8. Click Shippers, and then click Add again.

9. Click Close in the Show Table dialog box.

10. In the grid's first column, click the Field cell, click the arrow, and select Orders.* from the list.

11. In the grid's second column, click the Field cell, click the arrow, and select Employees.LastName from the list.

12. Clear the Show check box.

13. Click the Criteria cell, type *"Buchanan"*, and then press Enter.

14. In the grid's third column, click the Field cell, click the arrow, and select Employees.FirstName from the list.

15. Clear the Show check box.

16. Click the Criteria cell, type *"Steven"*, and then press Enter.

17. In the grid's fourth column, click the Field cell, click the arrow, and then select Orders.OrderDate from the list.

18. Clear the Show check box.

19. Click the Criteria cell, type *Between #01/01/1998# And #01/31/1998#*, and then press Enter.

20. In the grid's fifth column, click the Field cell, click the arrow, and select Shippers.CompanyName from the list.

21. Clear the Show check box.

22. Click the Criteria cell, type *"United Package"*, and then press Enter. Now compare your results to Figure 5-11.

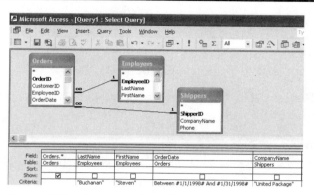

Figure 5-11   Designing the select query.

23.   On the Query menu, click Run. Compare your results to Figure 5-12. Two orders were booked by Steven Buchanan during January 1998 and shipped via United Package.

Order ID	Customer	Employee	Order Date	Required Date	Shipped Date	Ship Via
10823	LILA-Supermercado	Buchanan, Steven	09-Jan-1998	06-Feb-1998	13-Jan-1998	United Package
10841	Suprêmes délices	Buchanan, Steven	20-Jan-1998	17-Feb-1998	29-Jan-1998	United Package

Figure 5-12   Orders booked by Steven Buchanan during the month of January 1998 and shipped via United Package.

Crosstab queries are ideal for summarizing larger amounts of data than select queries. Select queries usually present all of the matching data records, whereas crosstab queries use rows and columns, similar to PivotTable reports, to summarize data. Generally, you use crosstab queries instead of select queries to calculate and restructure data for easier data analysis. Crosstab queries calculate a sum, average, count, or other type of total for data that is grouped by two types of information that you specify—one down the left side and another across the top.

To create and run a crosstab query by using a wizard, click Query on the Insert menu, click Crosstab Query Wizard, and then click OK. In the Which Table Or Query Contains The Fields You Want For The Cross Tab Query Results list, click a table or query containing the fields that you want to display in the crosstab report. Specify the fields that you want displayed in the crosstab report's rows and columns, and specify a summarization type. Specify a name for the crosstab query, click Finish, and the crosstab report is displayed.

Your Turn

In this exercise, you will create a crosstab report showing total order invoice amounts for all customers for the years 1996 to 1998.

1. If the Northwind.mdb file is not already open, start Access and open Northwind.mdb in the Chap05 folder.

2. On the Insert menu, click Query.

3. Click Crosstab Query Wizard, and then click OK.

4. Click the Queries option, click Query: Invoices, and then click Next.

5. Double-click Customers.CompanyName to add this field as a row heading, and then click Next.

6. Click Order Date to use this field as a column heading, and then click Next.

7. Click Year as the grouping interval, and then click Next.

8. In the Fields list, click Extended Price. This is the data that will be summarized. In the Functions list, click Sum, and then click Next.

9. Click Finish, and compare your results to Figure 5-13.

Company Name	Total Of ExtendedPrice	1996	1997	1998
Alfreds Futterkiste	$4,273.00		$2,022.50	$2,250.50
Ana Trujillo Emparedados y helados	$1,402.95	$88.80	$799.75	$514.40
Antonio Moreno Taquería	$7,023.97	$403.20	$5,960.77	$660.00
Around the Horn	$13,390.65	$1,379.00	$6,406.90	$5,604.75
Berglunds snabbköp	$24,927.58	$4,324.40	$13,849.01	$6,754.17
Blauer See Delikatessen	$3,239.80		$1,079.80	$2,160.00
Blondel père et fils	$18,534.08	$9,986.20	$7,817.88	$730.00
Bólido Comidas preparadas	$4,232.85	$982.00	$3,026.85	$224.00
Bon app'	$21,963.24	$4,074.28	$11,208.35	$6,680.61
Bottom-Dollar Markets	$20,801.61	$1,832.80	$7,630.25	$11,338.56
B's Beverages	$6,089.90	$479.40	$3,179.50	$2,431.00
Cactus Comidas para llevar	$1,814.80		$238.00	$1,576.80
Centro comercial Moctezuma	$100.80	$100.80		

Figure 5-13   Crosstab report displaying total order invoice amounts for all customers for the years 1996 to 1998.

Creating Reports

Access reports are much more robust than reports you can create for data in Excel worksheets. In fact, many data analysts like the Access report layouts and features so much that they create Access database files that do nothing more than link to Excel worksheet data and then create reports based on the data. The reports can be saved in the Access database or exported as HTML, XML, or other file formats.

Access reports do the following:

- Sort and group records for better visual data categorization.

- Display subtotals and grand totals.

- Provide report sections such as headers and footers.

- Provide additional information such as date and time.

- When based on filters or queries, display only the relevant subset of a larger group of records.

- Customize the windows that are used to display and navigate through reports.

To create and view a report, you should first create a table or query that contains the data that you want to display in the report. Then click Report on the Insert menu. Click Report Wizard, and then click OK. In the Tables/Queries list, select the table or query that contains the data you want to display in the report. After selecting each field you want in the report, specify how to display, sort, and organize the report's data. You can then provide a report title, click Finish, and the report is displayed.

Putting It Together

In this exercise, you will create an Access report that displays the results from a linked Excel worksheet. You will also practice grouping and sorting the report's details.

1. If the Northwind.mdb file is not already open, start Access and open the Northwind.mdb file in the Chap05 folder.

2. On the File menu, point to Get External Data and then click Link Tables.

3. In the Files Of Type list, select Microsoft Excel.

4. Select the Hotel.xls file in the Chap03 folder, and then click Link.

5. Click the Next button twice, click Finish, and then click OK.

6. On the Insert menu, click Report.

(continued)

7. Click Report Wizard, and then click OK.

8. In the Tables/Queries list, select Table:Sheet1.

9. In the Available Fields list, double-click the Gold Customer Name, Nights Booked, and Total Room Service fields, and then click Next.

10. Double-click Gold Customer Name to group the records by this field. Click Next.

11. Select Total Room Service as the field to sort by, and then click Ascending.

    Clicking Ascending changes the button's label to Descending and the sort order to a descending order. The records will be sorted so that the customer having the highest total room service will be at the beginning of the report.

12. Click Summary Options, select the Sum option for both Nights Booked and Total Room Service, select the Summary Only option, click OK, and then click Next.

13. Click the Stepped and Portrait options, and then click Next.

14. Click the Bold option, and then click Next.

15. In the What Title Do You Want For Your Report box, type Customer Room Service Summary, click the Modify The Report's Design option, and then click Finish.

16. On the View menu, select Sorting And Grouping.

17. Click the row selector for the Gold Customer Name row, and drag the row below the Total Room Service row.

    Making this change organizes the report's data so that details will be sorted in descending order by the sum of the Total Room Service field values. If the Gold Customer Name field was at the top of the list, the report details would be sorted in ascending order by the Gold Customer Name field values instead.

18. Close the Sorting And Grouping dialog box, and then, on the View menu, click Print Preview. Compare your results to Figure 5-14.

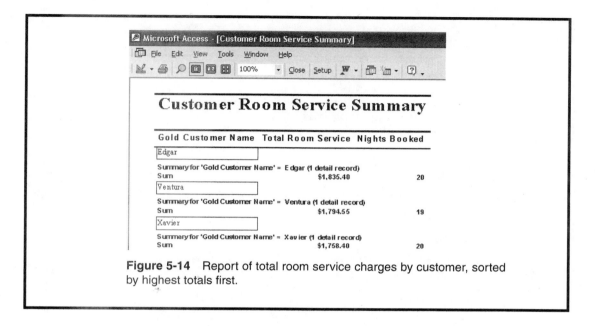

Figure 5-14   Report of total room service charges by customer, sorted by highest totals first.

Analyzing Data with PivotTable and PivotChart Views

In a manner similar to how Excel uses PivotTable reports and PivotChart reports, Access allows you to view and work with data in PivotTable views and PivotChart views. The PivotTable view and PivotChart view toolbars, shortcut menus, and other tools work almost identically to their Excel counterparts. For information about how to create and work with PivotTable reports and Pivot-Chart reports, see Chapter 4.

To create a PivotTable view or PivotChart view of a table, query, or form, open the table, query, or form and then click PivotTable or PivotChart on the View menu. You can then customize the PivotTable view or PivotChart view to fit your requirements.

> **Note**   PivotTable View and PivotChart View are not available in Access 2000.

Your Turn

In this exercise, you will create a PivotTable report and a PivotChart report based on the Invoices query.

1. If the Northwind.mdb file is not already open, start Access and open the Northwind.mdb file in the Chap05 folder.

2. On the View menu, point to Database Objects and then click Queries.

3. In the list of queries in the Database window, double-click the Invoices icon.

4. On the View menu, click PivotTable View.

5. From the PivotTable field list, drag the Company Name icon to the Drop Row Fields Here area.

6. In the PivotTable field list, click the Extended Price icon, select Data Area in the drop zone list, and then click Add To.

7. In the PivotTable field list, click the plus (+) symbol next to the Order Date By Month icon and then drag the Years icon to the Drop Column Fields Here area. Compare your results to Figure 5-15.

	Years ▾			
	⊞ 1996	⊞ 1997	⊞ 1998	Grand Total
	+ −	+ −	+ −	+ −
Company Name ▾	Sum of Extended Price	Sum of Extended Price	Sum of Extended Price	Sum of Extended Price
Alfreds Futterkiste		$2,022.50	$2,250.50	$4,273.00
Ana Trujillo Emparedados y helados	$88.80	$799.75	$514.40	$1,402.95
Antonio Moreno Taquería	$403.20	$5,960.77	$660.00	$7,023.97
Around the Horn	$1,379.00	$6,406.90	$5,604.75	$13,390.65
Berglunds snabbköp	$4,324.40	$13,849.01	$6,754.17	$24,927.58
Blauer See Delikatessen		$1,079.80	$2,160.00	$3,239.80
Blondel père et fils	$9,986.20	$7,817.88	$730.00	$18,534.08
Bólido Comidas preparadas	$982.00	$3,026.85	$224.00	$4,232.85
Bon app'	$4,074.28	$11,208.35	$6,680.61	$21,963.24
Bottom-Dollar Markets	$1,832.80	$7,630.25	$11,338.55	$20,801.60
B's Beverages	$479.40	$3,179.50	$2,431.00	$6,089.90
Cactus Comidas para llevar		$238.00	$1,576.80	$1,814.80
Centro comercial Moctezuma	$100.80			$100.80

Figure 5-15   PivotTable report based on the Invoices query.

8. On the View menu, click PivotChart View.

9. Click a blank area of the PivotChart View.

10. On the PivotChart menu, click Chart Type.

11. Click Area.

12. Click the 3D Area icon, and then close the Properties dialog box. Compare your results to Figure 5-16.

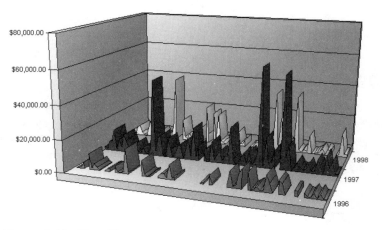

Figure 5-16   PivotChart report based on the Invoices query PivotTable report. (Company names have been removed for clarity.)

As you can quickly see, 1997 was a better year for sales than 1996 or 1998.

Using Access to Integrate with SQL Server Databases

Unlike an Access database (a file with the .mdb extension), which contains both data (in tables) and the database objects (such as forms and reports) that you use to work with the data, a Microsoft Access project (a file with the .adp extension) gets its data from a Microsoft SQL Server database and only contains forms, reports, and data access pages that display the data for analysis. You can connect an Access project to a remote SQL Server 2000 database, a local SQL Server 2000 database, or a local installation of the SQL Server 2000 Desktop Engine. The fact that an Access project does not contain any data itself allows you to use the features of SQL Server for very large databases or large numbers of concurrent users and use the familiar Access user interface for queries (called *views*, *functions*, and *stored procedures* in SQL Server terminology), data entry forms, reports, and so on.

To create an Access project and connect to a SQL Server database, click New on the File menu, click Project (Existing Data) if you're using Access 2002, or Microsoft Access Projects if you're using Access 2000. Provide a file name and location, and then click Create. On the Connection tab, select or enter a server name, provide your server logon credentials, select a database, and then click OK.

SQL Server uses different terms and data types than Access. You'll notice terms such as *identity seed*, *varchar*, and *stored procedure* when you create or modify data tables or queries. To understand these terms, as well as how to work in more detail with Access projects, refer to the book *Microsoft Access Projects with Microsoft SQL Server* (Microsoft Press, 2002).

SQL Server itself can seem somewhat intimidating to first-time users. The key point to remember is that with Access projects, you don't have to be an expert in the inner workings of SQL Server. You need to understand a few differences in terminology, but otherwise you can use the skills you've mastered in this chapter to analyze SQL Server data through Access projects.

Analyzing Access Data over the Web

Both Access 2000 and Access 2002 provide support for hosting Access data over the Web. *Data access pages* are Web pages that connect to and display data from an Access database. Users can then interact with and analyze the data over an intranet or the Internet. Because data access pages are Web pages, users need only a browser to work with them. Of course, if your users want to use the data analysis features of Access to work with data access pages, they must have Access installed on their computers.

Creating a data access page is very similar to creating a regular data entry form. In fact, the Page Wizard looks and behaves like the Form Wizard and Report Wizard. To create a data access page using the wizard, click Page on the Insert menu. Click Page Wizard, and then click OK. Select the table or query to use as the basis for the data access page, specify the fields you want to use, and specify any grouping levels, sort order, title, and theme.

Although the data access page looks similar to an Access data entry form, the data access page is actually stored outside the Access database or project. You save the data access page on either an intranet Web server or a Web server on the Internet where you have the appropriate access rights. A link to the data access page is stored in the Access database or project so that when you double-click the icon in the Database window's Pages tab, Access knows where to find the data access page.

For more information about using data access pages, consult the books about Access listed earlier in the chapter.

Summary

In this chapter, you learned the following:

- Relational and nonrelational data are different, primarily because with relational data you use multiple data tables to ascertain certain business facts.

- Importing data into an Access database creates a copy of the data, while linking data tables in an Access database to tables in an external data source lets you change and update the original date in Access. Commonly, you link data tables to an external data source if the data is updated frequently.

- The basic data analysis skills of filtering, sorting, and querying data in Access tables and forms are similar to the skills you learned for Excel except that the user interface components are slightly different.

- Access reports are in many cases superior to printing Excel spreadsheets. Use Access report features when you want sophisticated grouping or other visual design features not supported in Excel.

- Access PivotTable views and PivotChart views bring the power of Excel PivotTable reports and PivotChart reports to Access 2002 data tables.

- Access projects can connect directly to SQL Server data. This allows you to use the Access user interface and data analysis features, while still keeping the original data and other database objects in SQL Server for very large database support, more robust disaster recovery options, and to handle very large numbers of simultaneous users.

- Data access pages are Web pages that connect to and display Access data. Because they are Web pages, users can view them using a Web browser. Creating data access pages in Access is similar to creating Access data entry forms.

In the next chapter, "Analyzing Data with the Office Web Components," you will learn how to analyze data by using the various Office Web Components: the Spreadsheet Component, the PivotTable Component, and the Chart Component.

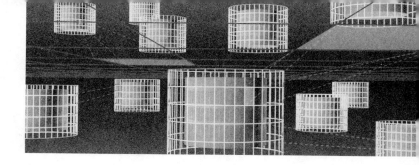

6

Analyzing Data with the Office Web Components

The data analysis techniques described so far in this book have focused on client applications such as Microsoft Excel and Microsoft Access. However, the data analysis requirements for many businesses have expanded beyond desktop applications. Businesses and organizations need to access and analyze up-to-date information from multiple, often distant, locations. You or an employee might be traveling or working from home or another remote location and need the latest sales figures or discounted price list. The Microsoft Office Web Components, introduced with Microsoft Office 2000, allow data to be published and analyzed interactively over the World Wide Web. Having your data available over the Web has several benefits. In most cases, users need little more than a compatible Web browser and a small set of downloadable software helper components. With these minimal requirements, the data is available to most any computer connected to the Web. The Office Web Components also provide toolbars and commands that are familiar to Office users, which makes performing data analysis tasks with them straightforward and lowers training requirements for users.

This chapter focuses on two main areas. Part of this chapter explains how to make data available through the Office Web Components, and the other part describes how to use the Office Web Components to work with the data. As you work through the exercises in this chapter, keep in mind that you'll need to address some issues that are not covered in this chapter when you make your data available over the Web. You might not want everyone viewing your data, which means you need to consider security. If your data will be accessed internationally, you should consider language and currency settings. Also, some users within an organization might not have a compatible Web browser or be able to download software components to their computers. You might need to review the hardware and software you have available before you can rely on accessing data regularly over the Web.

Objectives

In this chapter you will learn how to

- Analyze data with the Office Web Components: the Spreadsheet Component, the PivotTable Component, and the Chart Component.

- Create starter Office Web Components in Web pages by using Microsoft FrontPage.

- Publish data in Excel workbooks to Office Web Components in Web pages.

Introducing the Office Web Components

Although the Office Web Components do not have as many features as Excel or Access, they can still perform a great variety of data analysis tasks, including sorting, filtering, grouping, conditional formatting, and more. The Office XP Web Components also support named cell ranges, displaying multiple worksheets, and more. Also, they have the ability to handle larger amounts of data, can display three-dimensional charts, and have an improved chart wizard.

> **Note** Access 2000 does not support the Office Web Components. The Office XP Web Components, as indicated above, are designed to be more compatible with Excel than the Office 2000 Web Components.

To use the full functionality of the Office Web Components, users must have Office 2000 or Office XP installed on their computers, depending on the version of the components they want to use. Users without a license to run Office can still use the Office Web Components, although not all the features, provided they download the correct components. See the Microsoft Office Web site at *http://www.microsoft.com/office/ork/2000/one/05t2_3.htm* for more information on licensing for the Office 2000 Web Components, or *http://www.microsoft.com/office/developer/platform/owcfaq.asp* for more information on licensing for the Office XP Web Components.

You should note that there are differences in the layout and features of the Office 2000 Web Components and the Office XP Web Components. For simplicity's sake, only the behavior of the Office XP Web Components will be fully described in this chapter. I'll call out differences in the Office 2000 Web Components as appropriate.

Also be aware that the appearance and behavior of the Office Web Components are slightly different at *design time* than they are at *run time*. Design time represents when you are designing the appearance and behavior of a component in a Web-development application such as FrontPage. Run time marks the time you spend actually interacting with data in a component that's displayed in Microsoft Internet Explorer.

> **Note**   To take advantage of all the features of Office Web Components, you must have version 5 or higher of Internet Explorer installed on your computer. The components are supported somewhat in version 4.01 of Internet Explorer. The Office Web Components will not work with Web browsers other than Internet Explorer.

In this chapter, you will analyze data for a group of insurance agents in one of their company's branch offices. Before proceeding with the exercises in this chapter, take a moment to open the Sales.htm file, located in the Chap06 folder, in Internet Explorer. If you are using the Office 2000 Web Components, open the Sales2000.htm file, also located in the Chap06 folder, instead. Viewing this file will give you a sense of how data is displayed in the different Web components.

Creating Office Web Components

You can create a Spreadsheet Component, PivotTable Component, or Chart Component from scratch by using a graphical Web-page development application such as Microsoft FrontPage. (Version 2000 or a later version of FrontPage is required.) To create an Office Web Component in FrontPage, follow these steps:

1.   Start FrontPage.

2.   On the File menu, point to New and then click Page Or Web.

3.   In the New Page Or Web task pane, click Blank Page.

4.   On the Insert menu, click Web Component. The Insert Web Component dialog box appears.

5.   In the Component Type list, click Spreadsheets And Charts.

6.   In the Choose A Control list, click Office Spreadsheet, Office Pivot-Table, or Office Chart, and then click Finish.

         Once you've inserted the component you need, you can connect the component to a data source or enter data from scratch. You'll learn how to perform these steps later in the chapter.

7.   Save and view the file.

> **Note**   In FrontPage 2000, neither the task pane nor the Insert Web Component dialog box are available, but the steps are basically the same.

Using the Spreadsheet Component

The Spreadsheet Component brings the look and feel of Excel spreadsheets and some of a spreadsheet's features to Web pages. See Figure 6-1 for an example of a Spreadsheet Component.

	A	B	C	D	E	F	G	H	I
1	Month	Day	Year	Claim Date	Customer ID	Agent ID	Claim Amount		
2	9	1	2002	9/1/2002	55	6	$8,141.16		
3	9	2	2002	9/2/2002	98	2	$9,304.06		
4	9	3	2002	9/3/2002	43	3	$11,200.49		
5	9	4	2002	9/4/2002	8	1	$15,998.40		
6	9	5	2002	9/5/2002	25	5	$16,328.65		
7	9	6	2002	9/6/2002	98	5	$10,648.53		
8	9	9	2002	9/9/2002	81	1	$10,208.64		
9	9	10	2002	9/10/2002	6	6	$3,116.06		
10	9	11	2002	9/11/2002	40	3	$19,867.79		
11	9	12	2002	9/12/2002	22	4	$17,571.27		
12	9	13	2002	9/13/2002	64	3	$16,473.85		
13	9	16	2002	9/16/2002	67	2	$11,733.43		
14	9	17	2002	9/17/2002	93	6	$5,995.29		

Figure 6-1   The Microsoft Office XP Spreadsheet Component.

Many of the buttons on the Spreadsheet Component's toolbar, shown in Figure 6-2, perform familiar operations; for example, cutting and pasting data and sorting data in simple ascending or descending order. The following list describes the toolbar buttons that are more particular to the Spreadsheet Component:

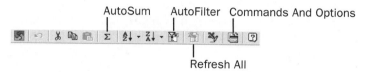

Figure 6-2   The Microsoft Office XP Spreadsheet Component's toolbar.

- AutoSum automatically inserts a sum for a group of cells.

- AutoFilter places a drop-down list in the top cell of each column. Clicking the arrow displays a list of values that you can use to filter the records in the spreadsheet.

- Refresh All (not available in Office 2000) retrieves the latest data from the data source.

- Commands And Options (Property Toolbox in Office 2000) displays the Commands And Options dialog box (named the Property Toolbox in Office 2000).

The tabs displayed on the Spreadsheet Component's Commands And Options dialog box at design time, shown in Figure 6-3, provide a number of options for managing the appearance and the use of the data in the component. The tabs include the following:

- The Format tab provides options for changing the appearance of text and cells.

- The Formula tab lets you view cell formulas and define named cell groups.

- The Sheet tab provides search capabilities and settings for other display options; for example hiding grid lines, freezing panes, defining viewable cells, and so on.

- The Workbook tab sets the calculation mode. Automatic calculation is more convenient than manual calculation, but this option can potentially slow down your computer's performance if a worksheet contains a lot of formulas. This tab also lets you display or hide scroll bars, row selectors, and the status bar, as well as rename, delete, hide, or reorder worksheets.

- The Import tab specifies the type of data to import (XML, HTML, or comma-separated value (CSV) data) from a Web address.

- The Protection tab supplies options that help you manage what users of the component can do when viewing data at run time. You can control whether a user can delete, insert, or resize columns or rows or filter and sort at run time. You can also enable the ability to insert, remove, or rename worksheets, as well as hide or display the Commands And Options dialog box at run time. These options give you greater control over what users can do with your data over the Web.

- The Advanced tab lets you set additional cell group and worksheet behaviors, such as having the spreadsheet expand or shrink on the Web page depending on how much data it holds.

- The Data Source tab defines data source connectivity information.

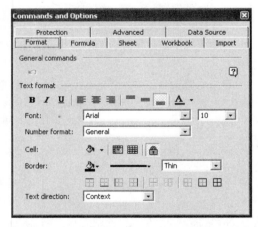

Figure 6-3   The Microsoft Office XP Spreadsheet Component's Commands And Options dialog box at design time.

At run time, the tabs on the Commands And Options dialog box include the Format, Formula, Sheet, and Workbook tabs, as shown in Figure 6-4.

> **Note**   The Office 2000 Spreadsheet Component's Property Toolbox tabs look different from the Office XP Spreadsheet Component's Commands And Options dialog box, but many of the features are the same.

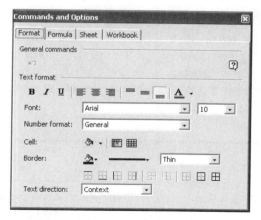

Figure 6-4   The Microsoft Office XP Spreadsheet Component's Commands And Options window at run time.

You can type data into a Spreadsheet Component, you can publish cell groups, worksheets, and workbooks to a Spreadsheet Component, or you can import data from another data source into a Spreadsheet Component.

To publish cell groups, worksheets, or workbooks to a Spreadsheet Component, on the File menu in Excel, click Save As Web Page. You can then select an option to save the entire workbook to the Web page or save a selection. The Add Interactivity option makes the data "live" in the Spreadsheet Component when it's displayed on a Web page. Without this option selected, you can't make any changes to the data at run time. The data is displayed in a static format. The Publish button provides additional control over the state of the data. This button opens a dialog box in which you can specify what portions of the workbook to publish and whether to automatically update the Web page hosting the Spreadsheet Component each time the original workbook is saved. Choosing this option means that users viewing the data on a Web site can have up-to-date information. In the Publish As Web Page dialog box, select the AutoRepublish Every Time This Workbook Is Saved option and then click Publish. When you save changes to the workbook containing the data you've published to the Web, Excel displays a dialog box with the option Enable The AutoRepublish Feature. Select this option and then click OK to update the data in the Spreadsheet Component as well. Keep in mind that changes that you make to the data in the Spreadsheet Component are not reflected in the original Excel workbook even if you choose the Add Interactivity option or the option to automatically republish the workbook.

> **Tip**   The Change Title button in the Save As dialog box lets you change the text that will be displayed in the title bar of the browser or, if the Add Interactivity option is selected, to provide a title for the published data. This title will appear on the Web page at the top of the selection.

Your Turn

In this exercise, you will publish data on an existing Excel worksheet to a Spreadsheet Component on a Web page.

1.   In Excel, open the InsClaim.xls file in the Chap06 folder.

2.   On the File menu, click Save As Web Page.

3.   Select the Add Interactivity check box to create an Office Spreadsheet Component on the Web page. (If you do not select the Add Interactivity check box, the data will be published as a list of data records that cannot be modified.)

4.   Click Save.

5.   Open the file (named Page.htm by default) in Internet Explorer. Compare your results to Figure 6-5.

	Month	Day	Year	Claim Date	Customer ID	Agent ID	Claim Amount		
2	9	1	2002	9/1/2002	55	6	$8,141.16		
3	9	2	2002	9/2/2002	98	2	$9,304.06		
4	9	3	2002	9/3/2002	43	3	$11,200.49		
5	9	4	2002	9/4/2002	8	1	$15,998.40		
6	9	5	2002	9/5/2002	25	5	$16,328.65		
7	9	6	2002	9/6/2002	98	5	$10,648.53		
8	9	9	2002	9/9/2002	81	1	$10,208.64		
9	9	10	2002	9/10/2002	6	6	$3,116.06		
10	9	11	2002	9/11/2002	40	3	$19,867.79		
11	9	12	2002	9/12/2002	22	4	$17,571.27		
12	9	13	2002	9/13/2002	64	3	$16,473.85		
13	9	16	2002	9/16/2002	67	2	$11,733.43		
14	9	17	2002	9/17/2002	93	6	$5,995.29		
15	9	18	2002	9/18/2002	15	2	$5,739.20		
16	9	19	2002	9/19/2002	96	1	$17,728.05		
17	9	20	2002	9/20/2002	39	4	$17,165.48		

Figure 6-5   Publishing the InsClaim.xls file as an Office XP Spreadsheet Component on a Web page.

It's important to remember when working with the Spreadsheet Component that while you can import external data into a Spreadsheet Component, any changes you make to data in a Spreadsheet Component will not be reflected in the original data source. Any changes you make to the appearance of a Spreadsheet Component at run time last only while the page with the component is open in your Web browser. If you need to save changes you've made to data on a Spreadsheet Component, you can export the data to a Microsoft Excel worksheet and save it there.

To import data from an external data source into an existing Spreadsheet Component on a Web page, follow these steps:

1.   With a Spreadsheet Component open in FrontPage (or another Web page designer), click the Commands And Options button.

2.   Click the Data Source tab.

3.   Complete the information in the Commands And Options dialog box to import the external data.

Creating a connection to an external data source is covered in more detail later in the chapter.

> **Note**   In the Office 2000 Spreadsheet Component in design time, click the Property Toolbox button, click the Import tab, and then complete the information in the Property Toolbox to import the external data.

Analyzing Data in the Spreadsheet Component

With the Spreadsheet Component, you insert worksheet formulas into cells, automatically sum data, sort data, and filter data. To insert a worksheet formula, you can type the formula in the applicable cell and then press Enter. To view a formula that's included in a cell, click the Commands And Options button and then click the Formula tab.

Your Turn

In this exercise, you will determine the average insurance claim amount.

1. Open the file Sales.htm (or Sales2000.htm if you are using Office 2000) in the Chap06 folder.

2. In the Sales.htm file's Spreadsheet Component, click cell G274.

3. Type =AVERAGE(G2:G273), and then press Enter. Compare your results with Figure 6-6. The average insurance claim amount is $10,216.84.

	A	B	C	D	E	F	G	H	I
264	1	20	2003	1/20/2003	59	5	$2,306.67		
265	1	21	2003	1/21/2003	55	3	$12,840.06		
266	1	22	2003	1/22/2003	63	5	$6,247.03		
267	1	23	2003	1/23/2003	81	5	$8,088.60		
268	1	24	2003	1/24/2003	19	4	$6,113.00		
269	1	27	2003	1/27/2003	26	4	$2,814.98		
270	1	28	2003	1/28/2003	72	5	$7,923.37		
271	1	29	2003	1/29/2003	24	2	$17,407.77		
272	1	30	2003	1/30/2003	45	5	$6,685.78		
273	1	31	2003	1/31/2003	5	3	$4,074.56		
274							$10,216.84		
275									
276									
277									

Sheet1

Figure 6-6   Average insurance claim amount.

To automatically sum data in the Spreadsheet Component, click the cell in which you want the summary formula, click the AutoSum button on the Spreadsheet Component's toolbar, and then press Enter.

Your Turn

In this exercise, you will determine the total amount for all insurance claims.

1. In the Sales.htm file's Spreadsheet Component, click cell G274.

2. Clear the AVERAGE worksheet function in cell G274 from the previous exercise.

3. On the Spreadsheet Component's toolbar, click the AutoSum button and then press Enter. Compare your results with Figure 6-7. The total amount for all of the insurance claims is $2,778,981.81.

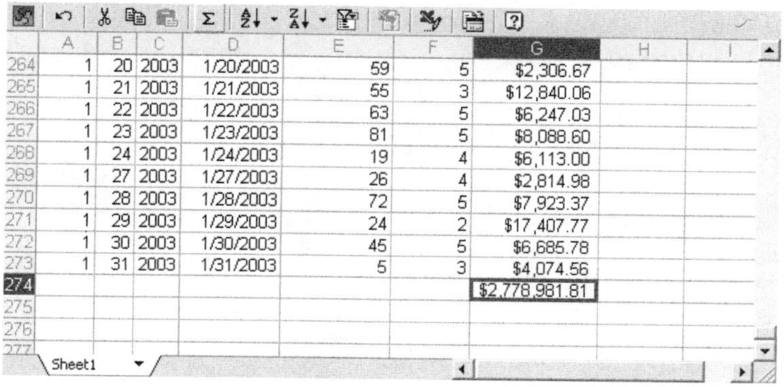

	A	B	C	D	E	F	G	H	I
264	1	20	2003	1/20/2003	59	5	$2,306.67		
265	1	21	2003	1/21/2003	55	3	$12,840.06		
266	1	22	2003	1/22/2003	63	5	$6,247.03		
267	1	23	2003	1/23/2003	81	5	$8,088.60		
268	1	24	2003	1/24/2003	19	4	$6,113.00		
269	1	27	2003	1/27/2003	26	4	$2,814.98		
270	1	28	2003	1/28/2003	72	5	$7,923.37		
271	1	29	2003	1/29/2003	24	2	$17,407.77		
272	1	30	2003	1/30/2003	45	5	$6,685.78		
273	1	31	2003	1/31/2003	5	3	$4,074.56		
274							$2,778,981.81		
275									
276									
277									

Sheet1

Figure 6-7   Total amount for all insurance claims.

To sort data in the Spreadsheet Component, click the arrow next to the Sort Ascending or Sort Descending button and then select the field by which you want to sort the data. Repeat these steps to further sort the records using other fields.

Note   In the Office 2000 Spreadsheet Component, you must click inside the field and then click the Sort Ascending or Sort Descending button. The arrows are not available.

To filter data in the Spreadsheet Component, on the Spreadsheet Component's toolbar, click the AutoFilter button. Click the arrow next to each field name by which you want to filter. Select or clear the check boxes to display or hide matching records by the specified field items. Then click OK.

Tip   Select or clear the Show All and Blanks check boxes to display or hide all items or blank field values, respectively.

Putting It Together

In this exercise, you want to find the highest October claim. To do so, you will filter the records to show just the October claims and then sort the claims in descending order.

1.   In the Sales.htm file's Spreadsheet Component's toolbar, click the AutoFilter button.

2.   Click the arrow in cell A1.

3.   Clear the Show All check box, select the 10 check box, and then click OK.

4.   Click cell G1, and then on the Spreadsheet Component's toolbar, click Sort Descending. The highest claim for October was $19,297.08, as you can see in Figure 6-8.

	Month	Day	Year	Claim Date	Customer	Agent	Claim Amount
24	10	29	2002	10/29/2002	37	1	$19,297.08
25	10	22	2002	10/22/2002	35	5	$18,430.37
26	10	11	2002	10/11/2002	87	2	$18,105.22
27	10	30	2002	10/30/2002	0	2	$17,679.98
28	10	23	2002	10/23/2002	61	2	$17,673.29
29	10	4	2002	10/4/2002	34	4	$17,495.02
30	10	1	2002	10/1/2002	66	2	$17,430.72
31	10	28	2002	10/28/2002	97	4	$17,293.76
32	10	30	2002	10/30/2002	75	4	$17,073.40
33	10	14	2002	10/14/2002	29	4	$16,396.68
34	10	17	2002	10/17/2002	51	1	$15,265.64
35	10	14	2002	10/14/2002	88	3	$14,199.71
36	10	15	2002	10/15/2002	22	5	$13,858.16

Figure 6-8 Data can be sorted and filtered in a Spreadsheet Component at run time.

Office XP Spreadsheet Component Features

The Office XP Spreadsheet Component has some features that the Office 2000 Spreadsheet Component lacks, such as support for XML Spreadsheet formatted data, displaying multiple worksheets in a single Spreadsheet Component, and data-bound sheets. This section briefly describes these features.

XML Spreadsheet Data Support

Excel can save a workbook's data and layout characteristics in the form of an XML file. This allows a workbook's data and layout to be saved as plain text using the XML Spreadsheet schema, enabling greater use of the data in other software applications. (For more information about the XML Spreadsheet schema and using XML data in Excel, see Chapter 10, "Working with XML Data in Excel and Access.") Additionally, other software applications that save XML data in the XML Spreadsheet schema format can provide instructions for presenting the data using different colors, cell borders, and so on.

To import data formatted in the XML Spreadsheet schema into a Spreadsheet Component, first open the Web page containing the Spreadsheet Component in FrontPage. Open the Commands And Options dialog box, and then click the Import tab. Select XML in the Data Type list, type the location of the XML file, and click Import Now.

Multiple Worksheets

Just like its Excel counterpart, the Office XP Spreadsheet Component supports multiple worksheets. To switch between worksheets, click the worksheet tab near the bottom of the component and then click the worksheet you want to display.

To rename a sheet, display the Commands And Options dialog box, click the Workbook tab, click a sheet in the Sheet Name list, and then rename the sheet in the box above the list of worksheets.

> **Note**   You can rename worksheets at run time only if the Insert, Remove, Or Rename Sheets option on the Protection tab of the Commands And Options dialog box was selected at design time.

Data-Bound Sheets

The Spreadsheet Component can connect to data stored in databases such as those maintained in Microsoft SQL Server 2000. A data-bound sheet gets its data from a database object such as a table or view. The data displayed in the component can easily be refreshed by the user.

To bind a Spreadsheet Component in this manner, you use the Data Source tab on the Commands And Options dialog box at design time. On the Data Source tab, click the Sheet Data Source option. In the Connection box, type the connection string for the data source or click Edit and follow the directions in the dialog box to connect to the data source you want to use. If necessary, type the command text or SQL string you want to use to retrieve specific data from the data source in the Command Text Or SQL box.

Here's an example of a connection string, using a computer running SQL Server 2000 named *Server_Name* and a database named *Database_Name*:

```
Provider=SQLOLEDB.1;Integrated Security=SSPI;Persist Security Info=True;Data
Source=Server_Name;Use Procedure for Prepare=1;Auto Translate=True;Packet Size=
4096;Workstation ID=Workstation_Name;Use Encryption for Data=False;Tag with
column collation when possible=False;Initial Catalog=Database_Name
```

Most of the information in this string is provided by default as you select connections in the various data source dialog boxes. An example of a command text or SQL string that selects the Product ID and Product Name fields from a table named Alphabetical List of Products would be:

```
SELECT 'Alphabetical List of Products'.ProductID, 'Alphabetical List of
Products'.ProductName  FROM 'Alphabetical List of Products'
```

Using the PivotTable Component

The PivotTable Component brings many of the features of PivotTable reports to Web pages. Figure 6-9 shows a sample of the PivotTable Component.

Month ▾	Day ▾	Year ▾	Customer ID ▾	
All	All	All	All	

	Drop Column Fields Here
Agent ID ▾	Sum of Claim Amount
1	$272,025.42
2	$663,723.20
3	$578,964.08
4	$558,591.43
5	$509,461.88
6	$196,215.80
Grand Total	$2,778,981.81

Microsoft Office PivotTable 10.0

Figure 6-9   The Office XP PivotTable Component.

Here's a list of some of the controls on the PivotTable Component's toolbar, shown in Figure 6-10:

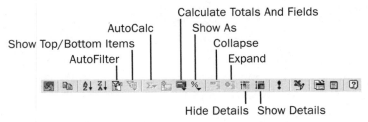

Figure 6-10   The Microsoft Office XP PivotTable Component's toolbar.

- AutoFilter places an arrow in each nondetail field. Clicking the arrow displays a list of values that you can use to select the records that match filter conditions.

- Show Top/Bottom Items (not available in Office 2000) displays only the top or bottom specified number of items.

- AutoCalc adds a field to the PivotTable field list that represents a summarization, such as Sum, Min, Max, Average, and so on. This field can be dragged to the Detail area of the PivotTable Component.

- Calculated Totals and Fields (not available in Office 2000) adds calculated totals and calculated detail fields.

- Show As (not available in Office 2000) displays numerical data as a percentage of totals or items.

- Collapse (not available in Office 2000) reduces the amount of detail displayed in the PivotTable Component for the selected field.

- Expand increases the amount of detail displayed in the PivotTable Component for the selected field.

- Hide Details (not available in Office 2000) hides detail in the Detail area of the PivotTable Component.

- Show Details (not available in Office 2000) shows detail in the Detail area of the PivotTable Component.

The PivotTable Component, like the SpreadSheet Component, uses the Commands And Options dialog box at design time to set up options for how data is displayed and managed in the PivotTable. Depending on which aspect of the PivotTable you are working with, not all the tabs are visible. Figure 6-11 shows some of the main tabs you'll work with.

- The Captions tab controls the appearance and text displayed in the PivotTable Component's title bar and drop zones. It also displays properties of the component, such as the name of the data provider.

- The Report tab defines subtotal display behaviors as well as other report display options.

- The Behavior tab shows or hides viewable display elements, automatically adjusts the size of the control, and determines items and display-expansion behaviors.

- The Protection tab provides you with greater flexibility for how users can modify the PivotTable Component's layout at run time by allowing or prohibiting users from interacting with certain portions of the PivotTable Component.

- The Data Source tab defines data source connectivity information.

- The Calculation tab (not shown in Figure 6-11) defines formulas for custom calculated totals and detail fields.

- The Filter And Group tab (also not shown) displays the top and bottom items and determines grouping behavior.

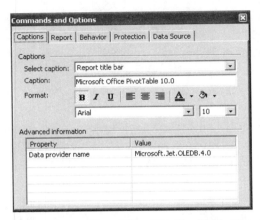

Figure 6-11   The Office XP PivotTable Component's Commands and Options window (at design time).

The PivotTable Component's Commands And Options dialog box has other tabs at run time. These tabs are shown in Figure 6-12.

Figure 6-12   The Office XP PivotTable Component's Commands And Options dialog box at run time. The appearance of the dialog box varies depending on the layout of the PivotTable Component.

> **Note**   The Office 2000 PivotTable Component's Property Toolbox looks slightly different from the Office XP PivotTable Component's Commands And Options dialog box, but many of the features are the same.

Linking to data from a PivotTable Component is similar to importing data into a Spreadsheet Component. Click the Data Source tab on the Commands And Options dialog box and complete the information to link to the external data.

> **Note**   In the Office 2000 PivotTable Component in design time, click the Property Toolbox button, click the Data Source tab, and then complete the information in the Property Toolbox to import the external data.

Analyzing PivotTable Component Data

With data displayed in a PivotTable component, you can perform data analysis tasks on the data. To sort data in the PivotTable Component, click the field name by which you want to sort and then click the Sort Ascending or Sort Descending button.

Your Turn

In this exercise, you want to sort insurance claim totals by agent number so that the highest total appears at the top of the list.

1.   In the Sales.htm file's PivotTable Component, click the Sum of Claim Amount field.

2.   On the PivotTable toolbar, click Sort Descending. Compare your results to Figure 6-13. Agent 2 had the highest insurance claim total of $663,723.20.

(continued)

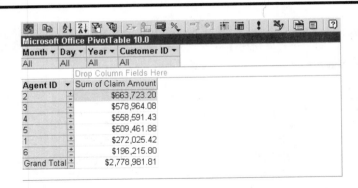

Figure 6-13   Claims by agent sorted by total claims in descending order.

To filter data in the PivotTable Component, click the arrow next to the field name by which you want to filter, select or clear the check boxes to display or hide matching items, and then click OK. Select or clear the All check box to display or hide all of the items.

Your Turn

In this exercise, you will display claims for agent 2 for only the month of January.

1.   In the Sales.htm file's PivotTable Component, click the arrow next to the Month field.

2.   Clear the All check box, select the 1 check box, and then click OK.

3.   Click the arrow next to the Agent ID field.

4.   Clear the All check box, select the 2 check box, and then click OK. Compare your results to Figure 6-14.

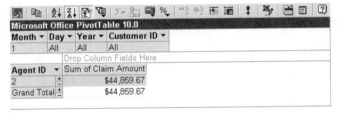

Figure 6-14   Claims for January for agent 2.

To show the top or bottom items in the PivotTable Component (Office XP only), click the field for which you want to show the top or bottom items. On the PivotTable Component's toolbar, click the Show Top/Bottom Items button, point to Show Only The Top or Show Only The Bottom, and then click the number of items you want to display.

> **Tip**   Click the Other menu option to provide more specific criteria for selecting top or bottom items.

Your Turn

In this exercise, you will display the three agents with the largest (top) total claim amounts.

1.   In the Sales.htm file's PivotTable Component, click the arrow next to the Agent ID field.

2.   Make sure that all agents are selected by selecting the All check box, and then click OK.

3.   Click the arrow next to the Month field, make sure that all months are selected by selecting the All check box, and then click OK.

4.   Click the Agent ID field, and then, on the PivotTable toolbar, click Show Top/Bottom Items, point to Show Only the Top, and click Other.

5.   In the Display The list, select Top.

6.   In the Items list, type *3*.

7.   In the Based On list, select Sum Of Claim Amount.

8.   Close the Commands And Options window.

9.   On the PivotTable toolbar, click the Sort Descending button, and compare your results to Figure 6-15.

(continued)

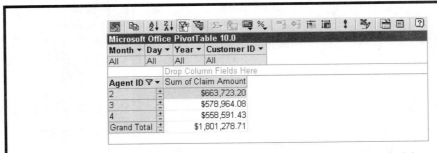

Figure 6-15   Top three agents as determined by total claims.

To insert a summary function into a PivotTable Component, click the field for which you want to insert the function. On the PivotTable Component's toolbar, click the AutoCalc button, and then click the summary function (Sum, Count, Min, Max, and so on).

Your Turn

In this exercise, you will display the number of claims processed by each agent.

1.   In the Sales.htm file's PivotTable Component, make sure that all items are showing; on the PivotTable Component's toolbar, click the Show Top/Bottom Items, and then click Show All.

2.   Click the Customer ID field.

3.   On the PivotTable Component's toolbar, click the AutoCalc field, and then click Count. Compare your results to Figure 6-16.

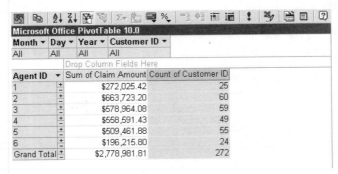

Figure 6-16   Number of claims processed by agent.

To insert a subtotal into a PivotTable Component, click the field for which you want to insert a subtotal. On the PivotTable Component's toolbar, click the Subtotal button.

Your Turn

In this exercise, you will add a total for all of the agent's insurance claim amounts.

1. In the Sales.htm file's PivotTable Component, click the Agent ID field.

2. On the PivotTable Component's toolbar, click the Subtotal button. Compare your results to Figure 6-17.

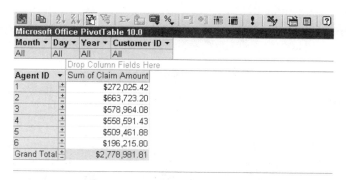

Figure 6-17   Total claim amount for all agents.

Calculated totals and detail fields (Office XP only) allow you to enhance data with summarizations and other fields that aren't available in the original data source. For instance, you might want to determine how a seasonal store-wide markdown in prices would affect profitability on specific products, but this type of analysis can't currently be made in the external data source.

To insert calculated totals and detail fields into the PivotTable Component, on the PivotTable Component's toolbar, click the Calculated Totals And Fields button. Click the option you want, either to create a calculated total or to create a calculated detail field. Assign the calculated total or calculated field a name and a formula, and then drag the total or field from the PivotTable field list to the PivotTable Component.

Your Turn

In this exercise, you will insert a calculated total representing administrative fees of 1.5 percent to process agents' claims.

1. In the Sales.htm file's PivotTable Component's toolbar, click the Calculated Totals And Fields button, and then click Create Calculated Total.

2. In the Name box, type Administrative Fees.

3. In the list next to the Insert Reference To button, select Sum Of Claim Amount (Total).

4. Click the Insert Reference To button.

5. In the formula that appears, type * 0.015 so that the formula looks like this: *[Measures].[Total1] * 0.015*.

6. Click Change.

7. Close the Commands And Options window, and compare your results to Figure 6-18.

> **Tip** To format the Administratives Fees field to look like currency, click the Administrative Fees field in the PivotTable Component, click Commands And Options on the PivotTable Component's toolbar, click the Format tab, and select Currency in the Number list.

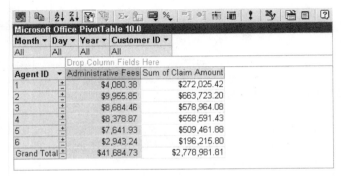

Figure 6-18 Total administrative fees to process insurance claims.

Additional Office XP PivotTable Component Features

The Office XP PivotTable Component has some features that the Office 2000 PivotTable Component does not support, such as custom grouping and custom grouping intervals and enhanced support for percentages as totals. This section briefly describes these features.

Custom Grouping and Custom Grouping Intervals

With custom grouping, you can randomly select items from a row or column field and group them into higher-level groups. For example, in the Sales.htm file, you can select from an Agent ID row field all of the sales agent IDs that exist in a particular geographic region and create a group. This would add a new row field named Agent ID1 with two members: Group1 and Other. You can change the caption of Group1 to West and Agent ID1 to Region in the Commands And Options dialog box. The Other group will contain all items that you did not include in the new West group. You can then rename the Other group to Other Regions, and the Region field will have two members: West and Other Regions.

To create a custom group, click the label of the parent field that contains the items you want to group, and then click Expand on the PivotTable Component's toolbar. Click the first item that you want to include in the group. To select more items, hold down the Ctrl key and click each item. Right-click a selected item, and then click Group Items. To remove a custom group from being displayed, right-click the group caption and then click Ungroup Items. To remove a custom group field altogether, right-click the field, and then click Delete.

You can also specify custom grouping intervals, such as to group Agent IDs 1 through 3 together, 4 through 6 together, and so on. To do so, select the row or column field whose items you want to group. On the PivotTable Component's toolbar, click Commands And Options, and then click the Filter And Group tab. Select an item in the Group Items By list (other than No Grouping). Set Interval to the value you want. To specify the value at which grouping begins, select the Start At check box and then type a value in the accompanying box. To specify the value at which grouping ends, select the End At check box and then type a value in the accompanying box. To remove a custom grouping interval, select No Grouping in the Group Items By list.

Percentages as Totals

Instead of summary totals, you can show totals as percentages. For instance, you can show the percentage that each sales agent contributed to total sales instead of showing the actual dollar amounts. Right-click the total field whose values you want to view as percentages, point to Show As, and then select one of the following options:

- Click Percent Of Row Total to display the values as a percentage of the total value of each row.

- Click Percent Of Column Total to display the values as a percentage of the total value of the selected column.

- Click Percent Of Parent Row Item to display the values as a percentage of the total value of the item's parent in the row field.

- Click Percent Of Parent Column Item to display the values as a percentage of the total value of the item's parent in the column field.

- Click Percent Of Grand Total to display the values as a percentage of the grand total.

Using the Chart Component

The Chart Component brings much of the PivotChart report features that you learned about in Chapter 4 to Web pages. Just like PivotChart reports, a Chart Component can synchronize its data and layout characteristics to match a linked PivotTable Component on the same Web page. Figure 6-19 shows a sample of the Chart Component.

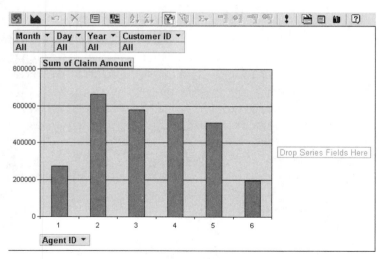

Figure 6-19   The Office XP Chart Component.

Here's a list of some of the controls on the PivotTable Component's toolbar, which is shown in Figure 6-20: :

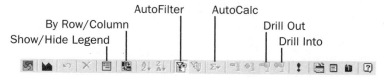

Figure 6-20   The Microsoft Office XP Chart Component's toolbar.

■ Show/Hide Legend shows or hides the chart legend.

■ By Row/Column changes the emphasis on which aspects of data you want to compare by changing which parts of your data appear as categories and which appear as series.

■ AutoFilter places an arrow in each nondetail field. Clicking the arrow displays a list of values that you can use to select items that match filter conditions.

■ AutoCalc adds a field to the Chart field list that represents a summarization such as Sum, Min, Max, Average, and so on. This field can be dragged to the Data area of the Chart Component.

■ Drill Out removes detailed information for a particular item.

■ Drill Into focuses on more detailed information for a particular item.

> **Note**   The Office 2000 Chart Component does not support a toolbar.

The tabs on the Chart Component's Commands And Options dialog box at design time again include a series of options and settings that affect the data displayed in the chart. Some of the tabs aren't visible unless you are working with a specific aspect of the chart. Some of the main tabs in the dialog box are shown in Figure 6-21.

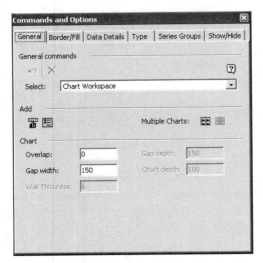

Figure 6-21 The Office XP Chart Component's Commands And Options dialog box at design time.

- The General tab selects chart items and determines widths, depths, and thicknesses of chart display elements.

- The Border/Fill tab determines the display of the chart borders and background fill.

- The Data Details tab defines data source connectivity information.

- The Type tab determines the chart display type.

- The Series Groups tab determines the behaviors of series fields and axes.

- The Show/Hide tab displays or hides chart display elements.

- The Conditional Format tab colors chart display elements based on data values.

- The Line/Marker tab changes the display of chart lines and data markers.

- The Axis tab changes the display of ticks, grid lines, and axes.

- The Scale tab changes the behavior and order of crossing axes and timescales.

The Chart Component displays many of the same tabs in the Commands And Options window at run time.

> **Note**   The Office 2000 Chart Component's Property Toolbox looks slightly different from the Office XP Chart Component's Commands And Options dialog box, but many of the features are the same. To display the Office 2000 Chart Component's Property Toolbox in design time, right-click a blank area of the Chart Component and click Property Toolbox. The Office 2000 Chart Component does not support a run-time version of the Property Toolbox.

Linking a Chart Component to data is slightly different from linking a PivotTable Component to data or importing data into a Spreadsheet Component. To link a Chart Component to data you use the Chart Wizard at design time. The Chart Wizard opens another version of the Commands And Options dialog box, which provides the Data Source tab on which you complete the information about the data you are linking to.

> **Note**   For the Office 2000 Chart Component, you link to existing data when you create the Chart Component through the Chart Wizard. You cannot switch to another data source unless you create another Chart Component from scratch.

Analyzing Chart Component Data

The Chart Component allows you to switch its chart type and also to sort, filter, insert summary functions, and drill into or out of data.

> **Note**   The rest of the procedures and exercises in this section can be performed only in Office XP.

To change a Chart Component's chart type, on the Chart Component's toolbar, click the Chart Type button. Then select the new chart type.

Your Turn

In this exercise, you will change the chart type from a column chart to a line chart.

1. Click anywhere inside the Sales.htm file's Chart Component.

2. On the Chart Component's toolbar, click the Chart Type button.

3. Click SmoothLine, and then click the sample chart for "Smooth Line. Displays Trend Over Time or Categories," the first item in the first row on the Type tab.

4. Compare your results to Figure 6-22.

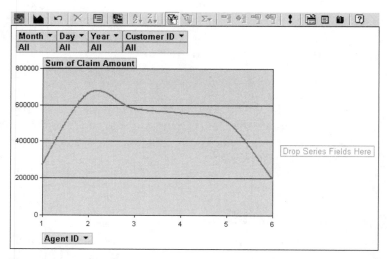

Figure 6-22 The smooth line chart type.

To return to the original chart type, in the Commands And Options dialog box, click Column and then click the sample chart for "Clustered Column. Compares Values Across Categories."

To sort data in a Chart Component, select the detail items by which you want to sort and then click the Sort Ascending or Sort Descending button.

Your Turn

In this exercise, you will display claim totals in descending order, from left to right, on the Chart Component.

1.   On the Sales.htm file's Chart Component, click inside a column.

2.   On the Chart Component's toolbar, click the Sort Descending button. Compare your results to Figure 6-23.

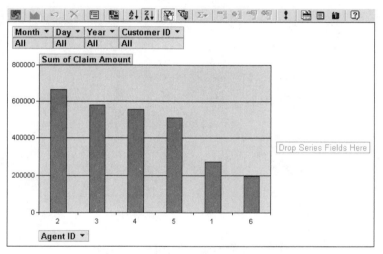

Figure 6-23   Claim totals in descending order from left to right.

To filter data in a Chart Component, click the arrow next to the field name you want to filter by. Select or clear the check boxes to display or hide matching items. Then click OK. Select or clear the All check box to display or hide all of the items.

Your Turn

In this exercise, you will display only December's claim totals in the Chart Component.

1. In the Sales.htm file's Chart Component, click the arrow next to the Month field.

2. Clear the All check box, select the 12 check box, and click OK. Compare your results to Figure 6-24, which shows the claims amounts sorted in ascending order by agent ID.

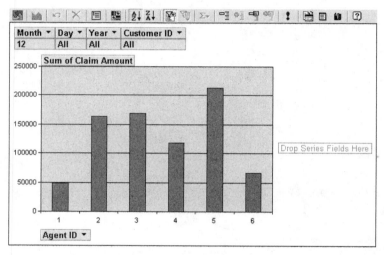

Figure 6-24   Claim totals for December only.

To undo the filter, click the arrow next to the Month field, select the All check box, and then click OK.

To show the top or bottom number of items in a Chart Component, click the detail item for which you want to show the top or bottom items. On the Chart Component's toolbar, click the Show Top/Bottom Items button, point to the Show Only The Top or Show Only The Bottom, and then click the number of items you want to show. Use the Other menu option to provide more specific top and bottom criteria.

Your Turn

In this exercise, you will display the three agents with the lowest total claim amounts.

1. In the Sales.htm file's Chart Component, click a column.

2. On the Chart Component's toolbar, click Show Top/Bottom Items, point to Show Only The Bottom, and then click Other.

3. In the Display The list, select Bottom.

4. In the Items list, type *3*.

5. In the Based On list, select Sum Of Claim Amount.

6. Close the Commands And Options window.

7. Click a column, and on the Chart Component toolbar, click the Sort Descending button. Compare your results to Figure 6-25.

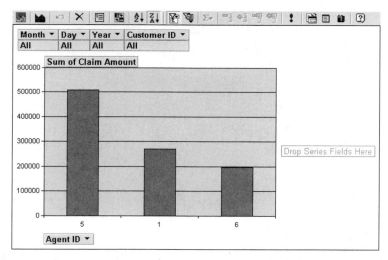

Figure 6-25 Bottom three agents as determined by total claims for all months.

To restore the chart's full data, click the Show Top/Bottom Items button and then click Show All.

To insert a summary function into a Chart Component, click the detail field for which you want to insert a function. Click the AutoCalc button, and then click the summary function (Sum, Count, Min, Max, and so on).

Your Turn

In this exercise, you will display in the Chart Component the total number of claims processed by each agent.

1. In the Sales.htm file's Chart Component, click the Sum Of Claim Amount field.

2. On the Chart Component's toolbar, click the AutoCalc button and then click Count. Compare your results to Figure 6-26.

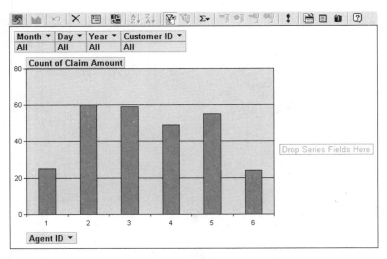

Figure 6-26   Number of claims processed by agent.

To return back to where you started, open the Commands And Options dialog box, click the Format tab, click a number in the vertical axis, and then select Currency in the Number list. Click the Count Of Claim Amount field, click the AutoCalc button, and then click Sum.

To show or hide detailed data (to drill out of or into data) in a Chart Component, click the item on the category axis that you want to examine. On the Chart Component's toolbar, click Drill Out or Drill Into.

Your Turn

In this exercise, you will drill into claim details for agent 5.

1.   In the Sales.htm file's Chart Component, drag the Month and Day fields next to the Agent ID field.

2.   In the category axis, click the number 5.

3.   On the Chart Component's toolbar, click the Drill Into button.

4.   On the category axis, click the number 12.

5.   On the Chart Component's toolbar, click the Drill Into button again.

6.   Click the arrow next to the Agent ID field, clear the All check box, check the 5 check box, and then click OK. Compare your results to Figure 6-27.

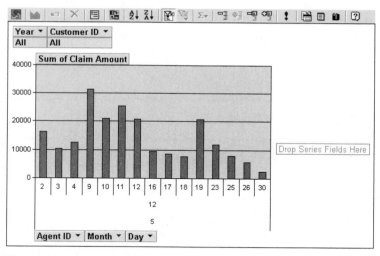

Figure 6-27   December claim amounts by day for agent 5.

Additional Office XP Chart Component Features

The Office XP Chart Component includes some features that the Office 2000 Chart Component does not support, such as a built-in datasheet and direct data binding. This section briefly describes these features.

Built-In Datasheet

The data source for a Chart Component is usually a database table or query, or data from another Web Component on the Web page. You can also create a Chart Component that gets its data from values you supply in a datasheet attached to the component.

To specify a datasheet as the Chart Component's data source, click Chart Wizard on the Chart Component's toolbar. On the Data Source tab, click Data Typed Into A Datasheet. Click the Data Sheet button, and then enter data for the category and the series of values. After typing values for the chart, press Enter to create additional rows and columns for chart values.

Direct Data Binding

Similar to the Spreadsheet Component, the Chart Component can connect to data stored in databases such as SQL Server 2000. To bind a Chart Component in this manner, click the Data Source tab in the Chart Component's Commands And Options dialog box. Click Data From A Database Table Or Query, and then click the Connection button. On the Data Details tab, type the connection string for the data source, or click Edit and follow the directions in the dialog box to connect to the data source you want to use. If necessary, type the command text or SQL string you want to use to retrieve specific data in the Command Text Or SQL box.

Summary

In this chapter, you learned the following:

- The Spreadsheet Component, the PivotTable Component, and the Chart Component can be used to sort, filter, group, conditionally format, and perform other data analysis tasks over the Web.

- You can use Microsoft FrontPage to create Office Web Components in Web pages. You can also use the Office Web Components to host data published from Microsoft Excel workbooks on Web pages.

    In the next chapter, "Introducing Online Analytical Processing," you will learn

- What online analytical processing (OLAP) and online transaction processing (OLTP) are, and why they are important in the data analysis field.

- How OLAP can be used to inform business decisions.

- How OLAP features are used in Microsoft Office.

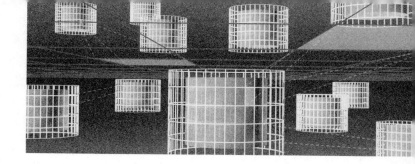

7

Introducing Online Analytical Processing

Until now, you have explored relational data, such as a set of data tables in a Microsoft Access database, and nonrelational data, such as groups of records in Microsoft Excel worksheets. This chapter introduces you to a different type of data, known as *multidimensional data* or *hierarchical data*. The technology field that deals with this type of data is known as *online analytical processing*, or OLAP.

Just about any relational or nonrelational data source with field values that can be organized hierarchically (time measurements such as years, months, and weeks; geographical areas such as countries, regions, and cities; business reporting structures such as executives, managers, and subordinates) can benefit from OLAP applications.

Objectives

In this chapter, you will learn

- How data can be structured hierarchically, making it different from relational and nonrelational data.

- How you can analyze multidimensional data with online analytical processing (OLAP) software applications to make better business decisions.

- How online transactional processing (OLTP) systems work in conjunction with OLAP systems to make the entry and storage of business transaction data easier and more efficient.

- Which Microsoft applications you can use to analyze multi-dimensional data.

The Case for OLAP

Online analytical processing (OLAP) refers to a category of business applications that are used to store and analyze large, relatively complex data sources in business disciplines such as sales and marketing analysis, budgeting, resource planning, performance measurement, and other types of business reporting. Although OLAP is not a new concept, it is still not widely understood.

Many organizations have anywhere from hundreds of megabytes to upward of several terabytes of related data, yet these organizations use software applications that are not optimized for analyzing this amount of data, or they don't use the data analysis software they have to their full benefit. It is impossible to load several hundred thousand records into a single Excel workbook or tens of gigabytes of data into a single Access database. Likewise, organizations might have dozens or even hundreds of employees entering data into a single database at the same time. When very large databases are being used by dozens or hundreds of both data-entry workers and data-analysis workers at the same time, the database systems' resources can be stretched to their operational limits, bringing entire systems to a standstill.

So what is the answer from a software perspective? Currently, many businesses use limited and inefficient approaches. For smaller data sources, several Excel workbooks might exist on a network computer, with each workbook containing only a portion of the data, typed in by a single employee. The problem with this approach is that there is no straightforward way to combine or aggregate the data from the separate workbooks into a single workbook, where analysis of the complete set of data can occur. Also, subtotals and PivotTable reports work very slowly when a lot of data is being analyzed because Excel has to calculate summarizations every time new figures are needed. And, if any single workbook is compromised for some reason, it is difficult if not impossible to recover the data.

For larger data sources, several Access databases might exist on a network computer, with each database containing a portion of the data, and several employees entering data into each database. This approach is better than using

Excel workbooks because you don't have to require users to stop working on the data when you want to analyze data or build reports, you have built-in features to handle relational data, and you have more options for data disaster recovery. However, Access limits the number of simultaneous users per database and imposes a limit of two gigabytes of data per database.

For very large data sources of several gigabytes or more—as well as for databases that require several dozens, hundreds, or thousands or users—organizations often use server-based database management systems such as Microsoft SQL Server. SQL Server databases have a lot of headroom; they can handle terabytes of data and thousands of simultaneous users, and they have a high degree of data disaster recovery, including the ability to recover individual data records that have been compromised.

However, even with SQL Server, there can be scenarios in which a database designed primarily to record business transactions responds very slowly to simultaneous data entry and data analysis requests. For instance, some travel agents might be accessing a database to book flights and reserve hotel rooms at the same time that a marketing specialist is using the database to analyze sales for the last quarter. The travel agents have to put customers on hold because the database server is responding too slowly. Likewise, the marketing specialist may complain that her tasks take too long. The travel agents cannot tell the marketing specialist to do her work only during off-peak hours, and the marketing specialist obviously cannot tell the travel agents to stop helping customers..

The solution for analyzing data in very large databases, databases with many simultaneous users, or databases with several relational data tables, is to use an OLAP software application such as Microsoft SQL Server 2000 Analysis Services. Analysis Services can take a copy of an organization's data, efficiently organize the data, and calculate summarizations of the data ahead of time. This allows both data-entry and data-analysis workers to benefit from huge performance gains because data analysts are working with a copy of the data, using summarizations that have been calculated ahead of time in categories that data analysts need (fiscal quarters, net revenue, and so on). Even smaller databases can benefit from the data storage, data compression, and resource optimization features of Analysis Services.

What Is OLAP?

To understand how OLAP data and Analysis Services work, you need to understand a little bit of what happens behind the scenes, as well as some of the terminology used to describe portions of the data and the summarizations that are generated in OLAP.

To help introduce the principles of OLAP, a small sample database is provided in the form of an Excel workbook, named CarSales.xls, in the Chap07 folder. This sample database lists the sales of 1000 cars over two years' time for a regional specialty automotive dealership. The first 10 records of the database are shown in Figure 7-1.

	A	B	C	D	E	F	G	H	I	J	K	L	M
1	Day	Month	Year	Quarter	Customer Sales Region	Customer State	Sales Manager ID	Salesperson ID	Car Series	Car Type	Color	Payment Type	Price
2	27	10	2001	4	West	CA	100	2	Standard	Station Wagon	Blue	60 Monthly Payments	26000
3	10	2	2002	1	West	WA	100	2	Standard	Coupe	Blue	48 Monthly Payments	31000
4	28	8	2002	3	West	WA	101	4	Deluxe	Sport Utility	Black	60 Monthly Payments	24000
5	31	10	2002	4	West	CA	101	4	Standard	Sedan	Black	48 Monthly Payments	35000
6	18	12	2002	4	West	WA	101	4	Deluxe	Minivan	Blue	36 Month Lease	34000
7	30	10	2002	4	West	CA	101	5	Deluxe	Sedan	Green	36 Month Lease	27000
8	10	8	2002	3	West	WA	101	4	Standard	Minivan	White	60 Monthly Payments	24000
9	9	9	2002	3	West	CA	102	8	Standard	Minivan	Blue	60 Monthly Payments	25000
10	11	2	2002	1	West	OR	101	5	Standard	Minivan	White	48 Monthly Payments	20000

Figure 7-1   First 10 records of the sample car sales OLAP database.

As you look at the data, notice that each record, or row, contains a lot of data. The more data, or facts, available, the more specific the business questions are that you can ask of the data. In OLAP terms, this group of records is called a *fact table* because it contains the detailed business facts you'll use in meaningful business analysis.

Also notice that the data is separated into its most basic components. For example, the date is separated into day, month, year, and quarter, unlike in many databases, in which a date is presented as a single field. Using our example, in a non-OLAP database, the car information might be stored in one field for the car series and type. In the fact table, the car series and type are stored in two separate fields. Information is stored in this detailed fashion so that an OLAP software application can return data summarizations for a wide range of potential business questions in the least amount of time. With data separated into its most basic parts, the OLAP software application can quickly interchange these parts depending on the data analysis task or business question at hand.

The third thing to notice in the sample database is that the data can be organized by relating fields to each other in a hierarchical fashion. For instance

- The Day, Month, Year, and Quarter fields can be organized into a Time category.

- The Customer Sales Region and Customer State fields can be organized into a Sales Geography category.

- The Sales Manager ID and Salesperson ID fields can be organized into a Sales Staff category.

- The Car Series, Car Type, and Color fields can be organized into a Car Information category.

These categories are known as *dimensions* in OLAP terminology. Dimensions, the basic organizational unit of OLAP, are typically presented in terms of dates, geographical areas, product and service offerings, employee reporting structures, and other organizational hierarchies. For instance, the Customer State field could be split further into cities, counties, or sales districts.

You can classify the data in each dimension by using groupings called *levels*. Levels describe groupings from the most summarized (highest) to the most detailed (lowest) level of data in a dimension. For example, the Time dimension contains Year, Quarter, Month, and Day levels because you can look at summarizations by year, then by quarter, then by month, and finally by day. In this example, other levels include the following:

- The Region level contains states.

- The Sales Manager ID level contains salespeople's IDs—one or more salespeople report to a particular sales manager.

- The Car Series level contains car types, which in turn contains car colors.

The individual collections of unique values contained in a level are known as *members*. A dimension that does not contain other levels, such as the Payment Type dimension, has one level with the same name as the dimension. Every member has a parent level, and every level contains child levels, child members, or both. Members at the bottom-most level of a dimension are sometimes referred to as *leaf members*. In our sample database, note the following:

- The Year level has 2 child members—2000 and 2001—as well as a child level (Quarter).

- The Quarter level has 4 child members (1, 2, 3, and 4) as well as a child level (Month).

- The Month level has 12 child members (the months numbered 1 through 12) as well as a child level (Day).

- The Day level contains 31 child members, or leaf members (1 through 31).

- The Customer Sales Region level contains only 1 member in this case (West) and a child level (Customer State).

- The Customer State level contains 3 leaf members (CA, OR, and WA).

- The Sales Manager ID level contains 4 members (100, 101, 102, and 103) as well as a child level (Salesperson ID).

- The Salesperson ID level contains 10 leaf members, numbered 1 through 10.

- The Car Series level contains 2 members (Standard and Deluxe) and the Car Type child level.

- The Car Type level contains 5 members (Coupe, Minivan, Sedan, Sport Utility, and Station Wagon), as well as a child level (Color).

- The Color level contains 5 leaf members (Black, Blue, Green, Red, and White).

- The Payment Type level contains 4 leaf members (36 Month Lease, 48 Monthly Payments, 60 Monthly Payments, and Cash).

Where does this leave the fields with numerical measurements, such as the Price field? These fields are called *measures* because, in a sense, we are measuring data in terms of how much money or another numerical measurement. In this sample database, we do not consider the sales manager IDs or salesperson IDs measures because you would never ask a business question such as what is the sum of all of the salesperson IDs? Instead you might ask a business question such as what is the sum of all car sales for the salesperson with the ID of 9? Every OLAP database must contain at least one measure. An OLAP database's dimensions, levels, members, measures, and summarizations are stored in what OLAP calls a *cube*.

To review, the sample database contains the following OLAP components:

- The Time dimension, which contains the Year, Quarter, Month, and Day levels

- The Sales Geography dimension, which contains the Customer Sales Region and Customer State levels

- The Sales Staff dimension, which contains the Sales Manager ID and Salesperson ID levels

- The Car Information dimension, which contains the Car Series, Car Type, and Color levels

- The Payment Type dimension, which contains a single Payment Type level

- The Price measure, which is the only measure in the sample database

For a graphical approximation of this sample database, see Figure 7-2.

Figure 7-2   Visual representation of the sample car sales OLAP database.

In the next section, you will learn how to put these concepts to use in analyzing OLAP data.

Using OLAP Data to Make Better Business Decisions

If you know the names of the dimensions, levels, and measures in an OLAP cube, you can ask some fairly complex business questions of the data. Using the sample car sales database as an example, you might want to ask business questions such as

- In which quarter were car sales the greatest when viewed by payment type?

- Year over year, what was the average standard car type sale in the individual states of the West region as compared to average deluxe car type sales?

- What was the best day of the month to sell sport utility vehicles for cash in Oregon, and how much income was generated from these sales compared to sport utility sales in Washington ?

- Month over month, what were the largest and smallest sticker prices for each of the combinations of car series, car types, colors, and payment types for California car buyers?

Knowing how your data is organized enables you to determine whether the business questions that you ask can actually be answered by the data. Using the car sales data example, you wouldn't be able to determine excise taxes collected as a portion of car sales; you could only determine total car sales.

> **Note**   If you determine that your questions cannot be answered by the way your data is organized, you have two options: revise your business questions, or collect and enter the missing data into the database. Make sure that you are collecting, entering, storing, and organizing as much data about your business activities as possible, both from a practical and legal perspective.

How many questions can you ask of the data in the sample car sales figures? If you multiply the number of possible sale dates by the number of possible sales regions, the number of possible sales manager and salesperson combinations, and so on, you can easily come up with hundreds or thousands of questions. But it does not end there. Now take each of these questions and multiply them by the number of available measures. Fortunately, this sample cube has only a Price measure. But if it also included a Sales Tax measure, an Odometer Reading measure, a Finance Percentage measure, and so on, the number of business questions you could ask could quickly grow to a staggeringly enormous number.

When you are working with a non-OLAP database, every time you ask a new business question, the data analysis software must perform a series of possibly complex calculations and summarizations to provide the answer. The need to perform these calculations is usually not an issue when up to a few thousand records are in the mix, but processing hundreds of thousands or more records could result in considerable waiting time while the data analysis application forms the answer. Just think what would happen if data-entry employees were using the same database to enter business data? You can see the implications for database downtime pretty easily.

In an OLAP database, the OLAP software takes snapshots of the data at selected time intervals. With a process known as *aggregation,* OLAP software can ask business questions ahead of any request and store the answers for retrieval. When you ask a question for which the answer has been calculated, the OLAP software immediately returns the answer to you. If the OLAP application hasn't yet addressed the question you pose, it should still be able to answer the question very quickly because it can calculate the answer from other aggregations already stored. For example, let's say I want to know the average car sales price for the sales manager with the ID of 101. If the OLAP application did not have the answer to this question already, but it did know the sum of the car sales for each salesperson, the application could quickly determine the sum of the car sales for the salespeople that report to the specific sales manager.

Even with small databases, transitioning data to an OLAP structure makes sense, especially if the amount of the data will grow.

Understanding Online Transaction Processing

OLAP applications are designed for data analysis. However, OLAP applications are not designed for recording the business transactions that make up the data. On the other hand, online transaction processing (OLTP) applications are designed for recording business transactions, but OLTP applications are not designed for data analysis. In this sense, OLAP and OLTP software applications complement each other and both types of applications are the foundation of sound data collection and data analysis systems.

It's easy to understand why OLTP software is important to a good data-gathering strategy. You know that every time you purchase goods or services, you participate in a sales transaction. For legal auditing purposes, every sales transaction must have a set of data, or business facts, associated with it. Often, sellers record the following facts about their sales transactions:

- Some portion of the buyer's personal information, such as a preferred customer number, a phone number, a name, and so on.

- Some portion of the seller's information, such as the location where the sale was made, the location's phone number and address, and so on.

- General information about the goods or services sold—descriptions, quantities purchased, the price charged per item.

- Whether the item was taxable, whether any discounts were applied, the payment type (cash, personal check, credit card), and so on.

- The date and time the sale was made.

To ensure that sales transactions are recorded in the least amount of time possible, OLTP applications are used to enable quick data entry. For instance, in most retail preferred-customer programs, a cashier asks for just the customer's phone number or requires the customer to swipe a preferred-customer card through a card reader. The phone number can be used to locate the customer's information, or the card's magnetic strip might contain all the information. If the cashier had to ask every person in line for their customer information before they could qualify for special purchase offers or discounts, many customers would probably stop doing business with that organization because of the inconvenience.

Likewise, a good OLTP software system can associate data with transactions when it needs to cross-reference sales prices, sales tax rates, applicable discounts, and so on. OLTP systems are important for any business or industry in which transactions are necessary, and when you think about it, finding a business or industry that does not record transactions of some type is pretty hard.

The reason that OLTP is an important counterpart to OLAP is that many organizations try to use the software applications they have to do too many data collection, storage, and analysis tasks that the applications weren't designed for. Most data collection and storage software applications cannot devote precious computer processing time to serve as data analysis systems, and almost all data analysis systems cannot handle the sheer volume of real-time transactions that need to be entered by data-entry workers.

For effective data collection, storage, and analysis computer systems, you need a combination of OLTP and OLAP software applications, and the tools to analyze the data:

- Excel is considered to be one of the best software applications for data analysis. It is not considered either an OLTP or OLAP solution, but it can be used to analyze OLAP data, as you'll see in the next chapter.

- Microsoft Data Analyzer is optimized for analyzing OLAP data, but it can't be used as either an OLTP or an OLAP system when it comes to collection or storage.

- Access can serve as a lightweight OLTP system, but it is not considered an OLAP solution.

- Microsoft SQL Server 2000 is regarded as an ideal OLTP solution, but it alone is not considered an OLAP solution.

- Microsoft SQL Server 2000 Analysis Services is considered the premier OLAP solution, but it cannot serve as an OLTP system.

For more information about OLTP systems, see Microsoft SQL Server 2000 Books Online, which is included with the product.

Data Storage Options

When organizations make the switch to a combination of OLTP and OLAP computer systems, they frequently do not plan their computer network architectures fully. Usually, these organizations go through a trial-and-error approach, in which they deploy their computer systems, realize that mistakes were made, and then deploy the same computer systems again. The results of redeployment are usually significant in both time and money. Planning a good data storage strategy is one of the most vital components to successfully deploying an efficient OLTP/OLAP system.

Storing large amounts of data on individual laptop and desktop computers, or on network computers without data recovery mechanisms such as backups in place, can lead to disaster if the data is ever compromised or lost. Products such as SQL Server provide for backups, transaction recovery and transaction rollbacks, advanced indexing for finding data more quickly, and automated database management wizards. (Chapter 12, "Maintaining Data Reporting and Analysis Systems," covers data management in more detail.)

A business environment in which a lot of simultaneous OLTP and OLAP tasks are performed requires both dedicated OLTP database server computers and dedicated OLAP database server computers. The OLTP databases are used strictly for data entry, and the OLAP databases are used strictly for data analysis. During time periods when the OLTP databases are inactive (for instance, nights and holidays), the OLAP database server computer can make a copy of the OLTP data and store it in a separate database, called a *data mart*. In practical terms, for smaller organizations this means that a server computer running SQL Server will accept OLTP data in a single database during business hours, another SQL Server database on the same server will warehouse the OLTP data during off-business hours, and an instance of SQL Server 2000 Analysis Services will analyze the warehoused OLTP data. This, of course, assumes that the SQL Server 2000 server computer has enough resources to handle these workloads. Medium to large organizations might have as many as three sets of database server computers: one set of computers running SQL Server that accept OLTP data during business hours, one set of SQL Server 2000 computers that warehouse the OLTP data during off-business hours, and a third set of computers with SQL Server 2000 Analysis Services that interact with the warehoused OLTP data whenever it is needed, day or night. Depending on your organization's budget and anticipated computer network traffic, you should deploy the most effective combination of OLTP and OLAP server computers.

There are three main data warehouse storage types: multidimensional OLAP (MOLAP), relational OLAP (ROLAP), and hybrid OLAP (HOLAP). Understanding these data warehouse types will help you plan OLAP systems that are fast and efficient.

- MOLAP stores the data and the aggregations on the OLAP database server. If you want good overall performance and data compression, you should consider a MOLAP approach. MOLAP is good for OLAP databases that need to be queried frequently; the data and the aggregations are stored on the same database server, providing for the fastest performance.

- ROLAP stores the data and the aggregations in a relational database. If you already have a considerable investment in a relational database management system, if your OLAP data will potentially contain more than 10 million members, or if you have large databases that are infrequently queried, you should consider a ROLAP approach. Although ROLAP performance is generally the slowest of these three storage types, it in many cases can provide you with the ability to store larger amounts of data.

- HOLAP stores the data in a relational database, but it stores the aggregations on the OLAP database server. This approach provides the benefits of quick access to aggregations while minimizing duplicate data being stored. If you are concerned about database size, or you are frequently asking for summarizations from large amounts of data, you should consider a HOLAP approach.

For more information about MOLAP, ROLAP, and HOLAP, see Microsoft SQL Server 2000 Analysis Services Books Online, which is included with the product.

Using Microsoft Office to Analyze OLAP Data

Office applications such as Excel, Access, the Office Web Components, and Data Analyzer all contain features that are designed to analyze OLAP data. In Excel you can

- Analyze data stored in an OLAP database.

- Create PivotTable reports and PivotChart reports based on data in an OLAP database.

- Create offline "slices" of OLAP data, known as *offline cubes*, that can be stored and accessed without requiring a network connection to the originating OLAP database server.

- Open and analyze an offline cube (available only in Excel 2002).

- Create OLAP cubes from non-OLAP data. This feature allows you to work with larger amounts of data in a PivotTable report or PivotChart report than you could otherwise and also makes data retrieval and data aggregation faster.

In Access you can

- Import or link to data stored in a data warehouse on a SQL Server 2000 server computer or other compatible data warehouse.

- Create data-entry forms and reports based on data from a data warehouse.

- Create PivotTable reports or PivotChart reports using data from a data warehouse you've imported or linked to (available only in Access 2002).

With the Office Web Components, you can apply the same analysis capabilities that you have in Excel in a Web environment. You can quickly analyze business data in a Web browser using a PivotTable or PivotChart. You can also

- Import data from OLAP database server computers or offline cubes into Spreadsheet Components.

- Create Web-based PivotTable reports or PivotChart reports based on OLAP data stored in OLAP database servers or offline cubes.

With Microsoft Data Analyzer, you can

- Use a new, synchronized, color-coded bar chart to display OLAP data.

- Display bar charts, pie charts, and data grids at the same time, all synchronized to the same OLAP data.

- Export OLAP data to Excel worksheets, Excel PivotTable reports, and Microsoft PowerPoint slides.

In the next two chapters, you will learn how to access and analyze OLAP data by using these Microsoft products. Chapter 9, "Analyzing OLAP Data with Microsoft Data Analyzer," will describe the capabilities of Data Analyzer in more detail.

Summary

In this chapter, you learned the following:

- The multidimensional and hierarchical nature of OLAP data makes it different from relational data and other types of data. Multidimensional data has more interrelationships than relational data, and the terminology used to display these interrelationships is unique.

- OLAP data is highly summarized; you can cross-reference hundreds of thousands or even millions of data records very quickly to identify business trends. Using OLAP, your organization can broaden the scope of the data analysis that feeds into its business decisions.

- OLTP and OLAP computer systems can both write to and read from data marts to make data-entry and data-analysis workers' jobs easier and more efficient.

- Products such as Excel, Access, the Office Web Components, and Data Analyzer include features with which you can analyze OLAP data.

In the next chapter, "Analyzing OLAP Data with Microsoft Excel," you will learn

- How to connect to, query, and work with OLAP data in Excel.

- How to create offline OLAP data cubes and in which scenarios this is helpful.

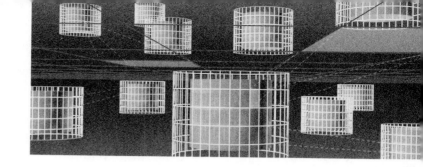

8

Analyzing OLAP Data with Microsoft Excel

In the last chapter, you learned about how OLAP databases structure data. In this chapter, you'll learn about the features in Microsoft Excel that make accessing and analyzing data stored in OLAP data cubes as straightforward as analyzing other types of data. Importing and linking to data; sorting, filtering, and querying data; and examining data in PivotTable reports and PivotChart reports—all these techniques and approaches are available with OLAP data sources.

Objectives

In this chapter, you will learn how to

- Use the features of Excel to connect to, query, and analyze data in OLAP databases.

- Use Excel to take portions of OLAP data off line for use "on-the-road" or at other times when you aren't connected to your network.

Connecting to OLAP Data

Before you can work with OLAP data, you need to connect to it. Connecting to OLAP data with Microsoft data analysis software is very similar to connecting to other types of data; the only difference is that you connect to data that resides in a cube on an OLAP database server computer or in an offline cube file. To connect to an OLAP database, you need to know the OLAP server name, the OLAP database name, and the OLAP cube name. To connect to an offline cube file, you need to know the path to the offline cube file. Although OLAP data cubes can be built from any data source, including Oracle, DB2, and mainframe systems, in the examples in this chapter, we'll assume that cubes are stored on computers running Microsoft SQL Server 2000 Analysis Services or are offline cube files stored on the local computer.

> **Note**   Most OLAP databases house too much data to store in a single offline cube file. An offline cube file contains, in most cases, only a portion of the data stored in a cube on an OLAP database server or a portion of the data stored in a relational database on a network server computer.

Connecting to OLAP Data with Microsoft Excel

You can use Excel to connect to an OLAP data source and create a PivotTable report based on the data. The data can exist on an OLAP database server or in an offline cube file. The data is presented in a PivotTable report instead of as a simple series of records because OLAP data and OLAP database servers are optimized for fetching aggregated or summarized data—data that is presented best in a PivotTable—and not individual data records.

> **Note**   Because OLAP data sources contain summarizations of typically tens of thousands or even millions of data records, you cannot import the individual data records from which an OLAP data source gets its data.

To connect to an OLAP server or offline cube file, follow these steps:

1. On the Data menu, point to Import External Data and then click New Database Query. The Choose Data Source dialog box appears.

2. On the OLAP Cubes tab, click New Data Source and then click OK.

3. Enter a name for the data source, and then select Microsoft OLE DB Provider For OLAP Services 8.0 in the Select An OLAP Provider For The Database You Want To Access list.

> **Note**   If you are connecting to a Microsoft SQL Server 7.0 OLAP Services database, select the Microsoft OLE DB Provider For OLAP Services option.

4. Click the Connect button, and the Multidimensional Connection wizard appears.

5. Select the Analysis Server option if you want to connect to an OLAP server, or select the Cube File option if you want to connect to an offline cube file.

   If you select the Analysis Server option, type the name of the OLAP server in the Server box, click Next, select the name of the database that you want to access, and then click Finish. If you select the Cube File option, type the path and file name of the offline cube file, and then click Finish. After clicking Finish, the Create New Data Source dialog box reappears.

> **Note**   You may be able to connect to an OLAP server on the Web if your network administrator has enabled HTTP or HTTPS connectivity to an Analysis server running on Microsoft SQL Server 2000 Enterprise Edition. If so, type the user name and password assigned to you by your network administrator before you click Next. If you are connecting through a dedicated network, you do not need to provide a special user name and password because the Analysis server uses your Windows logon name and password to determine what level of access you have to the Analysis server.

> **Tip** SQL Server 2000 Analysis Services comes with a sample OLAP database named FoodMart 2000. If you want to experiment with OLAP data analysis but don't yet have an OLAP database, the FoodMart 2000 OLAP database is a good place to start.

6. If the cube name is not already selected, select it in the Select The Cube That Contains The Data You Want list, and then click OK. The Choose Data Source dialog box reappears.

7. Click the name of the data source that you just created, and then click OK. The PivotTable And PivotChart Wizard–Step 3 Of 3 page appears.

8. Select the New Worksheet option or the Existing Worksheet option. If you select the Existing Worksheet option, the PivotTable report begins at the cell referenced in the list below the Existing Worksheet option. Click Finish.

    Figure 8-1 shows the PivotTable report created after connecting Excel to the FoodMart 2000 sample OLAP database's Sales cube.

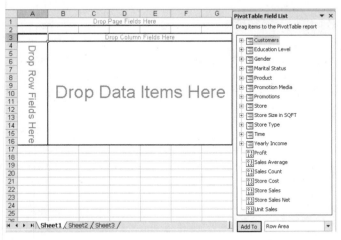

Figure 8-1   PivotTable report based on the Sales cube.

> **Tip** If you connected to the sample FoodMart 2000 OLAP database, selecting the Sales or Sales and Warehouse cubes will give you a sizeable amount of OLAP data to experiment with.

If you want to connect to and open an offline cube file in fewer steps, and you're using Excel 2002, you can skip the previous steps and use the following steps instead.

1. On the File menu, click Open.

2. In the Files Of Type list, select All Files.

3. Locate and select the .cub file you want to open, and then click Open. The OLAP cube data is presented as a PivotTable report in the current workbook. Figure 8-2 shows the PivotTable report set up after using Excel 2002 to open the CarSales.cub file in the Chap08 folder.

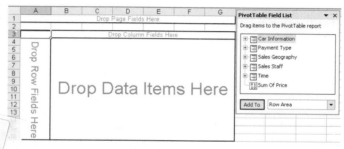

Figure 8-2   PivotTable report based on the CarSales.cub file.

to OLAP Data with the Office Web Components

st as you can use the Office Web Components to connect to data over an tranet, you can use the Office Web Components to connect to OLAP data. Connecting to OLAP data with the Office Web Components is helpful when you need to display data from an OLAP data source along with other types of data on a Web page. You might use such a configuration in a Web-based business management system. Connecting to OLAP data with the Office Web Components is similar to connecting to other types of data. You can connect to OLAP data using the PivotTable Component or the Chart Component. You can't use the Spreadsheet Component because the individual data records that make up the OLAP data are not available, only the summarized data is.

To connect to OLAP data from a PivotTable Component or Chart Component, follow these steps:

1. Using Microsoft FrontPage (or another Web page editor), insert a Pivot-Table Component or a Chart Component on the Web page where you want to view the data. (This might be a blank Web page at this point.)

2. On the PivotTable Component's toolbar, click the Commands And Options button. Or, on the Chart Component's toolbar, click the Chart Wizard button. The Commands And Options dialog box appears.

3.   For the PivotTable Component, click the Data Source tab, select the Connection option, and then click the Edit button. For the Chart Component, click the Data Source tab, select the Data From A Database Table Or Query option, click the Connection button, and then click the Edit button.

4.   In the Select Data Source dialog box, select a data source and click Open. You can then build the chart or PivotTable report using the field list.

     If you need to create a new data source, click the New Source button in the Select Data Source dialog box. The Welcome To The Data Connection Wizard page appears.

5.   In the list of data sources, select Microsoft SQL Server OLAP Services and then click Next. The Connect To Database Server page appears.

6.   In the Server Name box, type the name of your Microsoft SQL Server 2000 Analysis Services computer. Click the Use Windows 2000 Security option if your Analysis Services computer accepts your current network logon name and password for access to the OLAP data. Click the Use The Following User Name And Password option and enter your user name and password if your Analysis Services computer requires a different set of logon credentials.

> **Note**   If you are not sure whether your Analysis Services computer accepts your network logon name and password or requires a special user name and password, see your computer network's administrator.

7.   Click Next. The Select Database And Table page appears.

8.   In the Select The Database That Contains The Data You Want list, select the OLAP database.

9.   Select the Connect To A Specific Cube Or Table check box. (If you do not select this check box now, you will prompted to select a specific cube or table before connecting to the data.)

10. Click the cube you want to connect to, and then click Next. The Save Data Connection File And Finish page appears.

11. Click Finish. The connection details are saved to an .odc file, and the Select Data Source dialog box reappears.

12. Click the .odc file that was generated in the previous step, and then click Open. The PivotTable Component or Chart Component connects to the OLAP data.

> **Note**   In Office 2000, the Edit button is named the Connection Editor, and the Data Link Properties dialog box appears instead of the Select Data Source dialog box. However, the concepts behind this procedure are the same: you designate a connection type and the name of the OLAP server along with the database and cube name on the server, or the location of the offline cube file.

Data Connection File Types

There are various types of files that Office can use to get data connection information.

- XML-based Office Database Connection (.odc) files are the recommended method of retrieving external data when you don't need to combine data from more than one table in an external database or filter the data to select specific records before creating a report. This file type is also recommended for retrieving data from OLAP databases.

- Universal Data Link (.udl) files are text-based files that contain information to connect to OLE DB data sources.

- Open Database Connectivity (ODBC) File Data Source Name (.dsn) files are text-based files for the specific use of a local computer connecting to an ODBC data source.

- Database Query (.dqy and .rqy) files are text-based files created with Microsoft Query, a graphical data query program often used with Excel.

- Text-based OLAP Query (.oqy) files return data from any OLE DB for OLAP provider, such as Microsoft SQL Server 7.0 OLAP Services or Microsoft SQL Server 2000 Analysis Services.

- OLAP Cube (.cub) files are binary files that actually hold OLAP data.

Using the Office Web Components to analyze OLAP data is similar to analyzing non-OLAP data. You can use the PivotTable Component and Chart Component to pivot, group, summarize, and chart OLAP data over the Web just as you would with relational or nonrelational data. See Chapter 6, "Analyzing Data with the Office Web Components," for details on how to use the Office Web Components.

Working with OLAP Data

After you've connected to an OLAP data source, you can use Excel data analysis features to make faster and more informed business decisions based on the OLAP data. In general, the summarizations created in the OLAP database give you varied perspectives on the data that matters the most.

For example, with a large number of individual data records that are not summarized, you can't easily spot trends or business anomalies. Subtotals and worksheet functions help by grouping and summarizing data records in a more useful manner. But as you learned in earlier chapters, creating or revising subtotal groupings and worksheet functions can be a time-consuming process. To quickly spot trends and data anomalies, as well as quickly switch data analysis perspectives, you can instruct Excel to use PivotTable reports and PivotChart reports to summarize data records. When it comes to OLAP data, because the data is already summarized, less data needs to be retrieved by Excel when you create or change an OLAP-based PivotTable report or PivotChart report. Using Excel to analyze OLAP data lets you work with much larger amounts of data much more quickly than you could if the data was organized in a nonrelational or relational data source. Additionally, OLAP dimensions and levels such as Fiscal Year, Fiscal Quarter, West Region, Sales District, and so on, can be used to hierarchically organize and analyze summarized business data better than less intuitive field names in a flat series of data records. Hierarchical data allows you to ask more sophisticated questions of your data, enabling more complex business decisions in less time.

Earlier in this chapter you learned how to create a database query that results in a PivotTable report. You can also use the PivotTable And PivotChart wizard to do the same thing. Whether you choose the earlier approach or use the PivotTable And PivotChart wizard is up to you; it's simply a matter of preference. The following exercise demonstrates how to use the PivotTable And PivotChart wizard to connect to an OLAP data source, build a meaningful report, and analyze the results.

Your Turn

In this exercise, you will use Excel 2002 to connect to an offline cube file (CarSales.cub) and create a PivotTable report based on the data.

1. In Excel, with a blank workbook open, click PivotTable And PivotChart Report on the Data menu.

2. Click the External Data Source option, and then click Next.

3. Click Get Data.

4. Click the OLAP Cubes tab, click New Data Source, and then click OK.

5. In the What Name Do You Want To Give Your Data Source box, type *Car Sales Cube*.

6. In the Select An OLAP Provider For The Database You Want To Access list, click Microsoft OLE DB Provider For OLAP Services 8.0, and then click Connect.

7. Click the Cube File option.

8. Click the browse button (the button with the three dots), and then locate and select the CarSales.cub file in the Chap08 folder. Click Open.

9. Click Finish to close the Multidimensional Connection dialog box.

10. Click OK to close the Create Data Source dialog box, and then click OK to close the Choose Data Source dialog box.

11. Click Finish to close the PivotTable And PivotChart wizard and display the PivotTable report.

Now, create a PivotTable report to get an idea of what data is available for analysis.

1. From the PivotTable field list, drag the Time icon to the Drop Page Fields Here area of the PivotTable report. Drag the Sales Geography icon to the Drop Row Fields Here area, drag the Sales Staff icon to the right of the Customer Sales Region field, and drag the Sum Of Price icon to the Drop Data Items Here area.

(continued)

2. Next, format the sales figures as currency: double-click the Sum Of Price field in cell A3, click Number, click Currency, type a zero (0) in the Decimal Places list, and click OK twice. Compare your results to Figure 8-3.

	A	B	C	D	E	F	G
1	Time	All ▼		PivotTable Field List		▼ ×	
2				Drag items to the PivotTable report			
3	Sum Of Price						
4	Customer Sales Region ▼	Sales Manager ID ▼	Total	⊞ ▤ Car Information			
5	West	100	$7,795,000	⊞ ▤ Payment Type			
6		101	$9,234,000	▤ **Sales Geography**			
7		102	$8,548,000	▤ **Sales Staff**			
8		103	$1,380,000	⊞ ▤ **Time**			
9	West Total		$26,957,000	▤ **Sum Of Price**			
10	Grand Total		$26,957,000				
11							
12				Add To	Data Area	▼	
13							
14							

Figure 8-3 Completed PivotTable report based on the CarSales.cub file.

Now, with the PivotTable constructed, we can do some analysis. Let's display the first quarter's car sales in Washington State for 2001 and 2002 combined, for all sales managers, and see if we can spot any trends.

1. In the Time field, click the arrow, select the Select Multiple Items check box, and then click the plus sign (+) next to the All check box.

2. Click the plus signs next to the 2001 and 2002 check boxes, and then clear the check boxes except for those with the number 1 next to them. Compare your results to Figure 8-4, and then click OK.

    These check boxes show you the power of using PivotTable reports to analyze hierarchical data: Excel can translate the dimensions and levels of an OLAP cube into a series of nested check boxes mimicking the relationship of years to quarters to months to days defined in the OLAP cube.

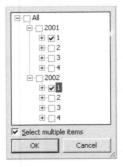

Figure 8-4 Check boxes for the Time field.

3. Click the arrow in the Customer Sales Region field, click the plus sign next to the West check box, and then select the WA check box. Compare your results to Figure 8-5, click OK, and then compare your results to Figure 8-6.

Figure 8-5   Check boxes for the Customer Sales Region field.

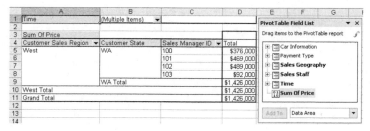

Figure 8-6   PivotTable report displaying car sales for the first quarter of both 2001 and 2002 for Washington State, for all sales managers.

The report doesn't currently tell us much, other than sales manager 103 had the least sales, and sales managers 101 and 102 had similar sales. Let's try to find out why sales manager 103 had the least sales by looking at the sales of each salesperson who reports to the managers.

1. Click the arrow in the Sales Manager ID field, and then click each of the four check boxes corresponding to the sales managers (100, 101, 102, and 103). The check symbol turns into a double-check symbol in each check box, signifying that one or more nested check boxes are also checked. (In this case, it means that all of the nested check boxes are checked.)

(continued)

> **2.** Click OK. You can quickly spot one possible reason why sales manager 103 had the least amount of sales—only one salesperson reports to sales manager 103, while the other sales managers each have three salespeople reporting to them. (Of course, this is not the only possible reason, but it's a good start.)

Creating Offline Cubes

As I mentioned earlier in this chapter, Excel can create offline cube files that contain a portion of the OLAP data stored on an OLAP database server. Offline cubes can also contain nonrelational data or relational data. In these cases, when Excel creates the offline cube file, it optimizes the data for analysis using an OLAP-like hierarchy. Offline cubes are effective when you need to package a portion of OLAP data for use when you don't have a network connection to the OLAP server. You can also create offline cube files to produce highly summarized non-OLAP data for faster performance with PivotTable reports and PivotChart reports.

There are two procedures you can use to create offline cube files in Excel. You follow one set of steps if you want to convert an OLAP cube stored in an OLAP database server to an offline cube file. You use a different procedure if you want to convert nonrelational or relational data into an offline cube file.

> **Note** You cannot create an offline cube file from another offline cube file.

To create an offline cube from OLAP data that resides on an OLAP database server, create a PivotTable report based on the cube using the steps presented earlier in this chapter. Then, on the PivotTable menu, click Offline OLAP. Click Create Offline Data File, and then follow the Create Cube File Wizard to choose the dimensions, levels, and measures that you want to include in your offline cube file. Specify a location for the offline cube file, click Finish, and then click OK in the Offline OLAP Settings dialog box. You can use the resulting .cub file in place of a live connection to an OLAP database server. When you can connect to the OLAP database server again, you can refresh the .cub file with the most recent OLAP data by clicking Refresh Data on the PivotTable menu. You can disconnect your computer from the network again at this point if you need to.

> **Note**   Refreshing an offline cube file might take a long time, depending on the size of the file. Be sure to allow adequate time and disk space before you try to refresh updated data from an OLAP database server.   .

To create an offline cube from nonrelational or relational data, point to Import External Data (Get External Data in Office 2000) on the Data menu and then click New Database Query. After you follow the steps to connect to a data source, select the Create An OLAP Cube From This Query option on the last page of the Query Wizard.

> **Note**   If you click the Save Query button before you click Finish, you can save your work as a .dqy file so that you can modify your offline cube later without needing to go through all the pages of the Query Wizard.

In the first step of the OLAP Cube Wizard, you select the fields you want to use as OLAP measures. For each field that you select, you designate a summarization type. In the second step of the wizard, you identify fields that will be used to create OLAP dimensions. You can also specify OLAP levels by dragging fields onto the fields you've already designated as dimensions. You can rename any dimension or level without changing the underlying data. In the last step of the wizard, you select an option for building or saving the cube. An offline cube file is stored with the extension .cub. You can then use any of the procedures presented earlier in this chapter to connect to and analyze OLAP data in the offline cube file.

Your Turn

In this exercise, you will create an offline cube file from data in an existing text file and then analyze the data in the offline cube file.

1. In Excel, with a blank worksheet open, point to Import External Data (Get External Data in Office 2000) on the Data menu and then click New Database Query.

2. Select the Use The Query Wizard To Create/Edit Queries option. On the Databases tab, click New Data Source and then click OK.

3. In the What Name Do You Want To Give Your External Data Source box, type *Car Sales CSV*.

4. In the Select A Driver For The Type Of Database You Want To Access list, select Microsoft Text Driver. Click Connect.

> **Tip**   If you do not select the Use The Query Wizard To Create/Edit Queries check box in step 2, an application named Microsoft Query appears after step 9 below. Use the Query Wizard when you want to create a simple query, such as you're doing in this exercise. Use Microsoft Query when you want to create a more complex query. Microsoft Query enables you to narrow your result set by creating advanced query expressions and complex filter criteria. You can also create offline cube files by clicking Create OLAP Cube on the File menu in Microsoft Query. To modify data connection details for an existing data source by using Microsoft Query, on the Data menu, point to Import External Data, and click New Database Query. Make sure the Use The Query Wizard To Create/Edit Queries check box is cleared, click the Databases tab, click an existing data source, and then click OK. For complete information about working with Microsoft Query, click Microsoft Query Help on the Help menu in the Microsoft Query window.

5. Clear the Use Current Directory check box, and then click Select Directory.

6. Locate and select the Chap08 folder.

7. Click OK to close the Select Directory dialog box, and then click OK to close the ODBC Text Setup dialog box.

8. In the Select A Default Table For Your Data Source list, select CarSales.csv.

9. Click OK to close the Create New Data Source dialog box, and then click OK to close the Choose Data Source dialog box.

10. Move the fields in the CarSales.csv file from the Available Tables And Columns list to the Columns In Your Query list, and then click Next.

11. Click Next until you get to the Query Wizard–Finish page, click the Create An OLAP Cube From This Query option, and then click Finish.

12. Click Next on the OLAP Cube Wizard welcome page to display the first step of the OLAP Cube Wizard.

13. Because the Price field is the only field that you will use as a measure, clear the check boxes for the fields in the Source Field list except for the check box next to Price. Compare your results to Figure 8-7, and then click Next.

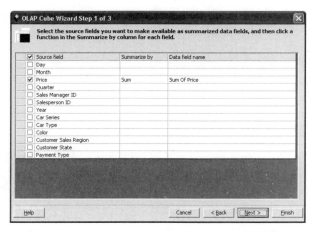

Figure 8-7   The Price field will be the measure in the cube file.

14. In the second step of the wizard, you identify the fields you'll use as dimensions. Drag the following fields from the Source Fields list to the Dimensions list: Car Series, Sales Manager ID, Year, Payment Type, and Customer Sales Region.

(continued)

15. To create additional levels within the cube's dimensions, drag the following fields from the Source Fields list to the corresponding dimensions:

❑   Drag the Car Type field to the Car Series level.

❑   Drag the Color field to the Car Type level.

❑   Drag the Salesperson ID field to the Sales Manager ID level.

❑   Drag the Quarter field to the Year level.

❑   Drag the Month field to the Quarter level.

❑   Drag the Day field to the Month level.

❑   Drag the Customer State field to the Customer Region level.

16. Rename the dimensions by right-clicking the dimension, selecting Rename from the shortcut menu, entering the new name, and pressing Enter. Change the names of the following dimensions:

❑   Rename the Car Series dimension to Car Information.

❑   Rename the Sales Manager ID dimension to Sales Staff.

❑   Rename the Year dimension to Time.

❑   Rename the Customer Sales Region dimension to Sales Geography.

17. Compare your results to Figure 8-8, and then click Next.

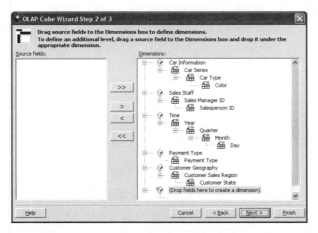

Figure 8-8   Completed details for the second step of the OLAP Cube Wizard, with dimensions and levels selected.

18. Select the option Save A Cube File Containing All Data For The Cube, and then click Finish to close the OLAP Cube Wizard.

> **Note**   On the last step of the OLAP Cube Wizard, you can select an option to rebuild the offline cube file every time the corresponding PivotTable report is opened and then retrieve the data for the cube all at once or only when you need it. Both of these options ensure that you have the latest data from the underlying data source, but these options can result in much slower performance than the option selected in step 18.

19. Click Save to save the settings as an .oqy file.

20. Click Finish to insert a PivotTable report referencing the new offline cube file. Compare your results to Figure 8-9.

Figure 8-9   The finished PivotTable report, ready for data analysis.

Let's use the resulting PivotTable report to analyze the data in the offline cube file. For this exercise, let's quickly determine which state had the most car sales for each year.

1. From the PivotTable field list, drag the Time icon to the Drop Page Fields Here area of the PivotTable report, drag the Sales Geography icon to the Drop Row Fields Here area, and drag the Sum Of Price icon to the Drop Data Items Here area.

(continued)

2. Click the arrow in the Customer Sales Region field, click the West check box (a double-check symbol appears in the check box), and then click OK. The Customer State field is displayed, showing data for the states in the West sales region.

3. We aren't concerned with seeing the Customer Sales Region field any more, so right-click the Customer Sales Region field and click Hide Levels. The Customer Sales Region field disappears.

4. In the Time field, click the arrow next to the word All, click the plus sign (+) next to the word All, click 2001, and then click OK. You'll see that Oregon had the most sales for 2001.

5. In the Time field, click the arrow next to 2001, click 2002, and then click OK. You'll see that Oregon also had the most sales for 2002.

Summary

In this chapter, you learned how to use Microsoft Excel and the Office Web Components to connect to and analyze OLAP data as well as how to use Excel to create an offline cube file. In the next chapter, "Analyzing OLAP Data with Microsoft Data Analyzer," you will learn all about Microsoft Data Analyzer and how it can connect to, view, and analyze OLAP data by using a unique graphical paradigm.

9

Analyzing OLAP Data with Microsoft Data Analyzer

Microsoft Data Analyzer, a member of the Microsoft Office family of data analysis applications, displays OLAP data in a unique way. It provides a highly graphical user interface and works with other Office applications, allowing you to quickly view and analyze data in ways you might not have imagined before. Data Analyzer is an ideal solution with which to present and analyze OLAP data in a more summarized manner than PivotTable reports.

Data Analyzer is also considered a member of the Microsoft family of *business intelligence* applications, which includes software products such as Microsoft SQL Server 2000 Analysis Services for data management and Microsoft Excel and the Office Web Components for data analysis. Business intelligence refers to the realm of data analysis tasks and software applications that enable organizations to quickly discern data trends, patterns, and relationships that represent the health of a business. Data Analyzer presents a view of multiple data dimensions, which can result in faster decision making. With this information, businesses might alter their direction in hours and minutes, rather than weeks or months.

Objectives

In this chapter, you will learn

- When it's best to use Microsoft Data Analyzer rather than PivotTable reports and PivotChart reports.

- How to connect to and view OLAP data with Data Analyzer.
- How to create custom measures with Data Analyzer.
- How to use Data Analyzer views to make better informed business decisions based on your OLAP data.

> **Note**   To use Data Analyzer effectively, you should be familiar with OLAP terms such as *cube*, *dimension*, *level*, *member*, and *measure*. If you are not, see Chapter 7, "Introducing Online Analytical Processing."

Introducing Microsoft Data Analyzer

Organizations that record and store data over long periods of time, or organizations that record and store hundreds of megabytes, gigabytes, or even terabytes of data face the daunting task of trying to make sense of the data so that they can inform and improve their business decisions. For instance, sales teams might have data gathered over several years that is dispersed throughout their corporate offices as well as in sales offices throughout several regions. A retail organization might need to figure out which products have sold the best during a peak shopping season and which poorly selling products should be discounted or discontinued in the future. Manufacturing organizations might need to analyze historical defect counts and other factors that could require the business to retrain workers or retool machinery. Insurance organizations might want to add new lines of coverage or face the reality of raising policy premiums because of the quantity and severity of past claims.

PivotTable reports and PivotChart reports can be great data analysis tools for these types of data analysis scenarios. However, when working with large data sources, data sources distributed geographically, or data collected over long periods of time, creating several reports, linking them together, and synchronizing their data can be time-consuming. And viewing such reports on line can be difficult because of a limited screen area in which to show these reports and perspectives on the data all at once. Displaying multiple business dimensions or measures on a PivotTable report or PivotChart report can result in visual clutter or even be confusing. Microsoft Data Analyzer addresses these issues and provides tools to show trends over time and locate similar members in a dimension for business data comparisons.

You should use Data Analyzer when you want to see a high-level, executive summary of your data. You can then export the data from Data Analyzer to PivotTable reports when you want to diagnose what is causing specific data trends or anomalies. For instance, you could use Data Analyzer to determine the sales for a particular product over the last three years, which you think have declined because of either poor marketing or by selling the product in the wrong geographical market. From there, you could use a PivotTable report to look at the details of each year's sales figures, comparing them to the amount spent on advertising campaigns in the geographical market and the volume of products stocked in each store in that market.

Microsoft Data Analyzer was specifically created to access OLAP data on an OLAP server or in an offline cube file. However, you can use the techniques described at the end of Chapter 8, "Analyzing OLAP Data with Microsoft Excel," to create an offline cube file in Excel from non-OLAP data. You can then use Data Analyzer to view the offline cube file's data.

Exploring the Data Analyzer User Interface

Before you connect to and analyze OLAP data with Microsoft Data Analyzer, you should become familiar with its special user interface components. The application's main window is shown in Figure 9-1. The data shown comes from a sample offline cube file (Airline.cub) provided with Data Analyzer.

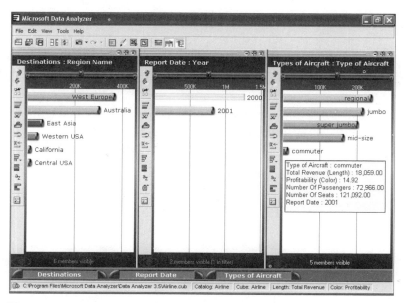

Figure 9-1   The Microsoft Data Analyzer main window.

Main User Interface Components

The Data Analyzer user interface consists of five main components, which include the menu bar, the toolbar, the status bar, the navigation bar, and a group of one or more dimension panes.

- The menu bar, located directly beneath the title bar, contains familiar Office-style menus such as File, Edit, View, Tools, and Help.

- The toolbar, located beneath the menu bar, contains shortcuts to menu commands.

- In Data Analyzer, the bar lengths and pie-slice sizes typically indicate numerical measurements, such as sales volumes, units produced, and so on. The colors of the bars and pie slices typically represent percentages or ratios such as profit margins, progress against sales quotas, manufacturing defect ratios, and so on. The status bar, located at the bottom of the screen, displays information about the current data source, including lengths and colors. From left to right, the status bar shows the OLAP server name or path to an offline cube file, the catalog name (the name of an OLAP database or offline cube file), the cube name, what the length of the bars or the size of the pie slices represents, and what the colors of the bars or the pie slices represent. (An OLAP database can contain more than one cube. In the case of offline cubes, the offline cube's file name is the same as the catalog name.)

- The navigation bar, located directly above the status bar, contains one button for each OLAP dimension that's displayed. Clicking these buttons (in this example Destinations, Report Date, and Types Of Aircraft) hides or displays the associated dimension.

- Dimension panes, a sample of which is shown in Figure 9-2, are located between the navigation bar and the toolbar.

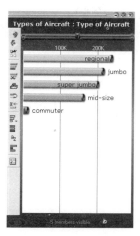

Figure 9-2   A Data Analyzer dimension pane.

Dimension Pane Components

Each dimension pane in Data Analyzer corresponds to a dimension in the OLAP source data. In addition to displaying data in bars, pie slices, or grids, the dimension pane includes components such as the handle, the label, the length scale, the Display Type toolbar, and the dimension toolbar.

■   The thin line at the top of the dimension pane, called the *handle*, can be used to drag the dimension pane to a new screen location. Next to the handle are Minimize, Maximize, and Close buttons that are included in typical Microsoft Office application windows.

■   Below the handle is a label showing the dimension's name and the current level. The names of the dimension and the level will be similar if the top level of a dimension's hierarchy is displayed, as is the case with the pane shown in Figure 9-2 (the Types Of Aircraft dimension and the Type Of Aircraft level).

■   The length scale, located directly below the dimension and level name, can be used to change the zoom level of the data. Sliding the magnifying glass icon to the left of the length scale zooms in on the level of data, showing smaller values, while sliding the magnifying icon to the right of the length scale zooms out on the level of data, showing values at the higher end of the range. In the sample, sliding the magnifying glass icon all the way to the left zooms in from 100K/200K to 20K/40K; sliding the magnifying glass icon all the way to the right zooms out from 100K/200K to 200K/400K. Length scales can be turned on or off by clicking Dimension Length Scales on the View menu.

- The Display Type toolbar, located at the bottom of the dimension pane, provides buttons with which you can switch the dimension pane's view to display bars, a grid, or a pie chart. To show the toolbar, rest your mouse pointer on the eye icon, and then click Bars, Grid, or Pie Chart.

- The dimension toolbar, located directly below the dimension and level name and to the left of the length scale, contains buttons to change the dimension pane's display characteristics. Dimension toolbars can be turned on or off by clicking Dimension Toolbars on the View menu.

Dimension Toolbar Buttons

From top to bottom, the buttons on the dimension toolbar include the following:

- Drill Up decreases the level of data details displayed by moving up one level in the dimension's hierarchy. In the sample, you can drill up from the Type Of Aircraft level to the All level.

- Drill Down increases the level of detail displayed by moving down one level in the dimension's hierarchy. For example, you could drill down from the All level to the Type Of Aircraft level.

- Default Members displays the default members as defined in the OLAP cube. For example, the OLAP cube creator can specify that the Type Of Aircraft level (instead of the All level) is the level that is initially displayed.

- Filter By All Visible Members selects all of the visible members in the dimension. You'll learn about how to select members later in this chapter.

- Hide Members Not In Filter hides the members that are not selected.

- Filter By Criteria allows you to define criteria by which to select members to display.

- Reverse Filter selects members that are not selected and removes members that are selected from the selection.

- Hide Empty hides members that have no data.

- Length sorts members by bar length, pie slice size, or grid figure.

- Color sorts members by bar or pie-slice color.

- Name sorts members by name.

- Natural sorts members by any default sort order defined by the OLAP cube creator before the data source connection was first made.

- Properties can be used to set miscellaneous dimension pane properties, such as whether to respect the default sort order as defined by the OLAP cube creator or define your own sort order.

Your Turn

In this exercise, you will familiarize yourself with basic components of the Data Analyzer user interface.

1. Start Data Analyzer. If the Microsoft Data Analyzer Startup dialog box appears, click Cancel to close it.

2. On the toolbar, click the Open button.

3. Locate and click the file Airline.max, and then click Open.

   In a default installation of Data Analyzer, this file is located at C:\Program Files\Microsoft Data Analyzer\Data Analyzer 3.5\. The Airline.max file contains information for connecting to the Airline.cub offline cube file in the same folder as the Airline.max file.

4. On the navigation bar, click Types Of Aircraft to hide the Types Of Aircraft dimension pane.

5. On the status bar, notice the labels Length: Total Revenue and Color: Profitability. The bar lengths (or pie-slice sizes) represent the total revenue; the bar and pie-slice colors represent the profitability percentage.

6. On the Report Date dimension pane, on the dimension toolbar, click the Drill Down button. This displays the next level in the Report Date dimension, moving from the Year level to the Month level. The Report Date dimension pane's text should now read Report Date: Month to reflect this operation.

7. The bars in the Report Date dimension pane are sorted by month with the earliest month (01/2001) at the top. On the Report Date dimension pane's dimension toolbar, click Length to sort the bars by length with the longest bar at the top. The bar for 07/2001 is now at the top.

(continued)

8.   In the Report Date dimension pane, rest your mouse pointer on the eye icon and then click Pie Chart to switch to a pie chart display. Click Grid to switch to a grid display. Click Bars to return to a bars display.

9.   On the File menu, click Close.

Connecting to OLAP Data

To connect to and display OLAP data in Microsoft Data Analyzer, you must first create a view file, which is a special text file with the extension .max. The view file itself does not include any data from the OLAP data source. Rather, it contains details about the OLAP data source connection and about how to initially display the data in Data Analyzer. You create one view file for each way in which you want to initially view a particular OLAP data source in Data Analyzer. For instance, you would create one view file to connect to a specific offline cube file and display a dimension's data initially as bars; you would create a different view file to connect to the same offline cube file and display the dimension's data initially as a pie chart.

> **Note**   You can also distribute a view file to other Data Analyzer users, provided the users have access to the associated OLAP data source. The view file contains information to connect to the data source; if other users cannot access the target OLAP data source with an application such as Excel, they won't be able to use Data Analyzer to access the target OLAP data source either.

To create a view file in Data Analyzer, click New on the File menu. Click Next and then click Add. You'll see the Connection Properties dialog box, shown in Figure 9-3.

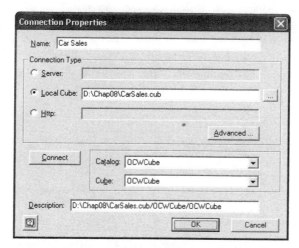

Figure 9-3   The Connection Properties dialog box.

In the Name box, type a descriptive name for the view, one that is easy for you to remember. In the Connection Type area, do one of the following:

- Click the Server option and type an OLAP server name if the OLAP data is stored on a Microsoft SQL Server 2000 Analysis Services server computer.

- Click the Local Cube option and type the full path to an offline cube file if the OLAP data is stored in an offline cube file.

- Click the HTTP option and type the Web address if the OLAP data is stored on a Microsoft SQL Server 2000 Analysis Services server computer available over the Internet. Click the Advanced button if you need to provide additional connection details such as a logon name (if the Web server requires one to access the OLAP data).

Click the Connect button to connect to the OLAP data. Select the OLAP catalog name in the Catalog list, and then select the OLAP cube name in the Cube list. Click OK to close the Connection Properties dialog box, and then click Next. Select the check box for each dimension that you want to display in a dimension pane in Data Analyzer.

Click Next. In the Display Type list, select Bars if you want to initially display member bars or select Grid if you want to initially display details in a grid. If you select Bars, in the Length list, select a measure that the bar lengths and pie-slice sizes will represent. In the Color list, select a ratio or percentage that the bar and pie-slice colors will represent. If you select Grid, select the measures as well as any ratios or percentages you want to appear in the grids and bar and pie-slice information tips.

> **Tip** If you forget to select a particular check box in the Define View—Dimensions page or you select the wrong choice in the Display Type, Length, or Color lists in the Define View—Measures page, you can modify your choices later after the view file is created.

Click Finish. The view file is created, Data Analyzer connects to the source data, and the data view is displayed according to the options that you specified.

Your Turn

In this exercise, you will create a Data Analyzer view based on the CarSales.cub offline cube file used in Chapter 8. You will also practice opening an existing view file in Data Analyzer.

1. Start Data Analyzer. If the Microsoft Data Analyzer Startup dialog box appears, click Cancel to close it.

2. On the File menu, click New.

3. If the Define View–Introduction page appears, click Next.

4. Click Add.

5. In the Name box, type *Car Sales*.

6. Click the Local Cube option, and then click the browse button (the button with the three dots on it).

7. Locate and select the CarSales.cub file located in the Chap08 folder, and then click Open.

8. Click Connect, click OK, and then click Next.

9. Select the Car Information, Sales Geography, Sales Staff, and Time check boxes, and then click Next.

10. Keep the Display Type and Length settings as is. In the Color list, select % Of Total Length Of Members In Filter, and then click Finish. Compare your results to Figure 9-4.

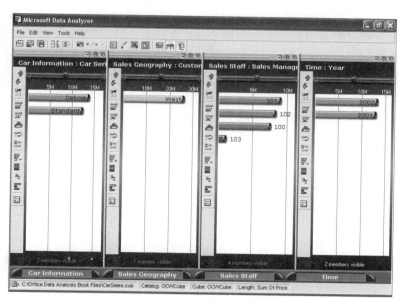

Figure 9-4   Initial view based on the Car Sales cube.

11. On the File menu, click Save As.

12. In the File Name box, type *CarSales*, and then click Save.

13. On the File menu, click Close.

14. To open the view file, on the File menu, click Open, locate and select the CarSales.max file, and then click Open.

Viewing and Analyzing Data with Data Analyzer

Now that you understand the basic Microsoft Data Analyzer user interface and know how to create a view, you will learn how to analyze the OLAP data by changing the display to answer important business questions.

If you open the CarSales.max file that you created in the previous section, you will notice four dimension panes: Car Information, Sales Geography, Sales Staff, and Time.

The first behavior to understand when working with dimension panes is that the information displayed in each pane is synchronized with the other panes. For example, if you rest your mouse pointer on the member bar labeled

101 in the Sales Staff dimension pane, you will discover that sales manager number 101 was responsible for $9,234,000 in car sales for both 2001 and 2002. Now, in the Time dimension pane, click the 2002 member bar once. Notice that the 2002 member bar changes color, the 2001 member bar turns into a striped bar to indicate that it is not included in any data results, and the member bars in the other dimension panes change lengths and colors. By selecting a member bar in one dimension pane, members in the other dimension panes change to reflect the data that relates to that member. To prove this, rest your mouse pointer on the 101 member bar in the Sales Staff dimension pane again. You will discover that the car sales change to $4,683,000 and that the text *Time: 2002* has been added to the information tip to indicate that this fact applies only to 2002.

To reset the lengths and colors in a Data Analyzer view, do one of the following:

■   Close and reopen the view file

■   Click Default Members on each visible dimension pane's toolbar

■   Right-click a blank area of each visible dimension pane, point to Go To, and click Default Members

To select multiple members in a dimension pane, you can click the first member, hold down the Ctrl key, and then click the other members; if the members are next to each other, you can click the first member, hold down the Shift key, and click the last member. You can also select all of a dimension pane's members by clicking Filter By All Visible Members in the dimension pane's toolbar.

The second thing to understand is how to navigate up and down the levels in a dimension. To do so, you click the Drill Up or Drill Down button to navigate to the next highest or next lowest level, respectively. You can double-click a member to show the member's child members. You can also go directly to a specific level by right-clicking a blank area in a dimension pane, pointing to Go To, and then clicking the level's name.

Tip   Although no element in the dimension pane easily identifies a child member's parent or child members, you can right-click a blank area in a dimension pane and then point to Go To to see how a dimension's levels are related to each other. You can also point to Drill Up To to see higher levels or point to Drill Down To to see lower levels in a dimension pane.

Third, you should understand how to change the colors of the bars and pie slices. To do so, on the View menu, click Color Scale. The Color Scale dialog box appears, as shown in Figure 9-5.

Tip   If you do not see the buttons in the Color Scale dialog box that are shown in Figure 9-5, click the Color Scale dialog box's Manual button.

Figure 9-5   The Color Scale dialog box.

From left to right, the Color Scale dialog box's buttons are:

■ Reset Values According To Data, which resets the colors based on the numbers you type in the Min, Mid, and Max boxes. (See the next bullet point.)

■ Automatic Mode. Switch To Manual Goal Settings, which displays the Min, Mid, and Max boxes. In these boxes, you can specify the data values on which to base the red, yellow, and green colors that are displayed in the bars and pie chart slices. To switch back to having Data Analyzer automatically decide on the meanings of the colors, click the Manual Mode. Switch To Automatic Goal Settings button.

■ Change The Meaning Of Green And Red, which determines whether low, middle, or high values are "good," or green. Green might not always signify a high number. For instance, in measuring manufacturing defects, green should probably represent lower numbers.

■ Change Color Scheme determines whether colors are based on filtered members (Use Highest And Lowest Values Of Significant Selected Members Only) or whether colors are based on all members in all of the dimensions (Choose Absolute High And Low Values).

Finally, you need to know how to quickly change which dimensions are displayed, as well as what the colors represent. To do so, on the Edit menu, click Change View. The Define View dialog box appears. On the Dimensions tab, shown in Figure 9-6, you can add or remove specific dimension panes by selecting or clearing the check box for a dimension. Use the controls on the Measures tab, shown in Figure 9-7, to change the type of display and what the view's bar lengths, pie-slice sizes, and colors represent. (I'll discuss the Define View dialog box's Template Measures tab later in this chapter.)

Figure 9-6   The Define View dialog box's Dimensions tab.

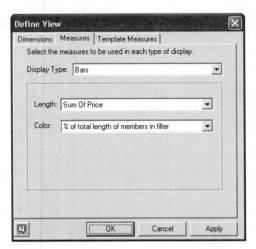

Figure 9-7   The Define View dialog box's Measures tab.

Your Turn

In this exercise, you will practice changing a view to answer simple business questions. To begin this exercise, open the CarSales.max file, located in Chap09 folder, or open the CarSales.max file that you created earlier in this chapter.

What was the total car sales figure for 2001 in Washington State? To answer this question, click the 2001 member bar in the Time dimension pane and then click the Drill Down button in the Sales Geography dimension pane. Rest your mouse pointer on the WA member bar. The total car sales figure is $3,132,000, as shown in Figure 9-8.

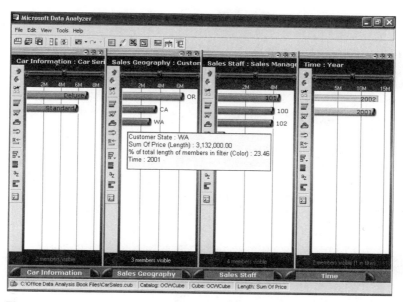

Figure 9-8   Car sales for 2001 in Washington State.

For each of the car series, which car type sold the most in 2002 for salesperson 8 in all states combined? To answer this question, first click the Default Members button in each of the dimension pane's toolbars. In the Time dimension pane, click the 2002 member bar. In the Sales Staff dimension pane's toolbar, click Drill Down, and then click the 8 member bar. In the Car Information dimension pane's toolbar, click Drill Down and notice that the sport utility car type sold the most in both the deluxe and standard car series, as shown in Figure 9-9.

(continued)

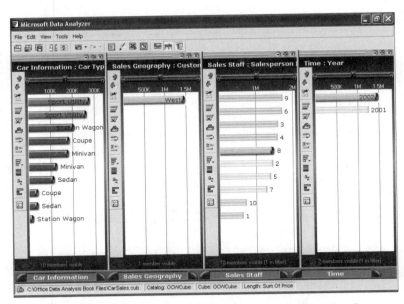

Figure 9-9 Top car types sold in 2002 for salesperson number 8.

Now change the meaning of green and red. First, click the Default Members button in each of the dimension pane's toolbars. On the View menu, click Color Scale. Next click Automatic Mode. Switch To Manual Goal Settings. Type *0* in the Min box, type *50* in the Mid box, and type *100* in the Max box, and then close the Color Scale dialog box. Notice the color changes on your computer's monitor, similar to Figure 9-10.

Who were the top three salespeople for the West region for 2001? To answer this question, click the Default Members button on each dimension pane's toolbar. Next, in the Time dimension pane, click 2001. In the Sales Staff dimension pane's toolbar, click Drill Down, and then click Filter By Criteria. In the box next to the In Top list, type *3*, and then click OK. Salespeople 6, 2, and 3 had the top sales in 2001, as shown in Figure 9-11.

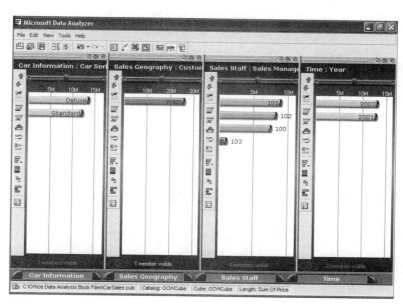

Figure 9-10   Color changes where 0 percent of the total lengths of the members in the filter are red and 100 percent is green.

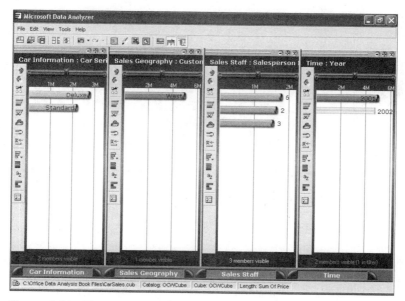

Figure 9-11   Top three salespeople for the West region in 2001.

(continued)

Now see whether you can change the view to arrive at the correct answer to these additional business questions:

Which year was better in terms of overall car sales for salesperson number 10? Answer: 2002. (See Figures 9-12 and 9-13.)

In which state were the most overall car sales for 2001? Answer: Oregon. (See Figure 9-14.)

Which salesperson sold the most deluxe sedans in California in 2002? Answer: Salesperson number 3. (See Figure 9-15.)

Which salesperson sold the most blue colored cars overall in Washington? Answer: Salesperson number 2. (See Figure 9-16.)

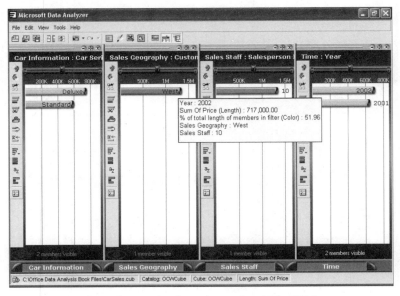

Figure 9-12   Overall car sales for salesperson 10 in 2002.

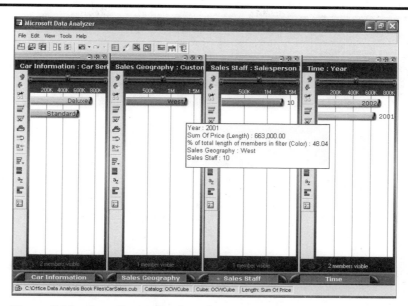

Figure 9-13   Overall car sales for salesperson 10 in 2001.

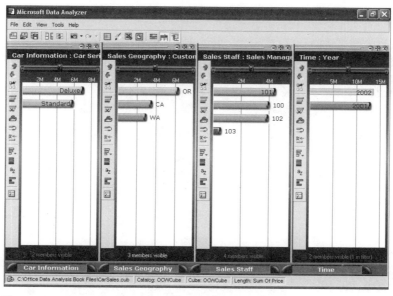

Figure 9-14   Overall car sales for 2001 by state.

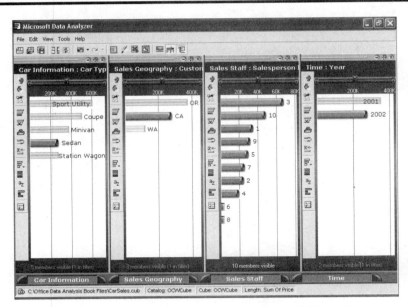

Figure 9-15 Deluxe sedan sales for California in 2002 by salesperson.

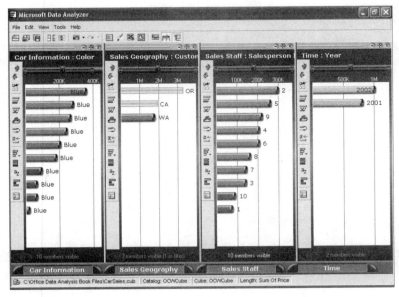

Figure 9-16 Overall blue car sales in Washington by salesperson.

Creating Custom Measures

You might have situations in which the measures that were defined in the original OLAP source data do not meet your business needs and the OLAP data source creator has not given you permissions to add measures to the original OLAP data source. For instance, you might not have the ability to add a measure to a read-only offline cube file, or your OLAP server administrator might not allow you to add a measure to the OLAP database on the server. In these situations, you can create a custom measure in Data Analyzer. The custom measure becomes part of the view file; it does not become part of either an offline cube file or an OLAP database on a server.

To create a custom measure in Data Analyzer, you use the Template Measure Editor, shown in Figure 9-17. To open the editor, click Add on the Template Measures tab of the Define View dialog box.

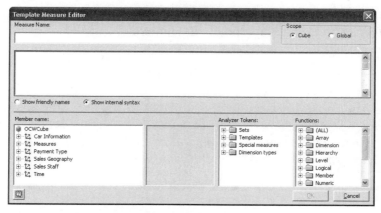

Figure 9-17   The Template Measure Editor.

In the Measure Name box, type a name that is easy for you to remember. In most cases you'll want to select the Show Internal Syntax option. The Show Friendly Names option hides the details of the underlying syntax that Data Analyzer uses to build custom measures. However, clicking the Show Friendly Names option prevents you from editing these expressions, which you need to do with practically all custom measures.

Multidimensional Expressions

The language used to construct custom measures in Data Analyzer is the *Multidimensional Expressions* (MDX) language. MDX syntax provides the means for retrieving and working with data stored in a cube. A few of the more frequently used MDX functions include

- The *Dimension* function, which returns the dimension that contains a specified member, level, or hierarchy.

- The *Level* function, which returns the level of a specified member.

- The *IsLeaf* function, which determines whether a specified member is a leaf member.

- The *Avg*, *Max*, *Median*, and *Min* functions, which return the average, maximum, midpoint, and minimum data values over a group of members.

For more in-depth information about how to use the various functions in the Template Measure Editor and MDX statements, consult the *MDX Function Reference* in the MSDN Library, located at *http:// msdn.microsoft.com/library/en-us/olapdmad/agmdxfunctintro_6n5f.asp*. You can also consult the *MDX Function List* in SQL Server Books Online at *http://www.microsoft.com/sql/techinfo/productdoc/2000/books.asp*.

For the Scope option, Cube is selected by default. With cube scope, a custom measure applies only to the current cube. Selecting the global scope option makes a custom measure available to all cubes viewed in Data Analyzer. You can create measures with either cube scope or global scope and run them against any cube, but if the custom measure doesn't make sense for a particular cube, Data Analyzer returns an error.

Construct the custom measure by dragging dimensions, members, tokens (which are shorthand versions of more advanced measures or member groups), and functions listed in the lower half of the dialog box to the expression box below the Measure Name box. To get a brief description of the functions in the Template Measure Editor's Functions list, you can rest your mouse pointer on any function in the list.

To add a measure you've defined to a view, you use the Measures tab of the Define View dialog box. If the Display Type list is set to Grid, check the box containing the name of the new custom measure. If the Display Type list is set to Bars, select the name of the new custom measure in either the Length or Color list, depending on whether you want the bar lengths or colors to represent the new custom measure.

Your Turn

In this exercise, you will create a custom measure that changes the lengths of the bars and the sizes of the pie slices in the CarSales.max view file to represent a 5 percent sales commission instead of total sales.

1. With the CarSales.max file open, click Change View on the Edit menu.

2. Click the Template Measures tab, and then click Add.

3. In the Measure Name box, type *Sales Commission*.

4. In the Member Name list, click the plus sign (+) next to the Measures icon, click the plus sign next to the MeasuresLevel icon, and then drag the Sum Of Price icon to the expression box.

5. In the expression box, following the text *[Measures].[Sum Of Price]*, type ** 0.05*. Compare your results to Figure 9-18, and then click OK.

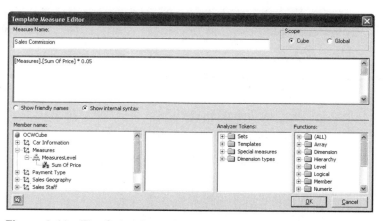

Figure 9-18   The Sales Commission custom measure definition.

(continued)

6. Click the Measures tab, select Sales Commission in the Length list, click OK, and compare your results to Figure 9-19. Rest your mouse pointer on any member bar to confirm that the bar lengths or pie-slice sizes now represent sales commission figures.

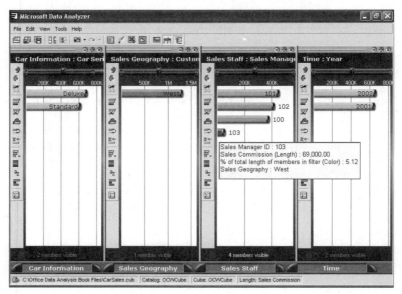

Figure 9-19   The bar lengths reflect the Sales Commission measure.

7. Switch the bar lengths and pie-slice sizes back to their original measures: on the Edit menu, click Change View, click the Measures tab, select Sum Of Price in the Length list, and then click OK. Compare your results to Figure 9-20.

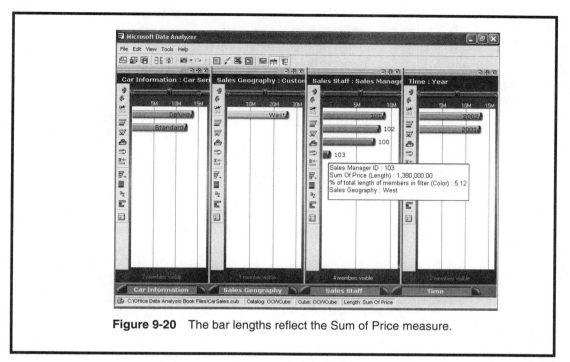

Figure 9-20   The bar lengths reflect the Sum of Price measure.

Here are a few additional custom measures that you can try in conjunction with the CarSales.max view file. To try these out, follow the steps in the previous Your Turn exercise and type the following expressions into the expression box below the Measure Name box. To learn more about how these expressions work, click the Show Names option after you type the expression into the expression box.

- Average Car Sales (the average of car sales for all of the visible members in a dimension pane): *Avg(~Set:$$CurrentAspect:Selected~, [Measures].[Sum Of Price])*. See Figures 9-21 and 9-22.

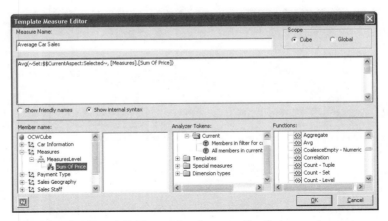

Figure 9-21 The definition of the Average Car Sales custom measure.

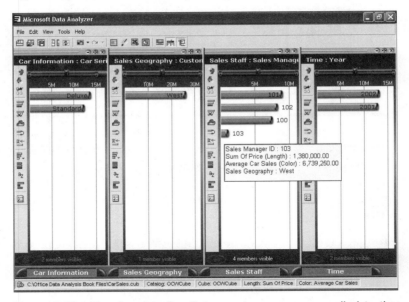

Figure 9-22 The Average Car Sales custom measure applied to the current view's colors. You can easily see that sales manager 103's sales were well below average.

■ Percent of Highest Car Sales Member (assuming that the members' lengths represent the Sum of Price measure, this measure is the ratio of the current member to the member with the longest length in the dimension pane): *~Trait:Core.Length~ / Max(~Set:$$CurrentAspect:Selected~, [Measures].[Sum Of Price])*. See Figures 9-23 and 9-24.

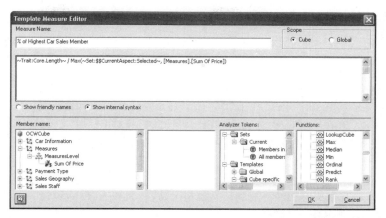

Figure 9-23   The definition of the Percent of Highest Car Sales Member custom measure.

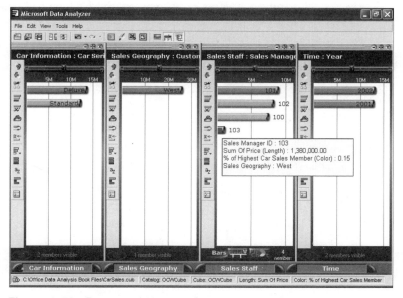

Figure 9-24   Percent of Highest Car Sales Member custom measure applied to the current view's colors.

Making Better Business Decisions

Microsoft Data Analyzer provides additional tools to enhance your data analysis tasks, including the BusinessCenter, the ability to export views to Excel as worksheets or PivotTable reports, and the ability to export view snapshots to Microsoft PowerPoint.

Using the BusinessCenter

The BusinessCenter displays a set of one or more common business questions, in a natural-language format, that can be asked of selected members or dimension panes. To use the BusinessCenter, right-click a member or dimension pane, click BusinessCenter, and follow the BusinessCenter's on-screen directions to customize one of the questions it poses. When you want to run a BusinessCenter question, click the BC icon next to the question. After you run a BusinessCenter question, you can turn off the BusinessCenter by clicking Undo BusinessCenter on the Edit menu.

Your Turn

In this exercise, you will use the BusinessCenter to discover which salespeople had the same car sales patterns over time as the top salesperson.

1. With the CarSales.max file open, in the Sales Staff dimension pane's toolbar, click Drill Down so that the Salesperson ID level is displayed.

2. Right-click the longest member bar (6), and then click Business-Center.

3. Click Car Information, click Time, and then click OK. The question should read "What other Salesperson ID have a distribution of Sum Of Price across Time similar to 6?"

4. Click the BC icon.

5. Notice that the pattern of sales for salesperson 7 is close to salesperson 6, as shown in Figure 9-25.

6. Slide the arrow icon near the bottom of the Find Similar Members dialog box to the right. You will notice that the member bar patterns look less and less like the member bar pattern for salesperson 6.

7. In the Find Similar Members dialog box, click the Select button. Data Analyzer selects the member bars for the two Salesperson IDs (for example, salespeople 6 and 7) and displays that view in its main window. Notice that information is displayed for only the two salespeople, as shown in Figure 9-26.

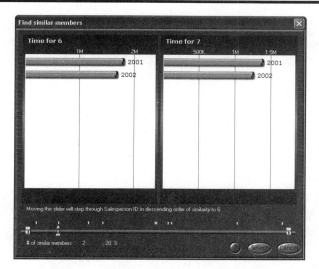

Figure 9-25   Business Center results comparing Sum of Price member bar patterns over time to salesperson 6.

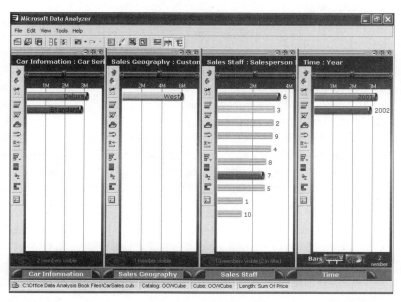

Figure 9-26   Clicking Select in the BusinessCenter filters the view in Data Analyzer

> **Note** You cannot modify the BusinessCenter's questions. You can, however use the Template Measure Editor to create your own measures that answer business questions.

Exporting Data Analyzer Views to Excel, PowerPoint, or the Web

You can export a copy of the information in a Data Analyzer view to an Excel worksheet or to a PivotTable report to work with a snapshot of more detailed data. You can also export a view to a PowerPoint slide to include a snapshot in a presentation or to a Web page to make a view snapshot available over an intranet or the Internet.

> **Tip** You can use Data Analyzer to view more detailed data in a cube by using a technique called *drill through*. Drill through allows you to see the actual data and transactions behind the bars or grids in a Data Analyzer view. However, drill through is not supported for data with values based on expressions such as calculated members or values associated with custom member formulas. Drill through permissions are granted by OLAP database administrators and are therefore not available for Data Analyzer views that connect to offline cube files. To drill through OLAP data sources that support this feature and for which you have permissions, on the Tools menu, click Drill Through. Note that the returned list of data records cannot be modified, grouped, or summarized. For more information about drill through, see the topic "View fields in the underlying data source" in Data Analyzer Help.

When exporting a snapshot of the information from Data Analyzer to an Excel worksheet, you use the Export To Microsoft Excel Workbook command on the Tools menu. The dimension panes and members you want to export must be visible in Data Analyzer. In the Excel workbook that's created, one worksheet is added to the workbook for each visible dimension pane. Each visible member in the dimension pane appears in a row, and the data that was represented by bar length and color in Data Analyzer appears in columns. Figure 9-27 shows the worksheet for the Time dimension from the car sales view. (To display the criteria—known as *slicers*—that was used to create each worksheet, click the plus sign in each worksheet's left margin.) You can then use the data analysis tools in Excel to work with the data without worrying about changing the original data in either Data Analyzer or the OLAP data source.

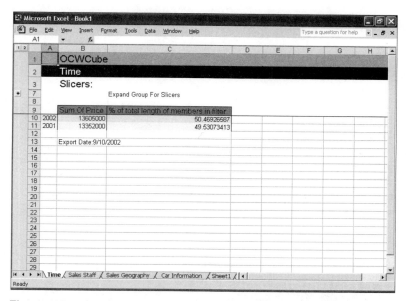

Figure 9-27   Results of exporting a copy of the CarSales.max view file to an Excel workbook.

You use the Export To Microsoft Excel PivotTable Report command on the Tools menu to export a snapshot of the information from Data Analyzer to an Excel PivotTable report. Here again, the dimension panes and members you want to export should be visible in Data Analyzer. (Minimized dimensions appear in the PivotTable report's page area.) Using a wizard, you assign dimensions to row or column areas and assign measures to the data area. Figure 9-28 shows an example of a PivotTable created from the car sales view in Data Analyzer. You can use the PivotTable report to work with the detailed data without worrying about changing the original data in either Data Analyzer or the OLAP data source.

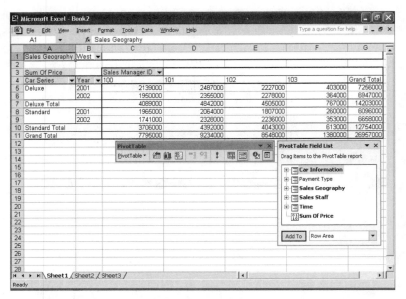

Figure 9-28 Results of exporting a copy of the CarSales.max view file to an Excel PivotTable report.

To export a Data Analyzer view snapshot as a PowerPoint slide, click Export To Microsoft PowerPoint on the Tools menu. A PowerPoint slide is created showing a snapshot of the dimension panes and members that were visible in Data Analyzer. See Figure 9-29 for an example.

To export a Data Analyzer view snapshot as a Web page, click HTML Report on the File menu. Specify whether you want to export the information in a bar or grid format (or in Unicode bar or grid format if you need to display non-English characters), type a report title, and specify where to publish the Web page. See Figure 9-30 for an example.

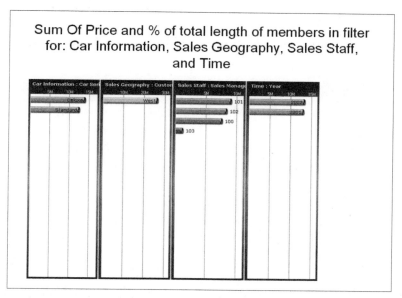

Figure 9-29   Results of exporting a copy of the CarSales.max view file to a PowerPoint slide.

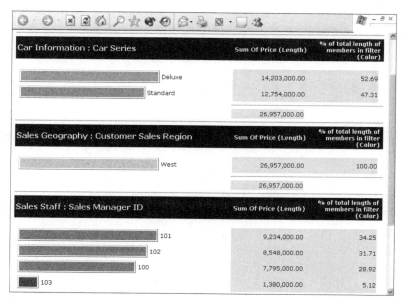

Figure 9-30   Results of exporting a copy of the CarSales.max view file to a Web page.

Summary

In this chapter, you learned the following:

■ Microsoft Data Analyzer is designed to analyze OLAP data. It provides an alternative to PivotTable reports and PivotChart reports. Data Analyzer can quickly drill up and drill down through levels in a cube, quickly isolate disparate members, and easily synchronize multiple views of the same data.

■ Data Analyzer uses a view file to connect to and render OLAP data graphically. In many cases, you can share your view files with others without worrying about moving the target OLAP data source.

■ If an OLAP data source doesn't contain the measures you need, and you don't have permissions to add measures to the original OLAP data source, you can create your own custom measures in Data Analyzer. These custom measures remain in your Data Analyzer view file for reuse and further customization.

■ Data Analyzer interacts with other Microsoft Office applications. You can use Data Analyzer in conjunction with Excel, PowerPoint, and Web browsers to analyze data and present the results of your analysis.

In the next chapter, "Analyzing XML Data," you will learn about the following:

■ What XML is and why it is gaining such broad acceptance in computing today.

■ How to understand and read XML data.

■ How to analyze XML data with Microsoft Excel and Microsoft Access.

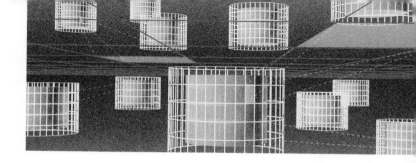

10

Working with XML Data in Excel and Access

Extensible Markup Language (XML) is a set of technologies that allows documents and data to be stored and shared in a file format that does not depend on a particular software application or computer operating system. With XML, organizations can exchange text-based data over the Web, through e-mail, or within a corporate intranet. An XML file's contents can be viewed, transformed, and analyzed regardless of the software applications an organization uses. For example, a manufacturing company might frequently order supplies from a vendor. The manufacturing company and the vendor agree on an XML format, or *XML schema*, they'll use to exchange their data, and now the manufacturing company can use Microsoft Excel 2002 to submit purchase orders to the vendor through e-mail. Using the agreed-upon XML schema, the manufacturing company need not be concerned about which software applications or computer operating systems the vendor uses to process the purchase orders. Microsoft Office XP is the first version of Office that enables XML-based data to be viewed, analyzed, and exchanged without undue modification of the original XML data.

Objectives

In this chapter, you will learn

- What XML is and how it can facilitate the exchange of data because of its nonproprietary nature.

■   How to interpret XML data.

■   How to work with XML data in Microsoft Excel 2002 and Microsoft Access 2002.

Note   The information in this chapter applies to Microsoft Office XP (specifically, Microsoft Excel 2002 and Microsoft Access 2002) only.

The Case for XML

With each version of a software application, manufacturers such as Microsoft add new features to enhance personal and organizational productivity. To enable the use of these features, software makers often need to change and fine-tune their file formats. If you open an Excel worksheet or a Microsoft Word document in a text editor such as Notepad, you'll notice a great number of unintelligible symbols. You see this jumble because the underlying information in the file is specifically designed to be read and interpreted by the program that created it, making it unreadable by a simple text editor. This information might contain special instructions for how the file's data is to be presented in the document window, how features such as versioning or pagination should be handled, and so on.

To help address this issue, software manufacturers create converters to perform operations such as changing files formatted for a different word-processing application into files that Word can read. But how can you accomplish something out of the ordinary, like viewing data stored on a proprietary mainframe computer in an Excel worksheet to do some data analysis? Then, after you've finished with the data, how can you send the results to another department or organization that doesn't have Excel on their computers for further analysis? Typically, this type of solution would involve expensive proprietary software converters and a lot of computer programming. These and other problems become easier to solve with XML.

The general rules about how to create and exchange XML-based data are defined and maintained by the World Wide Web Consortium (W3C), a product-neutral standards body. Based on the W3C rules, more and more software manufacturers, including Microsoft, are creating productivity enhancements in programs such as Excel and Access, with which users can create, view, analyze, and exchange XML data. More and more organizations are beginning to create, store, and exchange data in XML format, which provides flexibility in their choice of software solutions for data creation, data storage, data analysis, and data exchange. Even better, XML is plain text, so you can use applications such as Notepad to create XML data and browsers such as Microsoft Internet Explorer to view and navigate XML data.

Making Sense of XML Data

When you look at XML data for the first time, it can be somewhat confusing. XML data can run together in a big chunk or be indented with lots of white space, unlike Excel worksheets and Access data tables, which present data in well-defined rows, columns, and cells. Pieces of XML data can be defined by a vast number of symbols, such as greater-than (>), less-than (<), and division (/) symbols, foreign characters such as *&* and *>*, and lots of quotation marks. Understanding the W3C XML rules and how these symbols are used in XML is the first task you must master before you can create, read, analyze, and exchange XML data.

To familiarize yourself with what XML data looks like, use Internet Explorer to open and view the CustList.xml file in the Chap10 folder. We'll use this file in several of the exercises in this chapter. As you learn more, the structure and meaning of the XML document will become more clear.

> **Note**   To view XML files in Internet Explorer, you must be using version 5 or later.

> **Note**   For the definitive explanation of the XML rules, you can go to the World Wide Web Consortium's (W3C) Web site at *http://www.w3.org/xml*. You should be aware that these rules are written in a very precise, complex manner. Reading them is similar to reading architectural blueprints—if you aren't a trained architect, it takes some patience to understand blueprints, and unless you understand technical notation such as Backus-Naur form (BNF), reading the W3C XML rules can similarly test your patience!

Basic XML Terminology

As with any computing technology, XML includes terminology that describes and simplifies what can seem at first to be hard-to-understand concepts. In this section, I'll highlight some of the key XML terms that you should become familiar with.

The term *XML data* is used to define the letters, numbers, and symbols that follow the rules of XML. A group of XML data can be stored in an *XML document*, such as a text file with the file extension *.xml*. An XML document that contains XML data that adheres to the rules of XML is referred to as a *well-formed* XML document. When a well-formed XML document adheres to one or more XML schemas, the XML document is also known as a *valid* XML document.

XML documents consist of one or more *elements*. An XML element consists of the element's name, zero or more element characteristics (or properties) known as *attributes*, and possibly some *content*. Content can consist of data such as letters, numbers, or symbols, and possibly even more elements (known as *child elements*) that contain even more data, and so on. Every element is defined by a *start tag*, which begins with the symbol < and ends with the symbol >, and an *end tag*, which begins with the symbols </ and ends with the symbol >. For instance, a simple *firstname* element would be represented as *<firstname>*Paul*</firstname>*. A *language* attribute could be added to make the *firstname* element look like this: *<firstname language="us-en">*Paul*</firstname>*. Elements that contain only the element's name or just attributes (these elements are known as *empty elements*) can be defined by a single shorthand tag that begins with the symbol < and ends with the symbols /> instead of using adjoining start and end tags. For example, the simplest form of an empty address element would be represented as *<address></address>* or just *<address/>*.

Namespaces can be used to distinguish identical element names that are used by two or more schemas referred to by a single XML document. Namespaces consist of two required parts. The first is the *namespace prefix*, a series of characters that's used to identify the namespace. The namespace prefix, along with a colon symbol, precedes an element's name to indicate that the element is defined by that particular namespace. The second required part is a *Uniform Resource Identifier* (URI), which is a longer version of the namespace. A URI can be any series of letters, numbers, and symbols that are reasonably assured to be unique across all space and time. By convention, a URI consists of an organization's public Internet address for its home Web page, along with a unique series of letters, numbers, and symbols administered and handed out by the organization to its members for the purpose of defining namespaces.

Note   A URI doesn't necessarily match a real Web address. Some organizations, including Microsoft, have begun to use a special series of characters that do not even look like Web addresses, such as the namespace URI *urn:schemas-microsoft-com:officedata*, to be sure that no confusion exists about whether these URIs are real Web addresses.

Note   Some software applications require that specific namespaces and URIs be included in XML documents for the application's features to work correctly with the XML data. Unrecognized namespaces and URIs are either ignored or rejected back to the user for clarification by XML-aware software applications.

For example, a sample namespace could be *http://www.microsoft.com/schemas/12-01-2002* with a namespace prefix of *msft*. In XML, this would be represented as *xmlns:msft="http://www.microsoft.com/schemas/12-01-2002"*, and a *postalcode* element that's part of the *msft* namespace would be represented as *<msft:postalcode>98052</msft:postalcode>*.

Elements, which are also sometimes referred to as *nodes*, can be organized into a structure that looks much like a genealogical family tree. Elements can contain child elements, grandchild elements, great-grandchild elements, and so on. Elements can also have relationships with sibling elements, elements can be contained by parent elements, grandparent elements, great-grandparent elements, and so on. For example, a *customerlist* element might contain several *customer* child elements. Each *customer* element would have other *customer* sibling elements. Furthermore, each *customer* element might contain a *customername* child element. Each *customername* element's grandparent element is the *customerlist* element, as shown in this very simple XML document:

```
<customerlist>
    <customer>
        <customername>Paul Cornell</customername>
    </customer>
    <customer>
        <customername>Nancy Davolio</customername>
    </customer>
</customerlist>
```

Processing instructions are special XML elements that can be used by applications to carry out specific actions. Processing instructions are single XML statements that begin with the symbols *<?* and end with the symbols *?>*. For example, the processing instruction *<?xml version="1.0"?>* identifies to XML applications that the file's contents contain XML formatted data.

XML applications can change elements in XML documents from one schema into another schema by applying a style sheet. Style sheets are well-formed XML documents that adhere to the Extensible Stylesheet Language Transformations (XSLT) specification. For example, if one organization uses the *purchaseorder* element to describe a purchase order, and another organization uses the *requisition* element to describe the same purchase order, XSLT can transform all the *purchaseorder* elements to *requisition* elements.

> **Note** A complete discussion of XSLT is outside the scope of this book. For more information about XSLT, see the W3C Web site at *http://www.w3.org/tr/xslt*.

Basic XML Rules

Now that you understand some of the basic terminology of XML, you can learn some of its basic rules. Understanding the following eight rules will help you create, analyze, and exchange well-formed XML.

1. XML element names and attributes are case-sensitive. XML tags such as *<region></region>*, *<Region></Region>*, and *<REGION></REGION>* do not refer to the same element. The case-sensitivity of XML tags is different from the rules of Hypertext Markup Language (HTML), which does not have this requirement.

2. Every XML start tag must have a matching end tag. In HTML, you can type *<p>This is a paragraph* to represent a paragraph. However, in XML you must type *<p>This is a paragraph</p>*.

3. An empty XML element is represented as an adjoining start tag and end tag or a special XML tag known as an *empty-element tag*. For instance, an empty *list* element could be represented as *<list></list>* or just *<list/>*.

4. Every XML document should start with a special XML processing instruction called the *XML declaration*. This processing instruction should contain, at a minimum, the text *<?xml version="1.0"?>*. This declaration signals to XML-aware applications that any accompanying data should be treated as XML.

5. Every XML document must have one and only one root element, known also as the *document element*. The document element appears after the XML declaration and contains all the other elements in the XML document.

6. All attribute values must be enclosed within quotation marks. In HTML, you can type attributes such as *<table rows=5 cols=2></table>*. In XML, however, you must type attributes as *<table rows="5" cols="2"></table>*.

7. Certain keyboard characters and other symbols have special uses in XML, for example the < and > symbols used in element tags. When these characters or symbols are part of the content—when they are not used as part of the XML markup—they must be represented by replacement characters known as *escape sequences*. For example, using the greater-than (>) symbol other than to denote start, end, or empty tags is not allowed in XML (except in a CDATA section as described in the next item). Instead, you use the escape sequence *>*. Here's an example:

```
<sentence>This is how you represent a greater-than (&gt;) symbol.
</sentence>
```

Other symbols that require escape sequences include less-than (*<*), ampersand (*&*), quotation mark (*"*), and apostrophe (*'*).

8. If you want to type a series of letters, numbers, and symbols without worrying about escape sequences, you can enclose the content in a *CDATA section*. A CDATA section starts with the symbols *<![CDATA[* and ends with the symbols *]]>*. Here's an example

```
<![CDATA[Look, I can type whatever I want here,
including symbols such
as <, >, and &,
without breaking the XML rules!]]>
```

The XML rules are suspended for the most part inside CDATA sections. CDATA sections are typically used to exchange complex or precise series of letters, numbers, and symbols.

Analyzing XML Data with Microsoft Excel

XML and Microsoft Excel workbooks are both designed to handle structured data, which makes Excel a natural choice to present XML data in its familiar pattern of worksheet columns, rows, and cells. However, because XML documents contain elements that can be related to other elements that don't lend themselves to a row-and-column layout, Excel must use a special algorithm to "flatten" XML data into a two-dimensional representation. Excel can avoid using the flattening algorithm if the XML data you're working with adheres to a schema created by Microsoft. I'll describe this schema later in the chapter.

Understanding and Working with the XML Spreadsheet Flattener

You can open any well-formed XML file in Excel 2002. To do so, click Open on the File menu and then select XML Files in the Files Of Type list. Once you open the XML file in Excel, you can analyze the XML data as if it were native Excel data.

Excel worksheets are two-dimensional rows and columns, and because XML data can have more than two dimensions, a flattening algorithm is used to force the XML data into worksheet cells. When you open an XML file in Excel that is not provided in the XML Spreadsheet schema (described later in this chapter), Excel uses the algorithm to load the XML data into columns, rows, and cells. The XML tags appear as column headings, and the data appears in rows below the appropriate column headings. XML files are opened as read-only in Excel so that you do not accidentally save your original XML file in the XML Spreadsheet schema format.

To see how this works, if you have not done so already, use Internet Explorer to open the CustList.xml file in the Chap10 folder. With the file open in Internet Explorer, open the same file in Excel for comparison. You can see the differences in how the XML data is presented in Internet Explorer and Excel in Figure 10-1 and Figure 10-2.

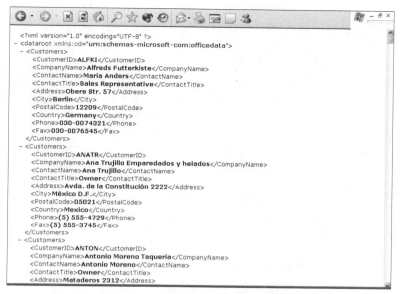

Figure 10-1 The CustList.xml file displayed in Internet Explorer 6.

	A	B	C	D	E
1	/dataroot				
2	/Customers/Address	/Customers/City	/Customers/CompanyName	/Customers/ContactName	/Customers/ContactTitle
3	Obere Str. 57	Berlin	Alfreds Futterkiste	Maria Anders	Sales Representative
4	Avda. de la Constitucio	México D.F.	Ana Trujillo Emparedados y hel	Ana Trujillo	Owner
5	Mataderos 2312	México D.F.	Antonio Moreno Taquería	Antonio Moreno	Owner
6	120 Hanover Sq.	London	Around the Horn	Thomas Hardy	Sales Representative
7	Berguvsvägen 8	Luleå	Berglunds snabbköp	Christina Berglund	Order Administrator
8	Forsterstr. 57	Mannheim	Blauer See Delikatessen	Hanna Moos	Sales Representative
9	24, place Kléber	Strasbourg	Blondel père et fils	Frédérique Citeaux	Marketing Manager
10	C/ Araquil, 67	Madrid	Bólido Comidas preparadas	Martín Sommer	Owner
11	12, rue des Bouchers	Marseille	Bon app'	Laurence Lebihan	Owner
12	23 Tsawassen Blvd.	Tsawassen	Bottom-Dollar Markets	Elizabeth Lincoln	Accounting Manager
13	Fauntleroy Circus	London	B's Beverages	Victoria Ashworth	Sales Representative
14	Cerrito 333	Buenos Aires	Cactus Comidas para llevar	Patricio Simpson	Sales Agent
15	Sierras de Granada 99	México D.F.	Centro comercial Moctezuma	Francisco Chang	Marketing Manager
16	Hauptstr. 29	Bern	Chop-suey Chinese	Yang Wang	Owner
17	Av. dos Lusíadas, 23	São Paulo	Comércio Mineiro	Pedro Afonso	Sales Associate
18	Berkeley Gardens 12 Brewery	London	Consolidated Holdings	Elizabeth Brown	Sales Representative
19	Walserweg 21	Aachen	Drachenblut Delikatessen	Sven Ottlieb	Order Administrator
20	67, rue des Cinquante	Nantes	Du monde entier	Janine Labrune	Owner
21	35 King George	London	Eastern Connection	Ann Devon	Sales Agent
22	Kirchgasse 6	Graz	Ernst Handel	Roland Mendel	Sales Manager
23	Rua Orós, 92	São Paulo	Familia Arquibaldo	Aria Cruz	Marketing Assistant
24	C/ Moralzarzal, 86	Madrid	FISSA Fabrica Inter. Salchicha	Diego Roel	Accounting Manager
25	184, chaussée de Tou	Lille	Folies gourmandes	Martine Rancé	Assistant Sales Agent
26	Åkergatan 24	Bräcke	Folk och fä HB	Maria Larsson	Owner
27	Berliner Platz 43	München	Frankenversand	Peter Franken	Marketing Manager

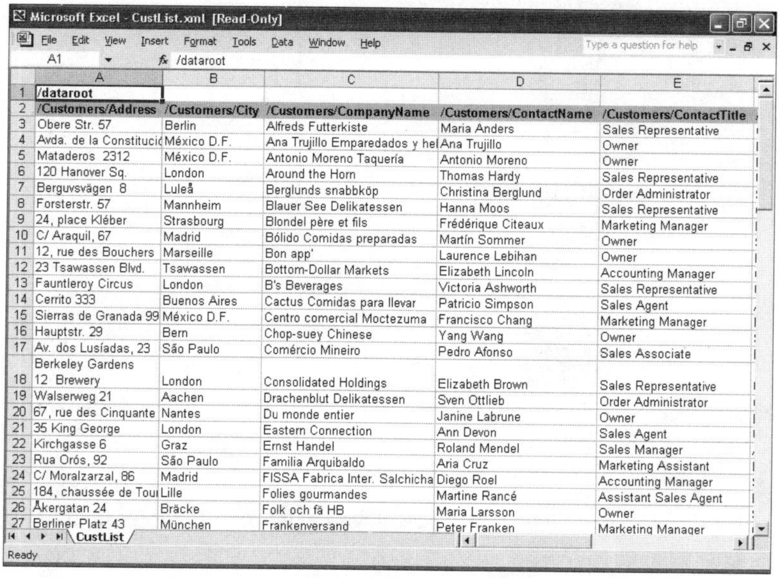

Figure 10-2 The CustList.xml file displayed in Excel 2002.

You should notice first that Excel presents the data from left to right in columns and rows, while Internet Explorer presents the data from top to bottom, with one element per line. The second difference to notice is that Internet Explorer presents the element names in XML notation, while Excel presents the element names in hierarchical notation. For instance, every *Customers* element in the XML file has a child element *CustomerID*. Excel represents the *CustomerID* element as */Customers/CustomerID*. Third, Internet Explorer presents elements in the order in which they occur in the XML file; Excel presents the element names in alphabetical order. Also of note, empty elements or missing elements appear as blank cells in Excel, and the document element (*dataroot* in this example) occurs on the first row by itself.

Finally, this XML file does not show how attributes and data summarizations are handled. To see how these work, use Internet Explorer to open the CustOrds.xml file in the Chap10 folder. With the file still open, open the file in Excel 2002 for comparison. The different views of the file are shown in Figure 10-3 and Figure 10-4.

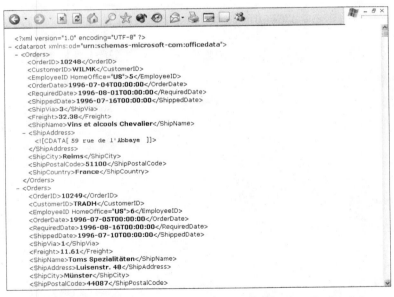

Figure 10-3   The CustOrds.xml file displayed in Internet Explorer 6.

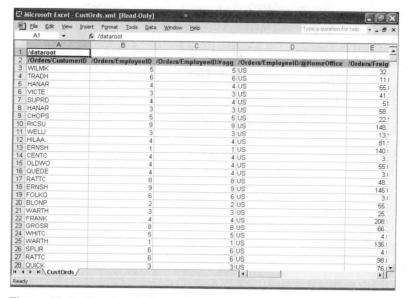

Figure 10-4   The CustOrds.xml file displayed in Excel 2002.

In the XML file, every *Orders* element contains an *EmployeeID* element with a *HomeOffice* attribute. In Excel, the attribute is preceded by an @ symbol; for example, */Orders/EmployeeID/@HomeOffice*. Also, whenever Excel sees an XML element that appears to include numerical data, Excel tries to perform a summarization (or *aggregation*) of the data values, with the result of the aggregation appearing with an *#agg* designation. (Notice in this case that Excel thinks the *EmployeeID*, *OrderID*, and *ShipVia* elements are numerical, but in reality they are just identifiers.)

Your Turn

In this exercise, you will see how you can use Excel data analysis features to work with XML data. You will use an XML file, flattened by Excel, to display only those rows from customer ALFKI. You will then look at the XML data presented in a PivotTable report.

1.   If you have not done so already, open the CustOrds.xml file (in the Chap10 folder) in Excel 2002.

2.   On the Data menu, point to Filter and then click AutoFilter.

(continued)

3. In cell A2, click the arrow, and then click ALFKI in the list. Only rows for customer ALFKI are displayed, as shown in Figure 10-5.

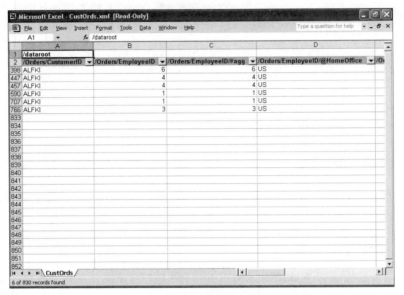

Figure 10-5   Orders for customer ALFKI only.

4. On the Data menu, click PivotTable And PivotChart Report, and then click Finish.

5. Drag the /Orders/CustomerID icon from the PivotTable field list to the Drop Page Fields Here area of the PivotTable report.

6. Drag the /Orders/EmployeeID icon from the PivotTable field list to the Drop Row Fields Here area of the PivotTable report.

7. Drag the /Orders/CustomerID icon from the PivotTable field list to the Drop Data Fields Here area of the PivotTable report.

8. Click the arrow in cell B1 (the /Orders/CustomerID page field value), click ALFKI, and then click OK. Notice that employees 1 and 4 booked 2 orders each, while employees 3 and 6 booked 1 order each.

Understanding and Working with the XML Spreadsheet Schema

To provide the highest fidelity and the best XML data import experience with Excel 2002, Excel worksheets and workbooks can be exported as XML documents by using a special XML schema called the *XML Spreadsheet schema* (XMLSS). The XMLSS schema, invented by Microsoft primarily for use in Excel 2002, comprises a particular set of XML elements and attributes that represent, in plain text format, most of the formatting and other features of an Excel worksheet or workbook. The XMLSS schema is often used by software applications that automatically create text files formatted as rich Excel worksheets or by two organizations, only one of which uses Excel, that need to output annotated information from Excel workbooks in a plain text format without retouching the data.

> **Note**   For complete information on the XMLSS schema's elements and attributes, see the article "XML Spreadsheet Reference" on the Microsoft Developer Network (MSDN) Web site at *http://msdn.microsoft.com*. For additional information, see Microsoft Knowledge Base Article Q288215 "INFO: Microsoft Excel 2002 and XML" at *http://support.microsoft.com/default.aspx?scid=KB;EN-US;Q288215&*.

To save the data in an Excel 2002 spreadsheet in the XMLSS schema format, select XML Spreadsheet in the Save As list when you save a file. You can open the XML file in Internet Explorer to examine the XMLSS schema output. To see how this works, open the Products.xml file in the Chap10 folder in Internet Explorer and in Excel. The different views of the file are shown in Figures 10-6 and 10-7.

First of all, notice that the XML data in Excel is very neat and clean. Element names don't appear with slash symbols, as they do in flattened Excel XML data, and columns created by the flattening algorithm for attributes and summarizations are gone as well. Second, notice that the Excel version of the XML data contains bold column headers and several cells that are colored red or green. Excel formatting features are available for XML data that follows the XMLSS schema format. Third, you should notice in Internet Explorer that the XML contains a lot of additional XML data. For example, you can see several namespace declarations in the *Workbook* element, overall document settings in the *DocumentProperties* and *OfficeDocumentSettings* elements, formatting characteristics in the *Styles* element, and so on. The trade-off for enabling Excel features in XML data is that a lot of Excel-specific information must be included in the XML data. Excel uses this information when it loads the XML file to present and format the XML data. You could theoretically create a full-fidelity Excel spreadsheet, including the data and formatting, by using a text editor such as Notepad. In most business scenarios, however, an XML file that includes the Excel schema information would most likely be created by some type of automatic XML report-generation program.

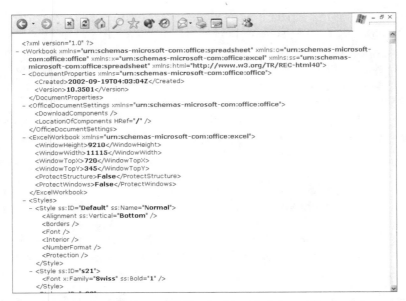

Figure 10-6   The Products.xml file displayed in Internet Explorer 6.

	A	B	C	D	E	F	G	
1	ProductID	CategoryID	ProductName	QuantityPerUnit	UnitPrice	UnitsInStock	UnitsOnOrder	Re
2	1	1	Chai	10 boxes x 20 bags	$18.00	39	0	
3	2	1	Chang	24 - 12 oz bottles	$19.00	17	40	
4	3	2	Aniseed Syrup	12 - 550 ml bottles	$10.00	13	70	
5	4	2	Chef Anton's Cajun Seasoning	48 - 6 oz jars	$22.00	53	0	
6	5	2	Chef Anton's Gumbo Mix	36 boxes	$21.35	0	0	
7	6	2	Grandma's Boysenberry Spread	12 - 8 oz jars	$25.00	120	0	
8	7	7	Uncle Bob's Organic Dried Pears	12 - 1 lb pkgs.	$30.00	15	0	
9	8	2	Northwoods Cranberry Sauce	12 - 12 oz jars	$40.00	6	0	
10	9	6	Mishi Kobe Niku	18 - 500 g pkgs.	$97.00	29	0	
11	10	8	Ikura	12 - 200 ml jars	$31.00	31	0	
12	11	4	Queso Cabrales	1 kg pkg.	$21.00	22	30	
13	12	4	Queso Manchego La Pastora	10 - 500 g pkgs.	$38.00	86	0	
14	13	8	Konbu	2 kg box	$6.00	24	0	
15	14	7	Tofu	40 - 100 g pkgs.	$23.25	35	0	
16	15	2	Genen Shouyu	24 - 250 ml bottles	$15.50	39	0	
17	16	3	Pavlova	32 - 500 g boxes	$17.45	29	0	
18	17	6	Alice Mutton	20 - 1 kg tins	$39.00	0	0	
19	18	8	Carnarvon Tigers	16 kg pkg.	$62.50	42	0	
20	19	3	Teatime Chocolate Biscuits	10 boxes x 12 pieces	$9.20	25	0	
21	20	3	Sir Rodney's Marmalade	30 gift boxes	$81.00	40	0	
22	21	3	Sir Rodney's Scones	24 pkgs. x 4 pieces	$10.00	3	40	
23	22	5	Gustaf's Knäckebröd	24 - 500 g pkgs.	$21.00	104	0	
24	23	5	Tunnbröd	12 - 250 g pkgs.	$9.00	61	0	
25	24	1	Guaraná Fantástica	12 - 355 ml cans	$4.50	20	0	
26	25	3	NuNuCa Nuß-Nougat-Creme	20 - 450 g glasses	$14.00	76	0	
27	26	3	Gumbär Gummibärchen	100 - 250 g bags	$31.23	15	0	
28	27	3	Schoggi Schokolade	100 - 100 g pieces	$43.90	49	0	

Figure 10-7   The Products.xml file displayed in Excel 2002.

Note   Microsoft Excel 2002 can save XML files only in the XMLSS schema format. It cannot save workbooks in any other type of XML schema.

By default, XML files are opened as read-only, leaving the original file unchanged for future use. When you open an XML file that references a style sheet, Excel gives you the opportunity to open the file without applying the style sheet, or to apply a specific stylesheet (if the file references more than one).

Tip   You can also save the data from a Microsoft Office XP Spreadsheet Component in the XMLSS schema format. To do so, click the Export To Microsoft Excel button on the Spreadsheet Component's toolbar. In the Save As list, select XML Spreadsheet.

The following Excel information and features are not saved in worksheets or workbooks that are saved as XML data:

- Charts, drawing layers, and other graphic objects
- Custom views, outlining, and grouping
- Data consolidation references and scenarios
- Shared workbook information
- User-defined function categories and Visual Basic for Applications projects

Note   Data in password-protected worksheets and workbooks cannot be saved as XML.

Your Turn

In this exercise, you will see that using Excel data analysis features with flattened XML is the same as XMLSS schema formatted data. You will use an XMLSS schema formatted file to display only those rows from Category ID 1. You will also see how easy it is to display this XML data in a Pivot-Table report, as you did in the last exercise.

1. If you have not done so already, in Excel 2002, open the Products.xml file in the Chap10 folder.

2. On the Data menu, point to Filter and then click AutoFilter.

3. In cell B1, click the arrow, and click 1 in the list. Only rows for Category ID 1 are displayed, as shown in Figure 10-8.

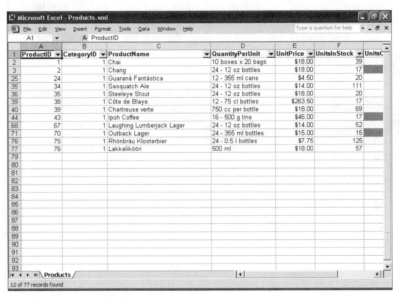

Figure 10-8   Products for category ID 1 only.

4. On the Data menu, click PivotTable And PivotChart Report, and then click Finish.

5. Drag the CategoryID icon from the PivotTable field list to the Drop Page Fields Here area of the PivotTable report.

6. Drag the ProductName icon from the PivotTable Field List to the Drop Row Fields Here area of the PivotTable report.

7. Drag the UnitsInStock icon from the PivotTable Field List to the Drop Data Fields Here area of the PivotTable report.

8. Click the arrow in cell B1 (the CategoryID page field value), click 1, and click OK.

9. Click cell A4 (the ProductName field). On the PivotTable toolbar, click PivotTable, and then click Sort And Top 10.

10. Click the Descending option, click Sum Of UnitsInStock in the Using Field list underneath the Descending option, and then click OK. Notice that the Rhönbräu Klosterbier has the most units in stock.

Understanding and Working with XML Data in Excel Web Queries

You now know that Excel 2002 supports reading and writing XML. Additionally, Excel 2002 can create refreshable Web queries to live XML files.

To create an Excel Web query to an XML file, in an Excel workbook, point to Import External Data on the Data menu and then click New Web Query. In the Address box, type the address of the XML file, and then click Go. Click the Click To Select The Entire Page icon (the icon with an arrow). Click Import. Select either the Existing Worksheet option or the New Worksheet option. (With the Existing Worksheet option, the XML data will be imported starting with the cell listed in the box directly below the option's label.) Finally, click OK. The XML data is imported into Excel as a Web query. You can now make changes to the original XML data file and reflect those changes in the Excel Web query by clicking Refresh Data on the Data menu in Excel.

Your Turn

In this exercise, you will create an Excel Web query to the Products.xml file, make a change to the Products.xml file, and see the change in the Web query.

1. Start Excel.

2. On the Data menu, point to Import External Data and then click New Web Query.

(continued)

3. In the Address box, type the address to the Products.xml file in the Chap10 folder, and then click Go. The address will take the form something like *file://c:/Microsoft Press/Excel Data Analysis/ Sample Files/Chap10/products.xml*.

4. Click the Click To Select The Entire Page icon (the icon with an arrow).

5. Compare your results to Figure 10-9, and then click Import.

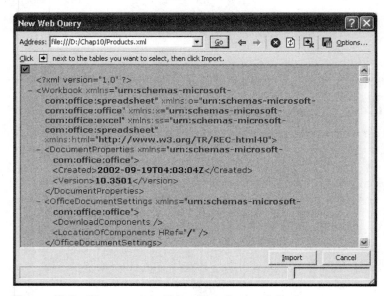

Figure 10-9   The completed New Web Query dialog box.

6. Click the Existing Worksheet option, and then click OK. The XML data is imported into Excel as a Web query.

7. Using Notepad, open the Products.xml file, change the single occurrence of the word *ProductID* to *ProductNumber* (use the Find command on the Edit menu to locate the text), and then save and close the file.

8. Back in Excel, click Refresh Data on the Data menu. Notice that the text in cell A1 changes from *ProductID* to *ProductNumber*.

Working with XML Data with Microsoft Access

Access 2002 can import XML files to Access tables. Once XML data is imported into Access, you can use the Access data analysis tools just as you would with native Access data. You can also export the data in Access tables, queries, forms, or reports to XML files. Access 2002 does not support importing XML schemas.

To import XML data into Access, on the File menu, point to Get External Data, and then click Import. In the Files Of Type list, select XML Documents, select the XML file, and then click Import. Follow any additional directions that Access specifies to complete the import.

To export data as XML, in the Database window, select the database object that contains the data you want to export, click Export on the File menu, and then select XML Documents in the Save As Type list. Click Export. Select the appropriate options to export the Access object's data as XML, the XML data's schema, and the XML data's presentation information. For example, you should consider exporting the XML data's schema if you want to create additional XML data files that adhere to that schema, and you should consider exporting the XML data's presentation information if you want to display the XML data on a Web site.

In the Export XML dialog box, the Data option must be selected for the Presentation Of Your Data (XSL) option to be available. Also, you can click the Advanced button to specify additional XML export options such as whether to include the XML schema information in the XML file, the encoding type, and so on.

> **Note**   XML can be *encoded* (this means how certain characters and symbols are displayed in different languages) in either the UTF-8 or UTF-16 format. Encoding is disabled if you are not exporting data or schema information.

Putting It Together

In this exercise, you will import and export XML data to and from Access 2002.

1.   Start Access and open the Northwind database in the Chap05 folder. If the Welcome screen appears, click OK to close it.

(continued)

2. On the Main Switchboard screen, click Display Database Window.

3. On the File menu, point to Get External Data and then click Import.

4. In the Files Of Type list, select XML Documents.

5. Locate and select the CustList.xml file in the Chap10 folder, and then click Import.

6. When the Import XML dialog box appears, click OK. Click OK to close the success message.

7. Open the Customers1 table and examine the imported XML to see that it looks just like Access data. For example, XML element names become field names in the table. Close the table when you've finished.

8. With the Customers1 table selected, on the File menu, click Export.

9. In the Save As Type list, select XML Documents, and then click Export.

10. Select the Data (XML), Schema Of The Data, and Presentation Of Your Data (XSL) options, and then click OK.

11. Use Internet Explorer to open and examine the three files that Access creates: Customers1.xml (the data file), Customers1.xsd (the schema file), and Customers1.xsl (the transform file).

In Figure 10-10, which shows the XML data in Customers1.xml, you can see a reference to the schema defined in the file Customers1.xsd. The *dataroot* element contains a *Customers1* element for each customer in the Customers1 table. Each *Customers1* element contains information about each customer.

Figure 10-11 shows Customers1.xsd. This schema defines the structure of the XML data that is exported from the Customers1 table. For instance, this schema states that the *dataroot* element can contain any number of *Customers1* child elements.

```
<?xml version="1.0" encoding="UTF-8" ?>
- <dataroot xmlns:od="urn:schemas-microsoft-com:officedata"
   xmlns:xsi="http://www.w3.org/2000/10/XMLSchema-instance"
   xsi:noNamespaceSchemaLocation="Customers1.xsd">
 - <Customers1>
     <CustomerID>ALFKI</CustomerID>
     <CompanyName>Alfreds Futterkiste</CompanyName>
     <ContactName>Maria Anders</ContactName>
     <ContactTitle>Sales Representative</ContactTitle>
     <Address>Obere Str. 57</Address>
     <City>Berlin</City>
     <PostalCode>12209</PostalCode>
     <Country>Germany</Country>
     <Phone>030-0074321</Phone>
     <Fax>030-0076545</Fax>
   </Customers1>
 - <Customers1>
     <CustomerID>ANATR</CustomerID>
     <CompanyName>Ana Trujillo Emparedados y helados</CompanyName>
     <ContactName>Ana Trujillo</ContactName>
     <ContactTitle>Owner</ContactTitle>
     <Address>Avda. de la Constitución 2222</Address>
     <City>México D.F.</City>
     <PostalCode>05021</PostalCode>
     <Country>Mexico</Country>
     <Phone>(5) 555-4729</Phone>
     <Fax>(5) 555-3745</Fax>
   </Customers1>
 - <Customers1>
     <CustomerID>ANTON</CustomerID>
     <CompanyName>Antonio Moreno Taquería</CompanyName>
     <ContactName>Antonio Moreno</ContactName>
```

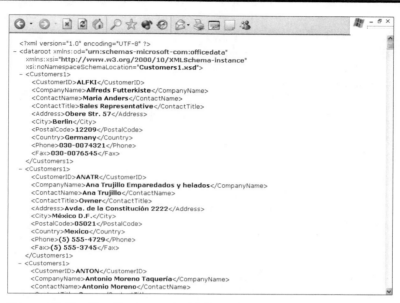

Figure 10-10 The Customers1.xml file.

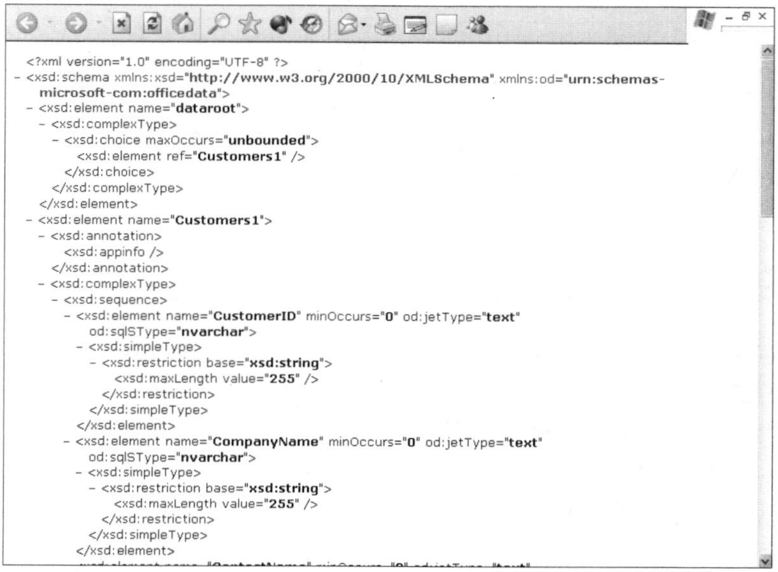

```
<?xml version="1.0" encoding="UTF-8" ?>
- <xsd:schema xmlns:xsd="http://www.w3.org/2000/10/XMLSchema" xmlns:od="urn:schemas-
   microsoft-com:officedata">
 - <xsd:element name="dataroot">
   - <xsd:complexType>
     - <xsd:choice maxOccurs="unbounded">
         <xsd:element ref="Customers1" />
       </xsd:choice>
     </xsd:complexType>
   </xsd:element>
 - <xsd:element name="Customers1">
   - <xsd:annotation>
       <xsd:appinfo />
     </xsd:annotation>
   - <xsd:complexType>
     - <xsd:sequence>
       - <xsd:element name="CustomerID" minOccurs="0" od:jetType="text"
           od:sqlSType="nvarchar">
         - <xsd:simpleType>
           - <xsd:restriction base="xsd:string">
               <xsd:maxLength value="255" />
             </xsd:restriction>
           </xsd:simpleType>
         </xsd:element>
       - <xsd:element name="CompanyName" minOccurs="0" od:jetType="text"
           od:sqlSType="nvarchar">
         - <xsd:simpleType>
           - <xsd:restriction base="xsd:string">
               <xsd:maxLength value="255" />
             </xsd:restriction>
           </xsd:simpleType>
         </xsd:element>
```

Figure 10-11 The Customers1.xsd file.

(continued)

Customers1.xls, shown in Figure 10-12, defines the layout of the XML data for presentation on a Web page. For example, the <TR> tag indicates that the XML data is to be displayed as an HTML-compliant table structure.

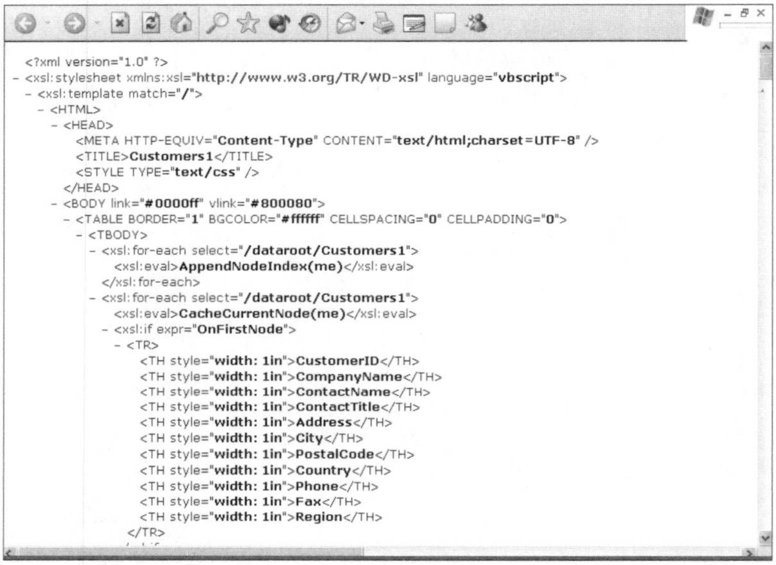

```
  <?xml version="1.0" ?>
- <xsl:stylesheet xmlns:xsl="http://www.w3.org/TR/WD-xsl" language="vbscript">
  - <xsl:template match="/">
    - <HTML>
      - <HEAD>
          <META HTTP-EQUIV="Content-Type" CONTENT="text/html;charset=UTF-8" />
          <TITLE>Customers1</TITLE>
          <STYLE TYPE="text/css" />
        </HEAD>
      - <BODY link="#0000ff" vlink="#800080">
        - <TABLE BORDER="1" BGCOLOR="#ffffff" CELLSPACING="0" CELLPADDING="0">
          - <TBODY>
            - <xsl:for-each select="/dataroot/Customers1">
                <xsl:eval>AppendNodeIndex(me)</xsl:eval>
              </xsl:for-each>
            - <xsl:for-each select="/dataroot/Customers1">
                <xsl:eval>CacheCurrentNode(me)</xsl:eval>
              - <xsl:if expr="OnFirstNode">
                - <TR>
                    <TH style="width: 1in">CustomerID</TH>
                    <TH style="width: 1in">CompanyName</TH>
                    <TH style="width: 1in">ContactName</TH>
                    <TH style="width: 1in">ContactTitle</TH>
                    <TH style="width: 1in">Address</TH>
                    <TH style="width: 1in">City</TH>
                    <TH style="width: 1in">PostalCode</TH>
                    <TH style="width: 1in">Country</TH>
                    <TH style="width: 1in">Phone</TH>
                    <TH style="width: 1in">Fax</TH>
                    <TH style="width: 1in">Region</TH>
                  </TR>
```

Figure 10-12 The Customers1.xsl file.

For more information on the data, schema, and transform files that Access generates and how you can work with them, see the topic "About XML data and Access" in Access Help.

Summary

In this chapter, you learned

- What XML is and how it can be used to create and exchange data with others, regardless of the computer systems or software applications that they use.

- How to use Excel 2002 to open, import, and analyze XML data.

- How to use Access 2002 to import and export XML data.

In the next chapter, "Extending Office Data Analysis Features with Code," you will learn how to work with code macros, procedures, and object models to create automated data analysis solutions using Excel, Access, the Microsoft Office Web Components, and Microsoft Data Analyzer.

11

Extending Office Data Analysis Features with Code

Many of the Microsoft Office data analysis features that you've read about and experimented with so far in this book can be automated through the use of programmatic code. Once you understand how to work with the Visual Basic Editor, the primary development environment used to write code for Office applications, you'll be better prepared to automate Office data analysis features.

To help lay a foundation for programming Office applications, this chapter begins with a discussion of Office code macros and procedures, which are collections of code that perform certain tasks, and then provides and explains code examples that relate to specific Office data analysis tasks and features. If you're familiar with at least one high-level programming language (Microsoft Visual Basic, for example), you will see some specific examples and gain some background about Office development. If you're not familiar with programming, while this chapter can't be a thorough introduction, you'll still gain an understanding of some fundamental concepts and see the direction that you need to go.

> **Note** The code samples in this chapter are written for Microsoft Office XP applications. For information about writing solutions for Office 2000, see the Office Visual Basic Help included with Office 2000 or visit the Microsoft Developer Network (MSDN) Web site at *http://msdn.microsoft.com*.

Objectives

In this chapter you will learn

- How Office code macros and procedures work.

- How the Office programmatic object models work.

- How to use code to access the data analysis features in Microsoft Excel, Microsoft Access, the Microsoft Office Web Components, and Microsoft Data Analyzer.

Understanding Office Code: Macros and Procedures

Microsoft data analysis solutions do not need to be complex, nor do they require a lot of effort to deploy. In many cases, a *macro* (a self-contained piece of code) can automate a data analysis task that involves several steps. For example, you could use macros to automate data analysis tasks such as the following:

- Sort and filter lists of records in Excel or Access.

- Insert standard Excel worksheet functions or Analysis ToolPak functions.

- Conditionally format Excel worksheet cells.

- Create Excel charts, PivotTable reports, or PivotChart reports from lists of records.

- Run Access queries.

- Display Access data tables or reports.

- Create Office Web Components on Web pages and connect them to a data source.

- Analyze OLAP data with Microsoft Data Analyzer views.

- Open and save XML data in Excel.

> **Note**   The code descriptions and examples in this chapter use the Visual Basic family of programming languages, which are the primary programming languages used by Office solution developers. Complete coverage of the Visual Basic family of programming languages is outside the scope of this chapter. For more information about Visual Basic, see the Microsoft Developer Network (MSDN) Visual Basic Web site at *http://msdn.microsoft.com/vbasic*. For more information on learning Visual Basic for Applications, see the MSDN Office Developer Center at *http://msdn.microsoft.com/office*. For more information on learning VBScript, see the MSDN Windows Script Developer Center at *http://msdn.microsoft.com/scripting*.

Each macro begins with one procedure. When you instruct an Office application to run a macro, the application starts with the first line of code contained within the macro's corresponding procedure.

If you're unsure what a procedure is, imagine performing a simple addition problem on a hand-held calculator, adding 3 to 5, for example. You first press the button for the number 3, then the addition symbol (+), and the number 5. When you press the equals sign (=), the calculator displays 8, as you'd expect. By following steps like this, you execute, or run, the procedure 3 + 5 = 8.

We can express a procedure such as this in symbolic terms as

```
intFirst + intSecond = AdditionResult
```

where *intFirst* represents the integer (a number without fractions) value 3, *intSecond* represents the integer value 5, and *AdditionResult* represents the integer value 8.

We can express this simple procedure in VBA code as follows:

```
Public Function AdditionResult(ByVal intFirst As Integer, _
        ByVal intSecond As Integer) As Integer

    AdditionResult = intFirst + intSecond

End Function
```

In programming terms, the parts of this procedure are defined as follows:

- The values *intFirst* and *intSecond* are the procedure's *arguments* or *input parameters*.

■ The *As Integer* keyword that follows the values *intFirst* and *intSecond* refers to the arguments' *input type*.

■ The *As Integer* keyword that follows the final parenthesis indicates the procedure's *return type*.

■ The *AdditionResult* statement before the keyword *End Function* is the procedure's *return value*.

A few additional items to note:

■ The *Public* keyword signifies the procedure's scope. Scope determines in what context a procedure can be executed. In this case, the *Public* keyword means that the procedure can be executed from other procedures in this code module or from other code modules within the same workbook or database, for example.

■ The *AdditionResult* portion following the *Function* keyword signifies the procedure's name. You can refer to this entire portion of code (or code block) as "the *AdditionResult* procedure."

■ The *ByVal* keyword indicates that the procedure is not modifying the actual values of *intFirst* or *intSecond* in any way. In this example, the *AdditionResult* procedure is using the values *intFirst* and *intSecond* to determine what the return value of *AdditionResult* will be. If you wanted to modify the actual values of *intFirst* and *intSecond*, you would use the *ByRef* keyword and write code that actually modifies the values of *intFirst* and *intSecond*.

■ The space-underscore (_) symbol at the end of the first line (following the code *ByVal intFirst As Integer*) is a *line continuation character*. This character is used for readability; it signifies that code on this line and the next line should be treated as a single line of code.

■ The *Function* keyword means that the procedure can return a value to any other procedure that *calls*, or refers to, it. There are two types of procedures: subroutines and functions. A subroutine does not return a value (although it can declare arguments) and is signified by the keywords *Sub* and *End Sub*.

■ The keyword *End Function* signifies the end of the function.

Your Turn

Now that you understand the basics of how procedures work, practice creating and running a simple procedure that calls the *AdditionResult* function.

1. Start Excel.

2. On the Tools menu, point to Macro and then click Macros.

3. In the Macro Name box, type *CallAdditionResult*.

4. In the Macros In box, select This Workbook.

5. Click Create. The Visual Basic Editor appears, and you'll see the following code:

    ```
    Sub CallAdditionResult()

    End Sub
    ```

6. Edit the code so that it looks like this:

    ```
    Sub CallAdditionResult()

        Dim intFirstNumber As Integer
        Dim intSecondNumber As Integer

        intFirstNumber = InputBox(Prompt:="Type the first integer.")
        intSecondNumber = InputBox(Prompt:="Type the second integer.")

        MsgBox Prompt:=intFirstNumber & " + " & _
            intSecondNumber & " = " & AdditionResult _
            (intFirst:=intFirstNumber, intSecond:=intSecondNumber)

    End Sub

    Public Function AdditionResult(ByVal intFirst As Integer, _
            ByVal intSecond As Integer) As Integer

        AdditionResult = intFirst + intSecond

    End Function
    ```

7. Click anywhere on the screen between the code *Sub CallAdditionResult()* and *End Sub*.

8. On the Run menu, click Run Sub/UserForm.

(continued)

9. When the first input box appears, type *3* and then click OK.

10. When the second input box appears, type *5* and then click OK. The message *3 + 5 = 8* appears.

Caution You will not be able to run the *CallAdditionResult* subroutine if your computer's Office security settings prohibit it. For example, if your Office security settings are set to High, the *CallAdditionResult* subroutine will not run. If your Office security settings are set to Medium, the *CallAdditionResult* subroutine will run only if you enable macros when prompted by Office. For more information on Office security settings, see the online help included with the application you are using.

Here's how the code you just wrote works:

■ VBA starts running the macro at the line *Sub CallAdditionResult()*.

■ The two *Dim* statements instruct VBA to create two locations in computer memory to store values. The first memory location is called *intFirstNumber*; the second memory location is called *intSecondNumber*. The two memory locations will be big enough to hold integer values.

■ The lines *intFirstNumber = InputBox(Prompt:="Type the first integer.")* and *intSecondNumber = InputBox(Prompt:="Type the second integer.")* are interpreted by VBA as follows:

a. Display an input box with the label *Type the first integer*.

b. After the user clicks OK, store in the memory location called *intFirstNumber* whatever the user has typed in the box.

c. Display an input box with the label *Type the second integer*.

d. After the user clicks OK, store in the memory location called *intSecondNumber* whatever the user has typed in the box.

- The line *MsgBox Prompt:=intFirstNumber & " + " & intSecondNumber & " = " & AdditionResult(intFirst:=intFirstNumber, intSecond:=intSecondNumber)* displays a message box with a label that is constructed as follows:

  a. Display the value that is stored in the memory location called *intFirstNumber*.

  b. Display the plus symbol (+).

  c. Display the value that is stored in the memory location called *intSecondNumber*.

  d. Display the equals symbol (=).

  e. Display the return value of the *AdditionResult* function.

- The value of the *AdditionResult* procedure is determined by passing the value that is stored in the memory location called *intFirstNumber*, followed by the value that is stored in the memory location called *intSecondNumber*. The *AdditionResult* procedure adds the values stored in the memory locations *intFirstNumber* and *intSecondNumber* (in our example, 3 and 5) and returns the result (8).

Understanding Office Code: Programmatic Object Models

To take full advantage of the ways you can automate Microsoft Office features by writing code, you need to understand the Office programmatic *object models*. An object model describes the relationships between application features that can be extended or automated using code. These features are exposed through type libraries, which are contained in files such as a dynamic-link library (DLL) files, executable (EXE) files, object library files (files with the extension .olb), or type library files (files with the extension .tlb). Some common type libraries are the Microsoft Excel Type Library (contained in the file Excel.exe) and the Microsoft Access Object Library (contained in the file Msacc.olb).

Object models include several components, namely *classes* (which include *objects*, *collections*, and *types*) and *members* (which include *properties*, *methods*, *events*, and *constants*).

- An object is an application component or feature. Examples of an object are an Excel *Worksheet* object, an Access *Report* object, and so on.

- A collection is a group of objects. Collections include the Excel *Worksheets* collection, the Access *Reports* collection, and so on.

- A property is a characteristic of an object or a collection. The Excel *Worksheet* object has a *Visible* property, which indicates whether the *Worksheet* object is visible or hidden.

- A method is an action that an object or collection can perform. One example is the *Worksheets* collection's *Add* method, which adds a *Worksheet* object to a *Workbook* object.

- An event is an action that a user or an application performs on an object or a collection. For instance, the *Workbook* object's *Open* event is triggered when the workbook file the object refers to is opened.

- A constant is text that substitutes for an integer. For example, the Excel constant *xlFillCopy* represents the integer 1. Computers think in terms of numbers, but we use constants as substitutes for numbers because words are easier for us to remember. Constants can be organized into groups of *types*.

The Visual Basic Editor

Excel and Access support the Visual Basic Editor, a tool that you can use to attach VBA macros or other code files (also called *modules*) to workbooks and databases. The code that you write runs in response to application or user actions such as a file opening, a mouse click on a particular screen location, and so on.

To display the Visual Basic Editor when you're working in an Office application, point to Macro on the Tools menu and then click Visual Basic Editor. The Visual Basic Editor consists of the following major components:

- The Project Explorer, which allows you to manage the VBA code accompanying an Office document. To display the Project Editor, click Project Explorer on the View menu.

- The Properties window, which allows you to view and modify VBA project and code properties such as code file names. You can display the Properties window by clicking Properties Window on the View menu.

- The Code window (on the View menu, click Code), which is the window in which you enter VBA code.

- The Immediate Window (on the View menu, click Immediate Window), which allows you to set and retrieve code properties while you're testing VBA code.

- The References dialog box (on the Tools menu, click References), which you use to add references to your VBA code to features and functions in other software applications and library files.

- The Object Browser (on the View menu, click Object Browser), which displays classes, properties, events, and so on from object libraries and procedures in your VBA project. You can also use the Object Browser to inspect the features and functions of other applications. The Object Browser is described in more detail in the next section.

You'll see these features illustrated and used in some of the procedures that follow. For more information on how to use the Visual Basic Editor and its components, see the Visual Basic Editor online help.

> **Note**   Data analysis solutions targeting the Office Web Components and Microsoft Data Analyzer use different coding approaches. Because the Office Web Components are hosted on Web pages, you use a Web scripting language such as Microsoft Visual Basic Scripting Edition (VBScript). Data Analyzer views can be hosted in a variety of solutions, such as Visual Basic forms, VBA UserForms, or Web pages. In these cases, the host application determines whether you can use a programming language such as Visual Basic, Visual Basic for Applications, or VBScript.

The Object Browser and Online Help

The Object Browser and the Office VBA Language Reference are tools you can use to help you understand the various Office object models. To display the Object Browser, first open the Visual Basic Editor (point to Macro on the Tools menu, and then click Visual Basic Editor). On the View menu, click Object Browser. The Object Browser is shown in Figure 11-1.

Figure 11-1   The Object Browser.

To reduce the amount of information the Object Browser displays, click a single type library in the Project/Library list near the top of the browser. The classes (objects, collections, and types) for that type library are displayed in the Classes pane. As you click an item in the Classes pane, the members (properties, methods, events, and constants) for that item are displayed in the Members pane. You can also type the name of an item you're looking for in the Search Text box, click Search, and then click an item in the Search Results pane.

To view the Office VBA Language Reference help topic associated with a class or member, click the class or member and then press F1. You can see the topic for the Excel *Application* object in Figure 11-2.

From this topic, you can access help topics for all the Excel *Application* object's members and child objects. You can also understand what the Excel *Application* object represents, learn how to use the Excel *Application* object in your code, and read usage remarks.

To change the entries in the Project/Library list, on the Tools menu, click References. In the References dialog box, shown in Figure 11-3, select or clear the check boxes for the type libraries you want to add or remove.

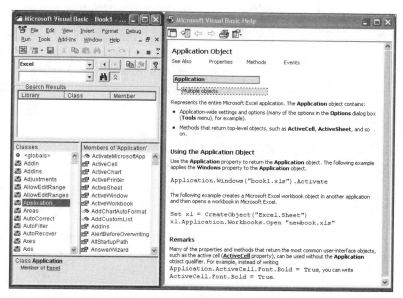

Figure 11-2   The Office VBA Language Reference online help provides information about the items in an object model.

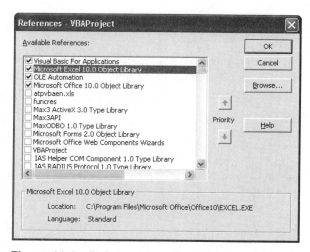

Figure 11-3   Referencing projects and programmatic libraries (object models).

> **Note**   Selecting items in the References dialog box increases the size of the Office file associated with the VBA project. If you are just exploring a type library's classes and members, be sure to clear the type library's corresponding check box when you are finished exploring it.

Working with the *Application* Object

Object models are organized into hierarchies of objects and collections, similar to family trees. Objects and collections can have parent and child objects and collections. To navigate through an object model, you usually start with the object model's *Application* object and then move through the object model from there. To start with the *Application* object, you declare (or dimension, using the *Dim* statement) an *Application* object, as shown in the following code snippet:

```
...
Dim acApp As Access.Application    ' For Access.
Dim xlApp As Excel.Application     ' For Excel.
...
```

In this code, I've used the standard letters *ac* and *xl*, along with the letters *App*, as the names of the variables (a variable is a computer memory location that stores objects) corresponding to an instance of each application's *Application* object (*acApp* and *xlApp*). Building on the Excel example above, you can reference the active Excel workbook with code similar to the following:

```
...
Dim xlApp As Excel.Application
Dim objWkb As Excel.Workbook

Set xlApp = Excel.Application
Set objWkb = xlApp.ActiveWorkbook
...
```

Rounding out this example, you can write code to list the names of the active workbook's worksheets as follows:

```
Public Sub WorksheetNames()

    Dim xlApp As Excel.Application
    Dim objWkb As Excel.Workbook
    Dim objWks As Excel.Worksheet
    Dim strMsg As String
```

```
Set xlApp = Excel.Application
Set objWkb = xlApp.ActiveWorkbook

strMsg = "This workbook's worksheets are named:" & vbCrLf

For Each objWks In objWkb.Sheets
    strMsg = strMsg & objWks.Name & vbCrLf
Next objWks

MsgBox Prompt:=strMsg

Set objWkb = Nothing
Set xlApp = Nothing

End Sub
```

Here's how the code works.

- The lines *Public Sub WorksheetNames()* and *End Sub* denote the beginning and end of the *WorksheetNames* procedure.

- The lines starting with the *Dim* keyword instruct the computer to reserve locations in memory to store program data and manipulate Excel features. The *Excel.Application* object (*xlApp*) represents an Excel application. The *Excel.Workbook* object (*objWkb*) represents an Excel workbook. The *Excel.Worksheet* object (*objWks*) represents a worksheet in a workbook. The *String* object (*strMsg*) represents some text that is constructed later in the procedure.

- The lines starting with the *Set* keyword instruct the computer to assign the reserved memory locations to Excel features. The *xlApp* object is assigned to the running Excel application. The *objWkb* object is assigned to the active workbook in the running Excel application.

- The *strMsg* object is set to the text "This workbook's worksheets are named:" followed by a carriage return.

- The *For Each…Next* keywords are used to iterate, or loop, through a collection of objects. In this case, the *Workbook* object's *Sheets* property provides access to all the workbook's worksheets. Each worksheet's name (found on the worksheet's tab and represented in the code as *objWks.Name*) is appended to the *strMsg* text, followed by a carriage return.

- The *MsgBox* function displays the *strMsg* text on the screen.

- Finally, to manage computer memory wisely, at the end of the subroutine, when the memory locations are no longer needed, the memory locations' contents are emptied and released to other computer processes by setting the object variables, such as *objWkb*, to *Nothing*. Then the procedure ends.

Your Turn

In this exercise, you'll run and test the *WorksheetNames* subroutine presented above.

1. Start Excel and create a new, blank workbook.

2. Open the Visual Basic Editor (on the Tools menu, point to Macro and then click Visual Basic Editor).

3. On the View menu, click Project Explorer.

4. Expand the project matching the name of your workbook; for example, VBAProject (Book 1).

5. Open the Microsoft Excel Objects folder.

6. Double-click the ThisWorkbook module.

7. Type the contents of the *WorksheetNames* procedure into the Code window (which is next to the Project Explorer).

8. Click anywhere between the lines of code *Public Sub WorksheetNames()* and *End Sub*.

9. On the Run menu, click Run Sub/UserForm. The workbook's worksheet names are displayed. Figure 11-4 shows the message box displayed for a default worksheet.

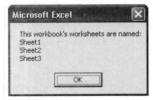

Figure 11-4   Results of running the *WorksheetNames* subroutine on a default worksheet.

Now that you are beginning to understand how Office solutions are created with macros, procedures, and an object model, you can start creating some of your own data analysis solutions. In the sections that follow, I'll show you some code that performs a data analysis task and explain how the code works. Try running the code samples, learn how the code works, and then customize and add to the code for your own needs.

Extending the Data Analysis Features in Microsoft Excel

Because many of the Excel data analysis tasks that you will do on a daily basis involve sorting, filtering, and subtotaling data records, let's start with an example of how to automate these straightforward tasks. The code we'll examine in the next several sections is attached to the BookSale.xls file in the Chap11 folder. If you want to run the code samples as you read, go ahead and open the file now.

Sort, Filter, and Subtotal Lists of Records

You can use code similar to the following *SortSales* subroutine to sort a list of data records. Using code such as this is a good way to ensure that records are always sorted when an Excel workbook is opened.

```
Public Sub SortSales()

    ' Purpose: Sorts a list of book store sales in descending order.

    Dim objWorksheet As Excel.Worksheet
    Dim objRange As Excel.Range

    ' Select the list.
    Set objWorksheet = Excel.Application.ActiveWorkbook.Sheets _
        (Index:="Book Store Sales")
    Set objRange = objWorksheet.Range(Cell1:="A1", Cell2:="D37")

    ' Sort the list.
    objRange.Sort Key1:=objWorksheet.Range(Cell1:="D1"), _
        Order1:=xlDescending, Header:=xlYes

    Set objRange = Nothing
    Set objWorksheet = Nothing

End Sub
```

Here's how the *SortSales* subroutine works:

■   As you've already learned, the keyword *Public* means that the sub-routine is available to any other procedures in the code project. The *Sub* keyword indicates that the procedure does not return any value to any calling procedure.

■   Here again, the *Dim* keyword reserves a memory location, using the name that follows each statement. Each memory location is dimensioned large enough to hold an object of the type following the *As* keyword. In this case, the memory locations are large enough to hold a *Worksheet* object and a *Range* object.

■   The *Set* keyword is used to put something inside the corresponding memory location. In this case, the code

```
Set objWorksheet = Excel.Application.ActiveWorkbook.Sheets _
    (Index:="Book Store Sales")
```

means that the memory location *objWorksheet*, representing a *Worksheet* object, will hold a reference to the worksheet named Book Store Sales in the active Excel workbook. At the end of the subroutine, the memory locations' contents are emptied and released to other computer processes by setting the object variables, such as *objWorksheet*, to *Nothing*.

> **Note**   The *Public*, *Sub*, *Dim*, *As*, *Set*, and *Nothing* keywords are used in the same manner as described here and earlier in the remaining code samples, so I'll no longer describe them in detail.

■   In Excel, a *Range* object can be used to refer to a group of cells on a worksheet; in this case, the cell range A1 to D37, inclusive. To refer to a single cell, use the *Worksheet* object's *Range* method with only the *Cell1* argument specified.

■   The *Range* object's *Sort* method can be used to sort the group of cells referred to in the *Range* object. In this code, the *Sort* method's *Key1* argument specifies that the column header in cell D1 (Sales) is the basis of the sort. The *Order1* argument specifies a descending sort order by using the *xlDescending* constant. The *Header* argument is set to *xlYes* to ensure that cell D1 is not sorted along with the rest of the column's cells.

You can run the *SortSales* subroutine by clicking anywhere inside the subroutine's code and clicking Run Sub/UserForm on the Run menu. You can also call the procedure from the ThisWorkbook module's *Workbook* object's *Open* event by adding the following code to the ThisWorkbook module:

```
Private Sub Workbook_Open()

    Call SortSales

End Sub
```

To run the *SortSales* subroutine using this method, close the workbook and then reopen it. When the workbook is opened, the *SortSales* subroutine automatically runs. Figure 11-5 shows the result of running the *SortSales* subroutine.

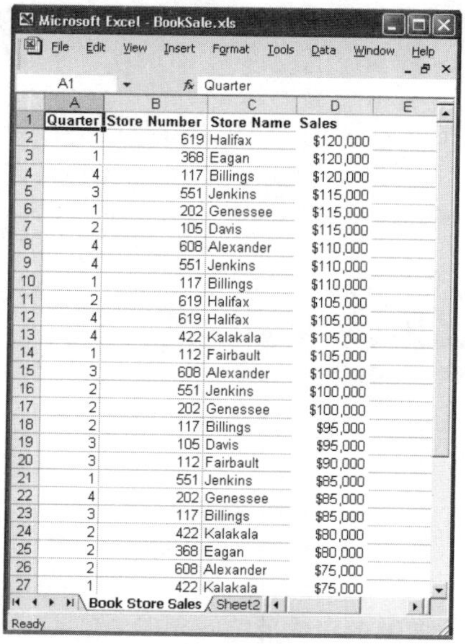

	A	B	C	D
1	Quarter	Store Number	Store Name	Sales
2	1	619	Halifax	$120,000
3	1	368	Eagan	$120,000
4	4	117	Billings	$120,000
5	3	551	Jenkins	$115,000
6	1	202	Genessee	$115,000
7	2	105	Davis	$115,000
8	4	608	Alexander	$110,000
9	4	551	Jenkins	$110,000
10	1	117	Billings	$110,000
11	2	619	Halifax	$105,000
12	4	619	Halifax	$105,000
13	4	422	Kalakala	$105,000
14	1	112	Fairbault	$105,000
15	3	608	Alexander	$100,000
16	2	551	Jenkins	$100,000
17	2	202	Genessee	$100,000
18	2	117	Billings	$95,000
19	3	105	Davis	$95,000
20	3	112	Fairbault	$90,000
21	1	551	Jenkins	$85,000
22	4	202	Genessee	$85,000
23	3	117	Billings	$85,000
24	2	422	Kalakala	$80,000
25	2	368	Eagan	$80,000
26	2	608	Alexander	$75,000
27	1	422	Kalakala	$75,000

Figure 11-5 Results of running the *SortSales* subroutine.

You can use code similar to the following subroutine, named *FilterSales*, to filter a list of data records. Like the *SortSales* subroutine, this subroutine is a good way to ensure that records appear as you need them when an Excel workbook is opened.

```
Public Sub FilterSales()

    ' Purpose: Filters a list of book store sales by displaying
    ' only sales above $100,000.
```

(continued)

```
Dim objWorksheet As Excel.Worksheet
Dim objRange As Excel.Range

' Select the list.
Set objWorksheet = Excel.Application.ActiveWorkbook.Sheets _
    (Index:="Book Store Sales")
Set objRange = objWorksheet.Range(Cell1:="A1", Cell2:="D37")

' Filter the list.
' 4 is the Sales column.
objRange.AutoFilter Field:=4, Criteria1:=">100000"

Set objRange = Nothing
Set objWorksheet = Nothing

End Sub
```

The *FilterSales* code is almost identical to the *SortSales* code. The exception is the line of code *objRange.AutoFilter Field:=4, Criteria1:=">100000"*. In this case, the *Range* object's *AutoFilter* method is using the *Field* argument to specify the column number to filter on (the 4th column, column D). The *Criteria1* argument specifies that only records with values of greater than 100,000 in column D should be displayed. The result of running the *FilterSales* subroutine is shown in Figure 11-6.

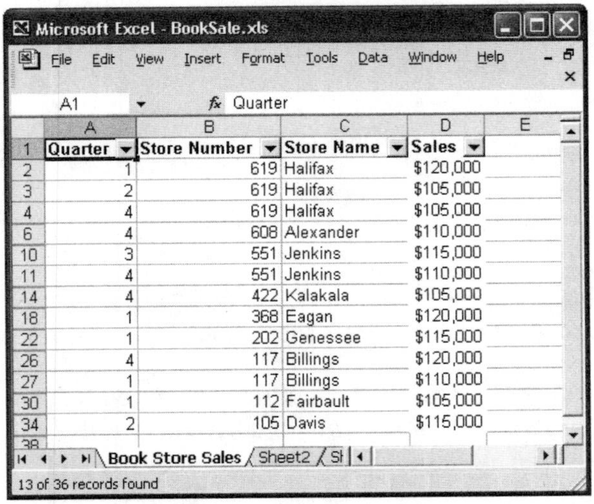

Figure 11-6   Records filtered by running the *FilterSales* subroutine.

In like manner, the *CreateSubtotals* subroutine, shown in the following code, can be used to automatically subtotal a list of records.

```
Public Sub CreateSubtotals()

    ' Purpose: Creates subtotals for a list of book store sales records.

    Dim objWorksheet As Excel.Worksheet
    Dim objRange As Excel.Range

    ' Select the list.
    Set objWorksheet = Excel.Application.ActiveWorkbook.Sheets _
        (Index:="Book Store Sales")
    Set objRange = objWorksheet.Range(Cell1:="A1", Cell2:="D37")

    ' Subtotal the list.
    ' 2 is the Store Number column, and 4 is the Sales column.
    objRange.Subtotal GroupBy:=2, Function:=xlSum, TotalList:=4
    ' Collapse the outline to show only the subtotals.
    objWorksheet.Outline.ShowLevels RowLevels:=2

    Set objRange = Nothing
    Set objWorksheet = Nothing

End Sub
```

Two lines of code differentiate the *CreateSubtotals* subroutine from the *SortSales* and *FilterSales* subroutines.

■ The line *objRange.Subtotal GroupBy:=2, Function:=xlSum, TotalList:=4* uses the *Range* object's *Subtotal* method to display the subtotals. The *GroupBy* argument specifies the second column (the Store Number column) as the record grouping for subtotals. The *Function* argument uses the *xlSum* constant to specify that the subtotals are sums. The *TotalList* argument specifies the fourth column (the Sales column) as the basis of the sums.

■ The line *objWorksheet.Outline.ShowLevels RowLevels:=2* is used to collapse the displayed subtotal level. The code uses the *Worksheet* object's *Outline* object, which contains a *ShowLevels* method; the method's *RowLevels* argument is set to 2, which specifies that the second subtotal level is to be displayed. Setting this argument to 2 is equivalent to clicking the 2 icon in the subtotals navigation column.

The result of running the *CreateSubtotals* subroutine is shown in Figure 11-7.

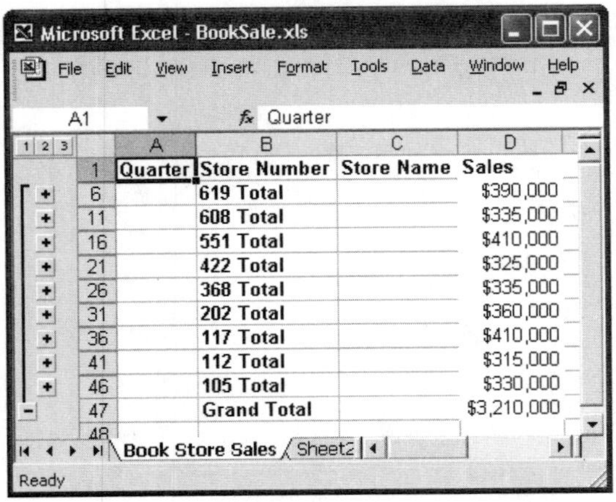

Figure 11-7   Subtotals added by running the *CreateSubtotals* subroutine.

Insert Standard Excel Worksheet Functions and Analysis ToolPak Functions

Worksheet and Analysis ToolPak functions bring a greater degree of analysis to your data than sorting, filtering, and subtotaling. For example, you might want to use code to insert and run a worksheet function or Analysis ToolPak function whenever a particular series of numbers changes or exceeds a certain threshold. The following subroutine (named *InsertWorksheetFunctions*) demonstrates how to insert a *SUM* and *AVERAGE* function into the Book Store Sales worksheet in the BookSale.xls file in the Chap11 folder.

```
Public Sub InsertWorksheetFunctions()

    ' Purpose: Inserts worksheet functions into the book store sales list.

    Dim objWorksheet As Excel.Worksheet
    Dim objRange As Excel.Range
    Dim objFunctionResult As Excel.Range
    Dim objLabel As Excel.Range

    ' Select the numbers to calculate.
    Set objWorksheet = Excel.Application.ActiveWorkbook.Sheets _
        (Index:="Book Store Sales")
    Set objRange = objWorksheet.Range(Cell1:="D2", Cell2:="D37")
    ' Indicate  where to insert the function's result.
    Set objFunctionResult = objWorksheet.Range(Cell1:="D38")

    ' Sum all of the sales in column D.
```

```
objFunctionResult.Value =_
    Excel.Application.WorksheetFunction.Sum(objRange)
' Insert a descriptive label.
Set objLabel = objFunctionResult.Offset(ColumnOffset:=-1)
objLabel.Value = "Sum of Sales"

' Average the sales in column D.
Set objFunctionResult = objWorksheet.Range(Cell1:="D39")
objFunctionResult.Value = _
    Excel.Application.WorksheetFunction.Average(objRange)
' Insert another descriptive label.
Set objLabel = objFunctionResult.Offset(ColumnOffset:=-1)
objLabel.Value = "Average of Sales"

Set objLabel = Nothing
Set objFunctionResult = Nothing
Set objRange = Nothing
Set objWorksheet = Nothing

End Sub
```

Although the *InsertWorksheetFunctions* subroutine has quite a few lines of code, the operations it performs are straightforward.

■ The lines of code starting with *Set objFunctionResult* specify the cells in which the results of each function will appear. The *SUM* function result will appear in cell D38, and the *AVERAGE* function result will appear in cell D39; the result is specified by the *Range* object's *Value* property. In this case, the *WorksheetFunction* object's *Sum* method calculates the sum of cells D2 through D37 (the Sales column) and places the result in cell D38. The *WorksheetFunction* object's *Average* method calculates the average of cells D2 through D37 and places the result in cell D39.

> **Note**   The *WorksheetFunction* object contains over 175 methods representing a wide array of Excel worksheet functions.

■ The lines of code starting with *Set objLabel* and *objLabel.Value* specify that a descriptive label for each function result be placed one cell to the left of the function result. The code performs this operation by setting the *ColumnOffset* argument of the *Range* object's *Offset* property to -1 (a value of 1 would offset one column to the right).

The result of running the *InsertWorksheetFunctions* subroutine is shown in Figure 11-8.

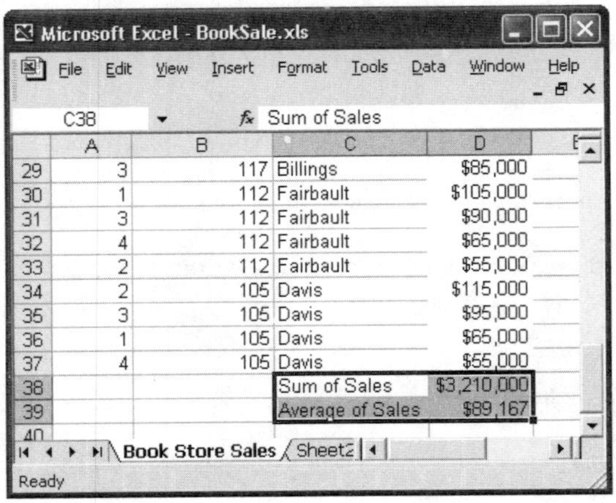

Figure 11-8   Results of running the *InsertWorksheetFunctions* subroutine.

For more sophisticated worksheet calculations, you can use the Analysis ToolPak functions. To do so, you must first set a reference to the Analysis Tool-Pak VBA functions. The steps to add the reference are described in the code comments below. The *InsertAnalysisToolPakFunctions* subroutine automatically runs the Descriptive Statistics and Rank and Percentile tools against data records in the BookSale.xls file.

```
Public Sub InsertAnalysisToolPakFunctions()

    ' Purpose: Inserts Analysis ToolPak functions into
    ' the book sales worksheet.

    ' Note: You must first reference the Analysis ToolPak VBA functions.
    '  To do so:
    ' In Excel, on the Tools menu, click Add-Ins.
    ' Select the Analysis ToolPak-VBA check box.
    ' In the Visual Basic Editor, on the Tools menu, click
    ' References. Select the atpvbaen.xls check box, and then click OK.

    Dim objWorksheet As Excel.Worksheet
    Dim objRange As Excel.Range
    Dim objOutput As Excel.Range
```

```
' Select the list and output location.
Set objWorksheet = Excel.Application.ActiveWorkbook.Sheets _
    (Index:="Book Store Sales")
Set objRange = objWorksheet.Range(Cell1:="D2", Cell2:="D37")
Set objOutput = objWorksheet.Range(Cell1:="F1")

' Display Descriptive Statistics.
Descr inprng:=objRange, outrng:=objOutput, Summary:=True

' Display Rank and Percentile information in a separate output location.
Set objOutput = objWorksheet.Range(Cell1:="I1")
RankPerc inprng:=objRange, outrng:=objOutput, Labels:=True

Set objOutput = Nothing
Set objRange = Nothing
Set objWorksheet = Nothing

End Sub
```

The two lines of code to point out here are the calls to the *Descr* and *RankPerc* methods, which represent the Analysis ToolPak's Descriptive Statistics and Rank and Percentile functions, respectively. The Analysis ToolPak's *Descr* method's *inprng* argument specifies the group of cells to use as an input to the Descriptive Statistics function, the *outrng* argument specifies the worksheet cell where the Descriptive Statistics function's results will begin to be displayed, and the *Summary* argument, when set to True, displays a list of the results of all the Descriptive Statistics function's summary statistics.

The Analysis ToolPak's *RankPerc* method's *inprng* and *outrng* arguments are used for the same purposes as in the *Descr* method, and the *Labels* argument is set to True to specify that the group of cells used as the input to the *RankPerc* method has column header labels.

The result of running the *InsertAnalysisToolPakFunctions* subroutine is shown in Figure 11-9.

Store Name	Sales		Column1			Point	120000	Rank	Percent
Halifax	$120,000					16	$120,000	1	97.00%
Halifax	$105,000		Mean	89166.66667		24	$120,000	1	97.00%
Halifax	$105,000		Standard Error	3615.991818		8	$115,000	3	88.20%
Halifax	$60,000		Median	92500		20	$115,000	3	88.20%
Alexander	$110,000		Mode	105000		32	$115,000	3	88.20%
Alexander	$100,000		Standard Deviation	21695.95091		4	$110,000	6	79.40%
Alexander	$75,000		Sample Variance	470714285.7		9	$110,000	6	79.40%
Alexander	$50,000		Kurtosis	-1.280921553		25	$110,000	6	79.40%
Jenkins	$115,000		Skewness	-0.21784768		1	$105,000	9	67.60%
Jenkins	$110,000		Range	70000		2	$105,000	9	67.60%
Jenkins	$100,000		Minimum	50000		12	$105,000	9	67.60%
Jenkins	$85,000		Maximum	120000		28	$105,000	9	67.60%
Kalakala	$105,000		Sum	3210000		5	$100,000	13	58.80%
Kalakala	$80,000		Count	36		10	$100,000	13	58.80%
Kalakala	$75,000					21	$100,000	13	58.80%
Kalakala	$65,000					26	$95,000	16	52.90%
Eagan	$120,000					33	$95,000	16	52.90%
Eagan	$80,000					29	$90,000	18	50.00%
Eagan	$70,000					11	$85,000	19	41.10%
Eagan	$65,000					22	$85,000	19	41.10%
Genessee	$115,000					27	$85,000	19	41.10%
Genessee	$100,000					13	$80,000	22	35.20%
Genessee	$85,000					17	$80,000	22	35.20%
Genessee	$60,000					6	$75,000	24	29.40%
Billings	$120,000					14	$75,000	24	29.40%
Billings	$110,000					18	$70,000	26	26.40%
Billings	$95,000					15	$65,000	27	14.70%

Figure 11-9   Data created by Analysis ToolPak functions run through the *InsertAnalysisToolPakFunctions* subroutine.

Conditionally Format Worksheet Cells

To this point, you have predominantly seen code that uses the Excel *Worksheet* and *Range* objects. To conditionally format worksheet cells programmatically, you must use the Excel *FormatCondition* object to both specify and apply conditional formats to cells. The following code sample applies conditional formatting to cells in the Sales column in the BookSale.xls file in the Chap11 folder.

```
Public Sub AddConditionalFormatting()

    ' Purpose: Adds conditional formatting to the Sales column.

    Dim objWorksheet As Excel.Worksheet
    Dim objRange As Excel.Range
    Dim objFormatCondition1 As Excel.FormatCondition
    Dim objFormatCondition2 As Excel.FormatCondition

    ' Select the list.
    Set objWorksheet = _
        Excel.Application.ActiveWorkbook.Sheets(Index:="Book Store Sales")
    Set objRange = objWorksheet.Range(Cell1:="D2", Cell2:="D37")
```

```
' Color the cell red if sales is less than or equal to $75,000.
Set objFormatCondition1 = objRange.FormatConditions.Add _
    (Type:=xlCellValue, _
    Operator:=xlLessEqual, Formula1:="75000")

objFormatCondition1.Interior.Color = RGB(255, 0, 0)

' Color the cell green if sales is greater than
' or equal to $100,000.
Set objFormatCondition2 = objRange.FormatConditions.Add _
    (Type:=xlCellValue, _
    Operator:=xlGreaterEqual, Formula1:="100000")

objFormatCondition2.Interior.Color = RGB(0, 255, 0)

Set objFormatCondition2 = Nothing
Set objFormatCondition1 = Nothing
Set objRange = Nothing
Set objWorksheet = Nothing

End Sub
```

To create a conditional cell format programmatically, you use the *Add* method of the *FormatConditions* collection to create an instance of a *FormatCondition* object. In this case, the *Add* method's *Type* argument is set to the *xlCellValue* constant to specify that the conditional cell format is based on cell values. The *Operator* argument is set to *xlLessEqual* in the first condition and *xlGreaterEqual* in the second condition. Both *xlLessEqual* and *xlGreaterEqual* are constants. They specify that the conditional cell format represents a less-than-or-equal-to or greater-than-or-equal-to test. The *Formula1* argument is set to 75000 in the first condition and 100000 in the second, specifying that cells will be tested against the $75,000 and $100,000 figures, respectively.

The *Color* property of the *FormatCondition* object's *Interior* object is set to a red-green-blue combination of *RGB(255, 0, 0)* and *RGB(0, 255, 0)*, respectively, to specify a red or green color.

In summary, any cell in the Sales column that is less than or equal to $75,000 will be colored red, and any cell in the Sales column that is greater than or equal to $100,000 will be colored green. The result of running the *AddConditionalFormatting* subroutine is shown in Figure 11-10.

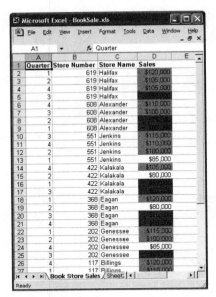

Figure 11-10   Result of running the *AddConditionalFormatting* sub-routine.

Create PivotTable Reports and PivotChart Reports

The code required to create PivotTable reports and PivotChart reports is not significantly more difficult than the code in the Excel solutions described to this point. However, several Excel programmatic objects must be created and managed in a solution that involves data pivoting, including objects that represent the Excel workbook's pivot cache, the PivotTable report object itself, PivotTable report fields, and an Excel *Chart* object that turns into a PivotChart report. The following code sample from the Chap11 folder's BookSale.xls file shows how to work with PivotTable reports and PivotChart reports.

```
Public Sub CreatePivotTableAndPivotChartReport()

    ' Purpose: Creates a PivotTable report and PivotChart report based on
    ' the book store sales data.

    Dim objWorksheet As Excel.Worksheet
    Dim objRange As Excel.Range
    Dim objPivotCache As Excel.PivotCache
    Dim objPivotTable As Excel.PivotTable
    Dim objRowField As Excel.PivotField
    Dim objPageField As Excel.PivotField
    Dim objDataField As Excel.PivotField
```

```
Dim objChart As Excel.Chart

' Select the list from which to create a PivotTable report.
Set objWorksheet = Excel.Application.ActiveWorkbook.Worksheets _
    (Index:="Book Store Sales")
Set objRange = objWorksheet.Range(Cell1:="A1", Cell2:="D37")

' Create the PivotTable report.
Set objPivotCache = Excel.Application.ActiveWorkbook.PivotCaches.Add _
    (SourceType:=xlDatabase, SourceData:=objRange)
Set objPivotTable = objPivotCache.CreatePivotTable _
    (TableDestination:="")

' Add the row, page, and data fields.
Set objRowField = objPivotTable.PivotFields(Index:="Store Name")

objRowField.Orientation = xlRowField

Set objPageField = objPivotTable.PivotFields(Index:="Quarter")

objPageField.Orientation = xlPageField

Set objDataField = objPivotTable.PivotFields(Index:="Sales")

objDataField.Orientation = xlDataField
' Format the Sales field as currency.
objDataField.NumberFormat = "$#,##0.00"

' Create a PivotChart column-style report using the PivotTable report.
Set objChart = _
    Excel.Application.ActiveWorkbook.Charts.Add(Before:=objWorksheet)

objChart.SetSourceData Source:=objPivotTable.TableRange2, PlotBy:=xlRows
objChart.ChartType = xlColumnClustered

Set objChart = Nothing
Set objDataField = Nothing
Set objPageField = Nothing
Set objRowField = Nothing
Set objPivotTable = Nothing
Set objPivotCache = Nothing
Set objRange = Nothing
Set objWorksheet = Nothing

End Sub
```

Here's an explanation of the key elements of the *CreatePivotTableAndPivotChartReport* subroutine.

■ The code calls the *Add* method of the *Workbook* object's *PivotCaches* collection to add a pivot cache, which represents the in-memory cache of a workbook's PivotTable report connections. In this instance, the *Add* method's *SourceType* argument is set to the *xlDatabase* constant to specify that the PivotTable report's data source is an internal data source. The *SourceData* argument specifies the list of data records on the Book Store Sales worksheet. After you programmatically create a pivot cache, you create a PivotTable report by calling the *PivotCache* object's *CreatePivotTable* method. The *TableDestination* argument specifies the cell where the upper-left corner of the PivotTable will appear.

■ The default *Item* property of the *PivotTable* object's *PivotFields* method is called to refer to individual *PivotField* objects representing PivotTable fields. The *objRowField*, *objPageField*, and *objDataField* objects represent PivotTable report row, page, and data fields. They are added to the appropriate areas of the PivotTable report by setting the objects' *Orientation* properties to the *xlRowField*, *xlPageField*, and *xlDataField* constants, respectively.

■ The *objDataField* object's *NumberFormat* property is set to "*$#,##0.00*" to specify a currency format for the sales figures. (For example, the number 1536.82 will be displayed as $1,536.82.)

■ To create a linked PivotTable chart, a generic Excel chart is programmatically created when the *Add* method of the Excel *Workbook* object's *Charts* collection is called. The *Add* method's *Before* argument specifies the sheet before which the new sheet is added. In this instance, this specifies that the chart should appear on a new worksheet as the first worksheet in the Excel workbook.

■ The *Chart* object's *SetSourceData* method turns the generic Excel chart into a PivotChart report by linking the PivotTable report object to the chart object. The *SetSourceData* method's *Source* argument is set to the PivotTable report object's *TableRange2* property, which returns all the PivotTable report's information to the chart (the *PivotTable* object's *TableRange1* property doesn't return the PivotTable report's page fields, so it is not used in this example). The *SetSourceData* method's *PlotBy* argument is set to the *xlRows* constant to indicate that the data should be plotted by rows instead of columns.

■ Finally, the *Chart* object's *ChartType* property is set to the *xlColumnClustered* constant to specify a clustered column chart layout.

The result of running the *CreatePivotTableAndPivotChartReport* subroutine is shown in Figure 11-11.

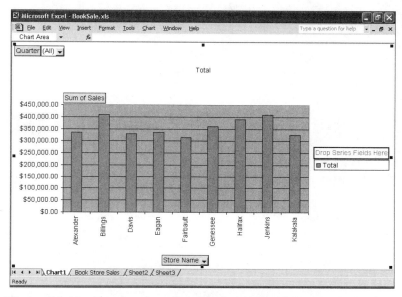

Figure 11-11   Results of running the *CreatePivotTableAndPivotChartReport* subroutine.

Opening and Saving XML Data in Excel

Using a program to open and save XML data in Excel is similar to opening and saving other types of data in Excel, as shown in the following two subroutines, included in the BookSale.xls file. The first subroutine opens an XML file.

```
Public Sub OpenAnXMLFile()

    ' Purpose: Opens an XML file.

    ' Change the Filename argument to match wherever you
    ' store the Customers1.xml file on your computer.
    Application.Workbooks.OpenXML Filename:= _
        "C:\Microsoft Press\Excel Data Analysis _
        \Sample Files\Chap10\Customers1.xml"

End Sub
```

In the *OpenAnXMLFile* subroutine, the *Workbooks* collection's *OpenXML* method simply opens the XML data file specified in its *Filename* argument.

(You can use the *OpenXML* method's optional *Stylesheets* argument to specify, with either a single value or an array of values, which XSLT stylesheet processing instructions to apply to the XML file's data before opening it in Excel.)

The following code saves data as an XML file.

```
Public Sub SaveXMLData()

    ' Purpose: Outputs the book store sales list as XML data
    ' in different XML formats.

    ' Save the active workbook as an XMLSS-formatted file.
    Excel.ActiveWorkbook.SaveAs Filename:="C:\BookSale.xml", _
        FileFormat:=xlXMLSpreadsheet

    Dim objWorksheet As Excel.Worksheet
    Dim objRange As Excel.Range

    ' Select just the first 10 rows of the book store sales list.
    Set objWorksheet = Excel.Application.ActiveWorkbook.Sheets _
        (Index:="Book Store Sales")
    Set objRange = objWorksheet.Range(Cell1:="A1", Cell2:="D10")

    ' Display the results in XDR format.
    Debug.Print objRange.Value(xlRangeValueMSPersistXML)

    ' Display the results in XMLSS format.
    Debug.Print objRange.Value(xlRangeValueXMLSpreadsheet)

    Set objRange = Nothing
    Set objWorksheet = Nothing

End Sub
```

In the *SaveXMLData* subroutine, the Excel *Workbook* object's *SaveAs* method saves the data at the path and file name specified by the *Filename* argument. To save the data using the Excel XML Spreadsheet Schema (XMLSS), the *FileFormat* argument is set to the constant *xlXMLSpreadsheet*. (There are over 40 different file formats that you can specify besides XML).

To return the results of a group of cells formatted as XML data, you can call the *Range* object's *Value* property. Use the constant *xlRangeValueMSPersistXML* to return the *Range* object's data formatted in the XML-Data Reduced (XDR) format, for example, if you were working with an older XML solution that requires data to be formatted in the XDR format. In most cases, however, you use the constant *xlRangeValueXMLSpreadsheet* to return the *Range* object's data formatted in the Excel XML Spreadsheet schema (XMLSS) format.

The results of running *SaveXMLData* are shown in Figure 11-12 and Figure 11-13.

```
Immediate
<xml xmlns:x="urn:schemas-microsoft-com:office:excel"
 xmlns:dt="uuid:C2F41010-65B3-11d1-A29F-00AA00C14882"
 xmlns:s="uuid:BDC6E3F0-6DA3-11d1-A2A3-00AA00C14882"
 xmlns:rs="urn:schemas-microsoft-com:rowset" xmlns:z="#RowsetSchema">
<x:PivotCache>
 <x:CacheIndex>1</x:CacheIndex>
 <s:Schema id="RowsetSchema">
  <s:ElementType name="row" content="eltOnly">
   <s:attribute type="Col1"/>
   <s:attribute type="Col2"/>
   <s:attribute type="Col3"/>
   <s:attribute type="Col4"/>
   <s:extends type="rs:rowbase"/>
  </s:ElementType>
  <s:AttributeType name="Col1" rs:name="Quarter">
   <s:datatype dt:type="int"/>
  </s:AttributeType>
  <s:AttributeType name="Col2" rs:name="Store Number">
   <s:datatype dt:type="int"/>
  </s:AttributeType>
  <s:AttributeType name="Col3" rs:name="Store Name">
   <s:datatype dt:maxLength="255"/>
  </s:AttributeType>
  <s:AttributeType name="Col4" rs:name="Sales">
   <s:datatype dt:type="int"/>
  </s:AttributeType>
 </s:Schema>
 <rs:data>
  <z:row Col1="1" Col2="619" Col3="Halifax" Col4="120000"/>
```

Figure 11-12   Results of running the *SaveXMLData* subroutine with XDR-formatted data.

```
Immediate
<?xml version="1.0"?>
<Workbook xmlns="urn:schemas-microsoft-com:office:spreadsheet"
 xmlns:o="urn:schemas-microsoft-com:office:office"
 xmlns:x="urn:schemas-microsoft-com:office:excel"
 xmlns:ss="urn:schemas-microsoft-com:office:spreadsheet"
 xmlns:html="http://www.w3.org/TR/REC-html40">
<Styles>
 <Style ss:ID="Default" ss:Name="Normal">
  <Alignment ss:Vertical="Bottom"/>
  <Borders/>
  <Font/>
  <Interior/>
  <NumberFormat/>
  <Protection/>
 </Style>
 <Style ss:ID="s21">
  <NumberFormat ss:Format="&quot;$&quot;#,##0"/>
 </Style>
 <Style ss:ID="s22">
  <Font x:Family="Swiss" ss:Bold="1"/>
 </Style>
 <Style ss:ID="s23">
  <Font x:Family="Swiss" ss:Bold="1"/>
  <Interior ss:Color="#FFFFFF" ss:Pattern="Solid"/>
  <NumberFormat ss:Format="&quot;$&quot;#,##0"/>
 </Style>
 <Style ss:ID="s24">
  <Interior ss:Color="#FFFFFF" ss:Pattern="Solid"/>
  <NumberFormat ss:Format="&quot;$&quot;#,##0"/>
```

Figure 11-13   Results of running the *SaveXMLData* subroutine with XMLSS-formatted data.

Programming the Data Analysis Features in Microsoft Access

Because Access does not have the breadth of data analysis features that Excel has, Access has no programmatic capabilities to do things such as insert worksheet functions or format table cells conditionally. Fortunately, the Access *DoCmd* object (accessible from the Access *Application* object) makes running most Access tasks through a program very easy. The following subroutines, included in the Chap11 folder's BookSale.mdb file, use three of the *DoCmd* object's methods: the *OpenTable* method opens a table, the *RunCommand* method runs a built-in Access command to sort data records in descending order, and the *ApplyFilter* method filters data records in the data table. The results of running these subroutines are shown in Figure 11-14 and Figure 11-15.

```
Public Sub SortBookSales()

    ' Purpose: Sorts the Book Store Sales table's records in descending
    ' order by quarter.

    Application.DoCmd.OpenTable TableName:="Book Store Sales"
    Application.DoCmd.RunCommand Command:=acCmdSortDescending

End Sub

Public Sub FilterBookSales()

    ' Purpose: Filters the Book Store Sales table's records
    ' in place so that only sales greater than $100,000
    ' are displayed.

    Application.DoCmd.OpenTable TableName:="Book Store Sales"
    Application.DoCmd.ApplyFilter WhereCondition:="Sales > 100000"

End Sub
```

Figure 11-14   Results of running the *SortBookSales* subroutine.

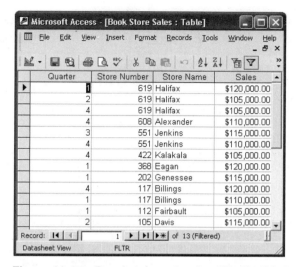

Figure 11-15   Results of running the *FilterBookSales* subroutine.

Extending the Data Analysis Features in the Microsoft Office Web Components

Typically, data analysis solutions that automate the Microsoft Office Web Components use code associated with Web pages. In the following example, available in the SalesPivotCode.htm file in the Chap11 folder, the Web page uses VBScript to create, customize, and display instances of the Spreadsheet Component, PivotTable Component, and Chart Component. The components connect to data in the BookSale.mdb file (also included in the Chap11 folder).

> **Note**   For brevity, only a code sample demonstrating the Office XP Web Components is featured in this section. For code samples demonstrating the Office 2000 Web Components, see the Office 2000 Web Components online help or the Microsoft Developer Network (MSDN) at *http://msdn.microsoft.com*.

```
<html>
<head>
<title>Office Web Components Code Examples</title>
</head>
<body>
<p>An invisible Microsoft Office Data Source Control connects to an Access
database in the background.</p>
<object id=MSODSC classid=CLSID:0002E553-0000-0000-C000-000000000046
VIEWASTEXT></object>

<p>Spreadsheet Component Code Example</p>
<object id=Spreadsheet1 classid=CLSID:0002E551-0000-0000-C000-000000000046
VIEWASTEXT></object>

<p>PivotTable Component Code Example</p>
<object id=PivotTable1 classid=clsid:0002E552-0000-0000-C000-000000000046
VIEWASTEXT></object>

<p>Chart Component Code Example</p>
<object id=ChartSpace1 classid=CLSID:0002E556-0000-0000-C000-000000000046
VIEWASTEXT></object>

<script id=clientEventHandlersVBS language=vbscript>
<!--

Sub window_onload

    Dim objPivotView
    Dim objTotal
    Dim objConstants
    Dim objChart


    ' Connect to the BookSale.mdb database.
    ' Change the ConnectionString property to match
    ' wherever you store the Booksale.mdb file on your computer.
    MSODSC.ConnectionString =
        "Provider=Microsoft.Jet.OLEDB.4.0;Password="""";
User ID=Admin;Data Source=C:\Microsoft Press\Excel Data  Analysis\Sample Files\
Chap11\BookSale.mdb;Mode=Share Deny None;Extended Properties="""";
        Jet OLEDB:System database="""";Jet OLEDB:Registry Path="""";
        Jet OLEDB:Database Password="""";Jet OLEDB:Engine Type=5;
        Jet OLEDB:Database Locking Mode=1;
        Jet OLEDB:Global Partial Bulk Ops=2;
        Jet OLEDB:Global Bulk Transactions=1;
        Jet OLEDB:New Database Password="""";
        Jet OLEDB:Create System Database=False;
        Jet OLEDB:Encrypt Database=False;
        Jet OLEDB:Don't Copy Locale on Compact=False;
```

```
        Jet OLEDB:Compact Without Replica Repair=False;
        Jet OLEDB:SFP=False"

' Connect the Spreadsheet Component to the Book Store Sales table in
' the Microsoft Office Data Source Control's referenced database.
Spreadsheet1.DataSource = MSODSC
Spreadsheet1.DataMember = "Book Store Sales"

' Connect the PivotTable Component to the Book Store Sales table in the
' Microsoft Office Data Source Control's referenced database.
PivotTable1.DataSource = MSODSC
PivotTable1.DataMember = "Book Store Sales"

Set objPivotView = PivotTable1.ActiveView
Set objConstants = PivotTable1.Constants
' Create the Sum of Sales field for the PivotTable Component.
Set objTotal = objPivotView.AddTotal("Sum of Sales", _
    objPivotView.FieldSets("Sales").Fields(0), _
    objConstants.plFunctionSum)

' Add the Store Name, Quarter, and Sales fields to the row, page, and
' data areas of the PivotTable Component.
objPivotView.RowAxis.InsertFieldSet objPivotView.FieldSets("Store Name")
objPivotView.FilterAxis.InsertFieldSet objPivotView.FieldSets("Quarter")
objPivotView.DataAxis.InsertFieldSet objPivotView.FieldSets("Sales")
objPivotView.DataAxis.InsertTotal objTotal

' Connect the Chart Component to the PivotTable Component
' as its data source.
ChartSpace1.DataSource = PivotTable1

' Change the Chart Component's view to a three-dimensional
' clustered column type.
Set objChart = ChartSpace1.Charts.Item(0)

objChart.Type = objConstants.chChartTypeColumnClustered3D

End Sub

-->
</script>
</body>
</html>
```

Let's review this code in more detail. To connect to the data, an instance of the Microsoft Office Data Source Control (MSODSC) is used. While the MSODSC has no visible representation on the Web page, it makes managing data source connections much easier when using code. The Office XP version of the MSODSC is identified by the class ID *0002E553-0000-0000-C000-000000000046.* (The computer uses this class ID along with the computer's registry to determine which specific ActiveX control to use.) To refer to the MSODSC in code, the MSODSC is given the friendly ID of *MSODSC*; the friendly ID is a more convenient way to refer to the ActiveX control in code than using the hard-to-remember class ID. The Spreadsheet component on the Web page is identified by the registry using the class ID *0002E551-0000-0000-C000-000000000046* and the friendly ID *Spreadsheet1* for coding purposes. Similarly, the PivotTable Component on the Web page is identified by the class ID *0002E552-0000-0000-C000-000000000046* and the friendly ID *PivotTable1*, and the Chart Component on the Web page is identified by the class ID *0002E556-0000-0000-C000-000000000046* and the friendly ID *ChartSpace1*.

The *<script>* tag is used to define code that will run when the Web page is displayed or when a user or a particular Web page component takes some sort of action. The *language* attribute is set to *vbscript*.

In this example, only one event subroutine, *window_onload*, will run when the Web page is initially displayed. In the *window_onload* event subroutine, objects are declared representing the PivotTable component (*objPivotView*), a PivotTable data field (*objTotal*), Office XP Web Components constants (*objConstants*), and a chart (*objChart*).

Note In VBScript, all object instances must be declared as the *Variant* data type. For example, in VBScript, the following code will cause an error:

```
Dim objChart As Excel.Chart
```

In most of the Office object models, you can use constants in code without declaring them first. In the Office Web Components object models and VBScript, you must declare constants before you use them in code.

Next the MSODSC object's *ConnectionString* property is set to reference the BookSale.mdb file in a folder named C:\Microsoft Press\Excel Data Analysis\Sample Files\Chap11. You should change this code in the SalesPivotCode.htm file to match the folder where you have your copy of BookSale.mdb.

Once the MSODSC connects to the BookSale.mdb file, the *DataSource* and *DataMember* properties of the Spreadsheet Component and PivotTable Component objects are set to the MSODSC object's data source (the BookSale.mdb file) and, specifically, the Book Store Sales table in the BookSale.mdb file. Later in the code, after the PivotTable view has been built, the Chart Component object's *DataSource* property is set to the PivotChart Component object to synchronize the Chart Component with the PivotTable Component.

The rest of the code that refers to the PivotTable Component object (*objPivotView*) is similar to the code in the *CreatePivotTableAndPivotChartReport* subroutine presented in the Excel code samples section earlier in this chapter:

■ The PivotTable Component object's *ActiveView* property refers to what is currently visible in the PivotTable Component on the Web page, which is known programmatically as a *PivotView* object. The *PivotView* object's *AddTotal* method creates a total field, and the *PivotDataAxis* object's *InsertTotal* method adds the total field to the PivotTable Component's data area. The basis of the total field, named Sum of Sales, consists of the Sales field's summary data.

■ To add fields to the PivotTable Component's row, page, and data areas, the *PivotView* object's *RowAxis*, *FilterAxis*, and *DataAxis* objects are first referenced. The *InsertFieldSet* method of each object references the corresponding field (the Store, Quarter, and Sales fields in this instance) to add the fields.

The results of running the code in the SalesPivotCode.htm file are shown in Figures 11-16, 11-17, and 11-18.

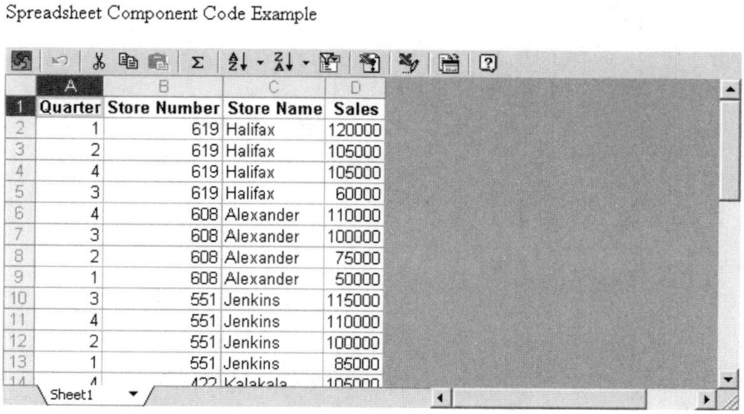

Spreadsheet Component Code Example

Figure 11-16 The SalesPivotCode.htm file's Spreadsheet Component.

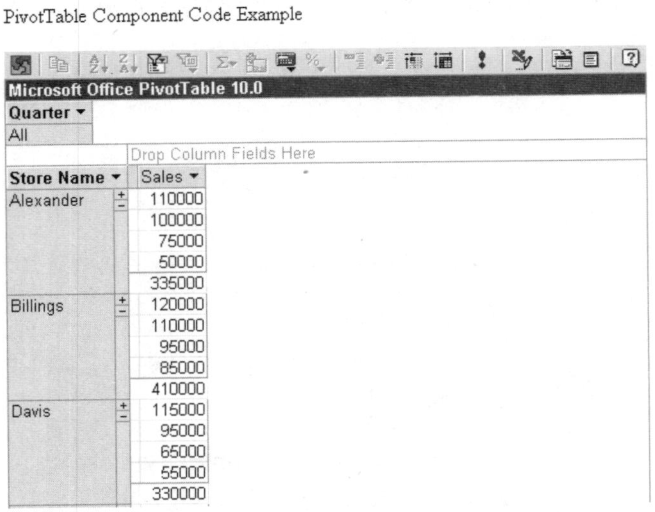

PivotTable Component Code Example

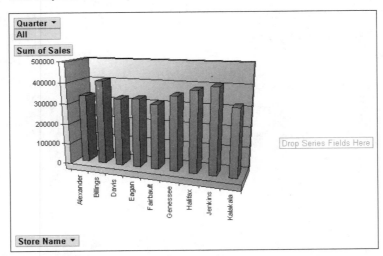

Figure 11-17 The SalesPivotCode.htm file's PivotTable Component.

Chart Component Code Example

Figure 11-18 The SalesPivotCode.htm file's Chart Component.

Extending the Data Analysis Features in Microsoft Data Analyzer

Microsoft Data Analyzer does not include the Visual Basic Editor that comes with most other Office applications. To program Data Analyzer, you must embed an instance of the Data Analyzer ActiveX control in an instance of a VBA UserForm, a 32-bit Windows form such as a Visual Basic or Microsoft Visual C++ form, or a Web page. You then write code using the hosting application's corresponding programming language. In the following code sample, included in the Chap11 folder's DACode.xls file, a VBA UserForm inside an Excel workbook hosts an instance of the Data Analyzer ActiveX control.

> **Note**   You must have Microsoft Data Analyzer and Microsoft SQL Server 2000 Analysis Services installed on your computer to run the following code sample. For complete information about programming the Data Analyzer ActiveX control, see the Microsoft Data Analyzer API help file included with Data Analyzer or the Microsoft Developer Network (MSDN) Web site at *http://msdn.microsoft.com*.

Here's the code:

```
Private Sub Workbook_Open()

    ' Open the frmDA VBA UserForm.
    frmDA.Show

End Sub
```

The *Workbook* object's *Open* event opens the VBA UserForm, referred to as *frmDA* in the code. The form contains an instance of the Data Analyzer ActiveX control.

```
' Note: You add the Microsoft Data Analyzer ActiveX Control to a
' VBA UserForm as follows:
' 1. Right-click a blank area of the Toolbox and click Additional Controls.
' 2. Select the Max3Ax Class check box, and then click OK.
' 3. Drag the Max3Ax icon from the Toolbox to the VBA UserForm.
' Note: To write code to customize the control, do the following:
' 1. On the Tools menu in the Visual Basic Editor, click References.
' 2. Select the Max3API check box, and then click OK.
' By default, the control is named "Max3Ax1".

' Global Data Analyzer Application object.
Public gdaApp As Max3API.Application
```

Similar to the other Office object models, Data Analyzer has an *Application* object that can be used to automate the application. The *Application* object instance (named *gdaApp* in this case) is declared in the General Declarations area of the VBA UserForm's code so that it can be accessed from several subroutines.

```
Private Sub UserForm_Activate()

    Set gdaApp = Max3Ax1.Application

    ' Connect to the sample FoodMart 2000 Sales cube.
    ' Change the next line of code to match the Microsoft SQL Server 2000
    ' Analysis Server name.
    gdaApp.ActiveView.Connect _
        ConnectionString:="location=localhost;provider=msolap"
    gdaApp.ActiveView.Catalog = "Foodmart 2000"
    gdaApp.ActiveView.Cube = "Sales"

    ' Determine the length and color of the bars and pie slices.
    ' In this case, length equals unit sales and color equals sales average.
    gdaApp.ActiveView.TraitsManager.Trait _
        (TraitID:=trtLength).SetSingleQuality _
        QualityType:=qtypMeasure, QualityID:="[Measures].[Unit Sales]"
    gdaApp.ActiveView.TraitsManager.Trait _
        (TraitID:=trtColor).SetSingleQuality _
        QualityType:=qtypMeasure, _
        QualityID:="[Measures].[Sales Average]"

    MsgBox Prompt:="Click one or more of the 'Display...' " & _
        "buttons at the bottom of the " & _
        "form to display a data view."

End Sub
```

The VBA UserForm's *Activate* event is triggered when the UserForm becomes active. Several operations occur inside the *Activate* event's code:

■ The Data Analyzer *Application* object's *ActiveView* property refers to the Data Analyzer ActiveX control's display area, referred to programmatically as a *View* object. The *View* object's *Connect* method's *ConnectionString* argument, along with its *Catalog* and *Cube* properties, is used to reference the data source to connect to. In this case, the data source is the Sales OLAP cube in the FoodMart 2000 OLAP database in the locally installed instance of Microsoft SQL Server 2000 Analysis Services.

■   To specify what the view's member bar lengths and colors represent, the *View* object's *TraitsManager* object is first referenced. The *Traits-Manager* object's *Trait* object is next referenced, specifying the *trtLength* or *trtColor* constants to indicate length or color settings, respectively. Finally, the specific *Trait* object's *SetSingleQuality* method sets the length or color settings by specifying an OLAP measure. This is done by setting the *SetSingleQuality* method's *Quality-Type* argument to the *qtypMeasure* enumerated constant and setting the *QualityID* argument to the measure name, using Multidimensional Expressions (MDX) syntax.

> **Note**   For more information about MDX syntax, see the Microsoft Developer Network (MSDN) Web site at *http://msdn.microsoft.com*.

In the next three subroutines, the UserForm's Display Advertising Data button, when clicked, clears any visible dimension panes from the display and then displays the Promotions and Promotion Media dimension panes, as shown in Figure 11-19. To clear all visible dimension panes, the *View* object's *Aspects* collection is referenced, and the *Aspects* collection's *Clear* method is called. To add a dimension pane, the *View* object's *Aspects* collection is referenced, and the *Aspects* collection's *Add* method is called, specifying the OLAP cube's dimension name for the ID argument.

```
Private Sub cmdAdvertising_Click()

    Call DisplayAdvertisingView

End Sub

Private Sub DisplayAdvertisingView()

    ' Purpose: Display time and promotional data.

    Call ReinitializeView
    gdaApp.ActiveView.Aspects.Add ID:="[Promotions]"
    gdaApp.ActiveView.Aspects.Add ID:="[Promotion Media]"

End Sub

Private Sub ReinitializeView()
```

(continued)

```
' Purpose: Clear any previous dimension panes
' and add the time dimension pane.

gdaApp.ActiveView.Aspects.Clear
gdaApp.ActiveView.Aspects.Add ID:="[Time]"
gdaApp.ActiveView.Aspects.Item _
    (v:="[Time]").GotoLevel LevelID:="[Time].[Year]"

End Sub
```

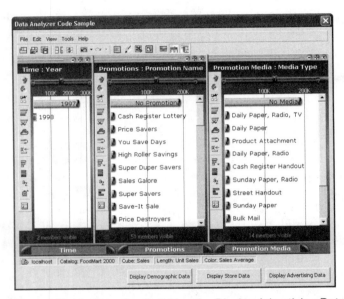

Figure 11-19   Results of clicking the Display Advertising Data button.

The next four subroutines contain code for the UserForm's Display Demographic Data and Display Store Data buttons, the results of which, when clicked, are shown in Figure 11-20 and Figure 11-21. The code for these subroutines is almost identical to the previous subroutines, except that different dimension panes are displayed in each case.

```
Private Sub cmdDemographics_Click()

    Call DisplayDemographicView

End Sub

Private Sub DisplayDemographicView()

    ' Purpose: Display time, education level, gender, and marital status.
```

```
      Call ReinitializeView
      gdaApp.ActiveView.Aspects.Add ID:="[Education Level]"
      gdaApp.ActiveView.Aspects.Add ID:="[Gender]"
      gdaApp.ActiveView.Aspects.Add ID:="[Marital Status]"

End Sub

Private Sub cmdStore_Click()

      Call DisplayStoresView

End Sub

Private Sub DisplayStoresView()

      ' Purpose: Display time, store location, store type,
      ' and store size in square feet.

      Call ReinitializeView
      gdaApp.ActiveView.Aspects.Add ID:="[Store]"
      gdaApp.ActiveView.Aspects.Add ID:="[Store Type]"
      gdaApp.ActiveView.Aspects.Add ID:="[Store Size in SQFT]"

End Sub
```

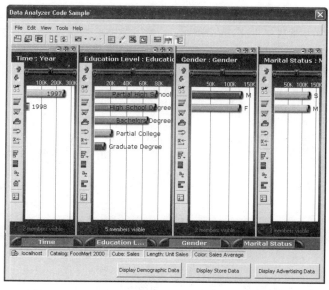

Figure 11-20   Results of clicking the Display Demographic Data button.

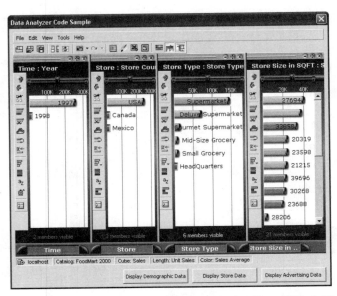

Figure 11-21 Results of clicking the Display Store Data button.

Summary

Many of the Office data analysis features can be extended through the use of code. For simple data analysis tasks, you can program macros, consisting of one or more procedures, in the Office Visual Basic Editor. Office macros are typically programmed using Visual Basic for Applications (VBA) code. The Microsoft Office Web Components and Microsoft Data Analyzer are two exceptions. In these cases, you host the Office Web Components on a Web page or you host Data Analyzer as an ActiveX control on a 32-bit form container or a Web page. For Office data analysis solutions based on Web pages, you can use Visual Basic Scripting Edition (VBScript) code. For other programmatic containers, you use the host application's programming language.

Before you can program Office data analysis solutions, you must understand the Office object models, including their objects, collections, properties, methods, events, types, and constants. You can explore the Office object models by using the Object Browser and the Office VBA Language Reference, both of which are accessed through the Visual Basic Editor. Before you can program any Office object model, you must set a reference to it. Most of the Office object models are traversed beginning with the *Application* object.

In the next chapter, "Maintaining Data Reporting and Analysis Systems," you will learn how to maintain Microsoft Access and Microsoft SQL Server 2000 databases.

12

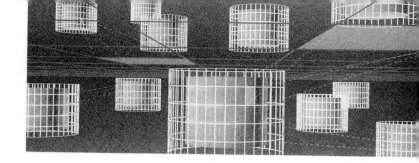

Maintaining Data Reporting and Analysis Systems

Continuous data availability and fast data-retrieval speed are two hallmarks of healthy data reporting and data analysis systems. When systems fail to provide access to their data, or data access is significantly slowed, organizations and individuals are hindered from making quality business decisions in a timely manner. You should make system maintenance a top priority—committing to the time, human resources, and budget it requires—when planning the design and implementation of data reporting and data analysis systems. Database maintenance is as important as the databases themselves.

This chapter introduces the requirements for maintaining data reporting and analysis systems and is written mostly for smaller organizations—organizations that use Access for their data storage or have just moved (or are planning to move) to Microsoft SQL Server 2000 for their data storage. Within organizations such as these, database maintenance is often performed by the same person or persons who perform data analysis. For information about maintaining data reporting and analysis systems in larger organizations, see the section "Additional Reading" at the end of this chapter.

Objectives

In this chapter, you will learn how to

- Go about creating and implementing database maintenance plans.

- Document, back up, and configure automatic maintenance plans for Microsoft SQL Server 2000 databases and how to secure these databases.

- Maintain Microsoft SQL Server 2000 Desktop Engine databases using Microsoft SQL Server 2000 tools.

- Document, analyze, repair, and secure Microsoft Access databases.

- Archive, restore, and process OLAP cubes in Microsoft SQL Server 2000 Analysis Services databases.

Creating and Implementing Database Maintenance Plans

Many organizations and businesses begin their data collection and analysis efforts without taking stock of what data already exists or is being analyzed. This omission usually leads to duplicate or conflicting data collection and analysis. The following questions will help you coordinate data collection and analysis efforts, which will make database maintenance tasks easier overall.

- Have you completed an inventory of your data? In larger organizations, this information includes the names and network locations of all the organization's data sources—the servers and the databases stored on them.

- From a general perspective, what purpose does each database serve? To preserve data and conserve resources, can any of these databases be archived to disk?

- Are the structure and relationships for each database documented? Is the documentation in electronic, paper, or some other format? After every significant change to a database's structure, has the new structure been documented? Where is the documentation stored?

- Do you have enough RAM, processing speed, and hard disk space on each of the computers you use for storing databases and making data available to users? Does your hardware meet not only your current needs but your estimates for future data storage and retrieval needs? When was the last time you defragmented your computers' hard disk drives?

- Do you have a plan in place to deal with possible data failure, such as nightly hard-disk backups. If any backups fail, how is your backup staff alerted? Are you using RAID (redundant array of independent disks), a system that distributes data over a group of disks to ensure that if one disk fails, no data is lost? (The "I" in RAID is sometimes considered an abbreviation for "inexpensive" instead of "independent.")

After your organization begins collecting and organizing its data, the following items will help ensure that data is always accurate and available.

- Backup schedules should be posted next to each computer that requires its data to be regularly backed up. Emergency contact names, phone numbers, pager numbers, and e-mail addresses should also be posted next to each of these computers in case an unexpected data loss or failure occurs.

- After every backup, a person should attest in some manner that the backup has been successfully completed and physically verified for accuracy.

- There should be a regular schedule for other database maintenance tasks, such as checking index performance, event logs, transaction logs, and data audits. There should be a chain of responsibility for physically checking and verifying that these tasks were completed successfully and any anomalies should be forwarded back up the chain.

- To plan for theft and natural disasters, at least one additional copy of each backup should be regularly archived to physical media, such as a magnetic tape or CD, and the media should be stored in a secure location (such as a fireproof floor safe or a climate-controlled vault) separate from your place of business. Only a few individuals should have access to the off-site media, and then only for emergency data retrieval purposes.

Maintaining SQL Server 2000 Databases

Microsoft SQL Server 2000 provides two tools, Enterprise Manager and Query Analyzer, that make basic database maintenance a snap. Both tools have graphical user interfaces that make working with databases much simpler.

To use Enterprise Manager on a computer with SQL Server 2000 installed, on the Start menu, click Programs, click Microsoft SQL Server, and then click Enterprise Manager. Once Enterprise Manager appears, you can access the database you want to maintain by opening the Console Root folder and then expanding the Microsoft SQL Servers group, the SQL Server group containing your database server, and the database server, as shown in Figure 12-1.

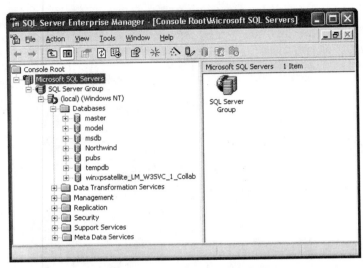

Figure 12-1   The SQL Server Enterprise Manager.

To connect to a SQL Server on a different computer, right-click the SQL Server group to which you want to add the SQL Server connection, click New SQL Server Registration, and then provide a server name, authentication details, and any other requested information in the dialog box shown in Figure 12-2.

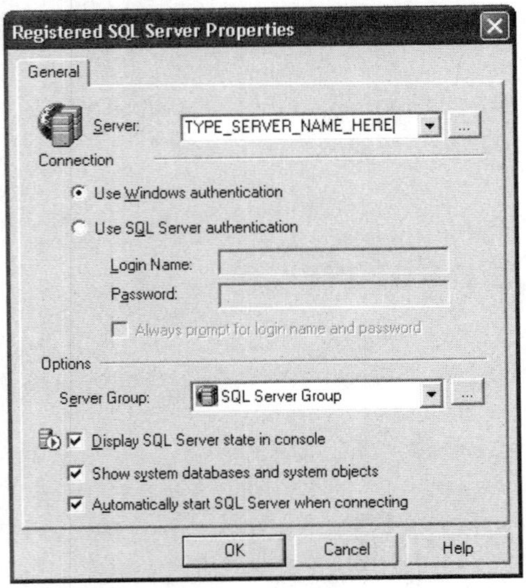

Figure 12-2   Connecting to SQL Server on a different computer.

To use Query Analyzer on a computer with SQL Server 2000 installed, on the Start menu, point to Programs, point to Microsoft SQL Server, and then click Query Analyzer. You then need to provide the information requested in the Connect To SQL Server dialog box, shown in Figure 12-3. (To connect to the SQL Server installed on the same computer, type *(local)* in the SQL Server list.)

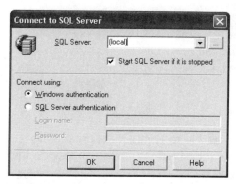

Figure 12-3   The Connect To SQL Server dialog box in Query Analyzer.

The following sections describe how to use Enterprise Manager and Query Analyzer to perform three important SQL Server 2000 database maintenance tasks:

- Documenting your databases.
- Backing up your databases.
- Using the SQL Server 2000 Maintenance Plan Wizard to automate common database maintenance tasks.

Documenting and Re-Creating SQL Server Databases

After you create a database, you should document the database in the event some type of unanticipated data failure requires you to re-create the structure of your database. To document a database, open Enterprise Manager, right-click the database you want to document, point to All Tasks, and then click Generate SQL Script. To thoroughly document a database, on the General tab of the Generate SQL Scripts dialog box, click the Show All button and then select the Script All Objects option. On the Formatting tab, select all the options except Only Script 7.0 Compatible Features. Also select all the check boxes on the Options tab. Clicking OK creates a text file that can be used to re-create the structure of the database from scratch.

> **Caution**   A SQL script created with the Generate SQL Scripts dialog box re-creates only the database's structure, not the database's data.

You use Query Analyzer to re-create a database's structure from scratch. After you connect to the server on which you want to re-create the database's structure, click Open on the File menu in Query Analyzer, click the SQL script file for the database, and then click Open. In the final step, click Execute on the Query menu.

> **Caution**   Using a SQL script file to re-create a database's structure on a SQL Server computer that includes a database with the same name will delete the existing database. Do not practice re-creating a database's structure on a computer that has an identically named database or you will lose the existing database.

Backing Up and Restoring SQL Server Databases

Backing up your databases is the most important database maintenance task. Losing data and having no way to recover it, needless to say, can be disastrous in terms of lost time, lost money, and missed business opportunities.

Although you can use the Database Maintenance Plan Wizard (described in the next section) to automate database backups, you should immediately set up automated backup tasks for your databases until you complete a formal database maintenance plan with the Database Maintenance Plan Wizard. To set up an automated backup task for a database, right-click the database icon in Enterprise Manager, point to All Tasks, and then click Backup Database. Provide the backup settings in the SQL Server Backup dialog box and then click OK. To restore a database from a backup, right-click the server's Database folder in Enterprise Manager, point to All Tasks, click Restore Database, and then provide the restore settings in the Restore Database dialog box.

For information about the settings in the SQL Server Backup or the Restore Database dialog box, click the General or the Options tab in the dialog box you want information about and then click the Help button.

Using the Database Maintenance Plan Wizard

The most convenient way to maintain SQL Server 2000 databases is to use the SQL Server 2000 Database Maintenance Plan Wizard. This wizard can regularly perform the following maintenance tasks:

- Reorganize databases to allow new data to be added more quickly.

- Compress databases to provide more database storage space.

- Update indexes to allow data to be located more quickly.

- Check databases to be sure they are not damaged.

- Back up databases and transaction logs to ensure that data can be restored to a specific point in time in the event of data loss.

- Duplicate transaction logs to another SQL Server to enable a standby server in case the first server is unavailable or busy. (This task is available only with SQL Server 2000 Enterprise Edition.)

To run the Database Maintenance Plan Wizard, once you have opened your database server, click the plus sign to open the Management folder, right-click the Database Maintenance Plans icon, and then click New Maintenance Plan. Complete the wizard's pages to create the maintenance plan. The following sections describe some of the terminology used in the Database Maintenance Plan Wizard. For help on any of the wizard's pages, click the Help button on that page.

System Databases Versus User Databases

System databases refer to databases that SQL Server uses internally to maintain data integrity across the server. System databases include information such as server login accounts, database templates, system alerts, and automated tasks. Some of the system databases you see in Enterprise Manager include the master, model, and msdb databases.

User databases refer to the databases in which you or your organization enter data for storage and analysis as part of conducting business. These databases generally include all databases except system databases. The best option to select on the Database Maintenance Plan Wizard's Select Databases page is All Databases, as it creates a maintenance plan for all the databases on the server.

Indexes

As the name implies, indexes are used by SQL Server to look up information when you need to find data. Indexes are stored on index pages. A certain amount of free space is desirable on index pages so that new index entries can be added. Creating lots of index pages with a small number of index entries on each page slows down search requests. The Database Maintenance Plan Wizard's Update Data Optimization Information page provides good default settings for optimizing database indexes. Selecting all the options on this page and using their default values provides good overall index optimization.

Backups and Transaction Logs

Backups are used to store copies of data in case the original data is lost or corrupted. Backups can be stored on storage media such as tape or in a folder on a drive connected to the SQL Server computer.

Transaction logs keep a record of data added, deleted, and changed in a database. When a database fails, SQL Server can use transaction logs to restore data as it was at a specific point in time. Without transaction logs, restoring a database to the state it was when the database failed can take much longer, and you might need to enter some of the data again.

When you create a database, you have the opportunity to create accompanying transaction logs. You should always create transaction logs at the same time you create a database, and you should always back up all your databases and transaction logs.

Securing SQL Server Databases

You should secure your SQL Server databases to prevent unauthorized access. You can also track SQL Server activity if you suspect you have a security issue with your SQL Server databases.

To secure the databases on a computer running SQL Server, depending on the type of security you want to allow, use Enterprise Manager to connect to the SQL Server and then do the following:

- Open the server's Security folder, and then add login credentials for one or more databases on the server. You can also add linked servers or remote servers to handle the distribution of data requests on your system.

- Open the server's Databases folder, expand a specific database icon, and add a user or security role to the individual database.

> **Note** For more information about SQL Server security, see SQL Server Books Online included with SQL Server.

You can use SQL Server Profiler to track SQL Server activities such as the success or failure of a login attempt or whether attempts to access database objects were successful. To use Profiler, point to Programs on the Start menu, point to Microsoft SQL Server, and then click Profiler. For help setting up event tracking in Profiler, click Contents And Index on the Help menu in Profiler.

Maintaining SQL Server 2000 Desktop Engine Databases

The SQL Server 2000 Desktop Engine does not include graphical database management tools. However, you can manage an instance of the SQL Server 2000 Desktop Engine from SQL Server 2000 Enterprise Manager if you can connect to the computer running SQL Server 2000 Desktop Engine from a computer with SQL Server 2000 installed. All the SQL Server 2000 tasks previously described can be completed using Enterprise Manager from a computer connected to an instance of SQL Server 2000 Desktop Engine.

Maintaining Access Databases

Many SQL Server 2000 database maintenance tasks have equivalent actions in Access databases. Similar to SQL Server 2000, important Access database maintenance tasks include documenting your databases and backing up your databases. Access also provides tools such as the Table Analyzer Wizard, the Performance Analyzer, and the Compact And Repair command that you can use to optimize your Access database (.mdb) files.

Documenting Access Databases

To document an Access database, on the Tools menu, point to Analyze and then click Documenter. Select the check boxes next to the database objects that you want to document, and then click OK. A series of reports that document the structure of the database's objects is created. The reports can be printed or saved to file formats such as Excel workbooks, HTML, Rich Text Format, or Access Snapshot Format by clicking Export on the File menu after Access creates the reports.

In the Documenter dialog box, click the Option button to include in the reports information such as table properties, relationships, and permissions; field names, data types, sizes, and properties; and index names, fields, and properties.

To thoroughly document a database, click the All Object Types tab and then click the Select All button. Be aware that the more objects you select, the longer it takes to generate the final report and the larger the final report becomes. For example, documenting the sample Northwind database can generate a report of more than 600 pages.

Backing Up and Restoring Access Databases

Access does not include any built-in database backup utilities. To back up an Access database, first close the database. (If you are using the Access database in a multiuser environment, confirm that all users have closed the database.) Then, using Microsoft Windows Explorer, the Microsoft Windows 2000 Backup And Recovery Tools, the Windows XP Backup Or Restore Wizard, or other backup software, copy the Access database to a backup medium of your choice. How you restore an Access database from a backup copy depends on which method you used to produce the backup copy. Using Windows Explorer or another backup tool, copy the backup Access database to your database folder.

If the Access database you are restoring and the backup copy have the same name, restoring the backup can replace the existing file. If you want to save the existing file, you should rename it before you copy the backup database. You can also back up individual database objects by creating a blank database and exporting the objects you want from the original database to the blank database by clicking Export on the File menu.

> **Caution**   If you are using user-level security, you should also create a backup of the workgroup information file. If you accidentally lose or damage the workgroup information file, you won't be able to start Access again until you restore or rebuild the workgroup information file. User-level security is covered in more detail later in this chapter in the section "Securing Access Databases."

> **Note**   Replicating a database is not the same operation as backing up a database. You replicate a database when you want to synchronize data in several copies of the same database across multiple computers. However, if a replica of a database is damaged and an undamaged backup of the database is not available (especially the master database replica), the damage could propagate through the connected databases with few or no recovery options. Database replication can be a somewhat complex subject, especially for new Access database administrators. For more information on replicating Access databases, see the Access online help.

Using the Table Analyzer Wizard

You can use the Table Analyzer Wizard to reduce duplicate data in Access database tables. Although the Table Analyzer Wizard doesn't tell you which tables need to be analyzed, the wizard can help you split data tables to create new tables in which each piece of data is stored only once. This allows you to update data in one place and use the data many times. The nice thing about using the Table Analyzer Wizard is that your original data table remains unchanged, which allows you to play with the wizard's settings until you get the results you want. To use the Table Analyzer Wizard, on the Tools menu, point to Analyze, click Table, and proceed through the wizard's steps.

Using the Performance Analyzer

The Performance Analyzer optimizes Access databases, recommending tasks that you can carry out automatically as well as making other suggestions that involve tradeoffs you must agree to before you carry out the suggested tasks. Finally, the Performance Analyzer can provide optimization ideas that you must carry out yourself. To use the Performance Analyzer, on the Tools menu, point to Analyze, click Performance, and proceed through the Performance Analyzer's steps.

You can practice using the Performance Analyzer to analyze the sample Northwind database. When you start Performance Analyzer, click the All Object Types tab, click the Select All button, and then click OK. Performance Analyzer suggests that you create an MDE file (a more secure copy of the databases), use fewer controls on the Employees and Orders forms, convert macros to Visual Basic code, and so on.

Compacting and Repairing Databases

If you delete data or objects from an Access database, you can leave gaps that the data or objects once occupied. These gaps result in inefficient disk space usage and longer data search times, especially with large files. Compacting Access files rearranges the files' contents to reduce or eliminate these gaps. You should regularly compact Access files for improved performance.

In most cases, Access detects whether an Access file is damaged when you try to open it; Access then gives you the option to repair the file before Access continues to try to open the file. If the damaged file contains a reference to another damaged Access file, Access does not attempt to repair the other damaged file. In some cases, Access may not detect that a file is damaged. If an

Access file behaves unpredictably, you should compact and repair the Access file at the same time.

To compact and repair an Access file, on the Tools menu, point to Database Utilities, and then click Compact And Repair Database. Access closes the file, compacts and repairs the file, and then reopens the file.

To help prevent Access files from being damaged, you should

- Compact and repair Access files regularly.

- Back up your Access files regularly to prevent having to deal with damaged files.

- Avoid quitting Access unexpectedly (for instance, by suddenly turning off your computer by using the power switch).

- Compact and repair all your Access files after rebooting your computer should your computer shut down unexpectedly.

Securing Access Databases

You have several options for securing an Access database and its associated objects (tables, forms, queries, and so on). Encrypting a database makes a database's data indecipherable by software applications such as word processors. Encryption is particularly useful when you transmit a database electronically. To encrypt an Access database, start Access but don't open any database. Point to Security on the Tools menu, click Encrypt/Decrypt Database, and then follow the directions displayed on your screen. Repeat these steps to decrypt an Access database by selecting a file with the extension .mde or .ade.

Encrypting an *unsecured* database has no effect, however, because anybody can open the database and gain full access to the data. One way to secure an Access database is to require a password to open the database file. After a password is set, a dialog box requesting the password is displayed whenever the database is opened. Only users who enter the correct password are allowed to open the database. After the database is open, all the database's objects are available to the user unless other types of security have been defined, as described later in this section. For a database that is shared among a small group of users or for a database on a single computer, setting a password is often all the security that is required.

To set a password for an Access database, you first need to open the database for exclusive use. Use the Open command on the File menu to open the database. In the Open dialog box, click the arrow beside the Open button and then click Open Exclusive. Then, on the Tools menu, point to Security, click Set Database Password, enter and confirm the password, click OK, and then close the database. To unset the password, open the database for exclusive use, enter the database password, and then click OK. With the database now open, point to Security on the Tools menu, click Unset Database Password, enter the password, click OK, and then close the database.

A more secure option is to implement Access user-level security. User-level security allows you to establish different levels of access to sensitive data and objects in a database. Users need a password to open the database, and then Access reads a workgroup information file in which each user is associated with a unique ID. The combination of unique ID and password determines which data and objects a user can access. The easiest way to implement user-level security is to point to Security on the Tools menu in Access, click User-Level Security Wizard, and then step through the wizard's pages.

For help completing the Security Wizard, click the Help button on any of the wizard's pages. For more information about Access security options, see the Access online help.

Maintaining SQL Server 2000 Analysis Services Systems

Microsoft SQL Server 2000 Analysis Services allows you to ensure data integrity by archiving and restoring OLAP cubes. Another key Analysis Services data integrity task you should perform is to process the OLAP cubes associated with a database whenever you update that database's data or structure so that the cubes reflect the changes.

Archiving and Restoring OLAP Cubes

To archive an Analysis Services database, right-click a database icon in the Analysis Manager window and then click Archive Database. Provide the archive settings in the Archive Database dialog box, and then click Archive to archive the database.

To restore an archived database, right-click a server icon in the Analysis Manager window and then click Restore Database. Select the archive database file, and then click Open to restore the file.

Processing OLAP Cubes

Analysis Services creates OLAP cubes from source data. These cubes contain summarized data, fact tables, and dimension tables that depend on the source data's specific structure. Changes to the structure of your source data affect the integrity and accuracy of the source data's associated cubes. Because Analysis

Services provides continuous access to cubes, any changes to an underlying data source must be made with the integrity of the cubes in mind. Many of the changes you make to cube structure within Analysis Manager and all the changes to an OLAP cube's underlying source data require the cube to be updated so that the changes can be reflected in the cube's data.

You can update OLAP cubes in the following ways:

■ An *incremental* update appends data in an OLAP cube but does not update the OLAP cube's summarized data. This update method does not process changes to a cube's structure or make changes to its existing source data. You should use this method only if you want to keep your data current.

■ A *refresh data* update clears and reloads an OLAP cube's data and recalculates its summarized data. You should use this method if the OLAP cube's source data has changed but its structure has not.

■ A *full process* update completely restructures an OLAP cube based on its current definition and then recalculates its data.

To manually process an OLAP cube, right-click an OLAP cube icon in the Analysis Manager window, click Process, select an update processing method, and then click OK. If you select an incremental update, provide any additional information required by the Incremental Update Wizard.

To automate OLAP cube processing, you must create a recurring SQL Server 2000 scheduled Data Transformation Services task as follows:

1. Open SQL Server 2000 Enterprise Manager. (On the Start menu, point to Programs, point to Microsoft SQL Server, and then click Enterprise Manager.)

2. Expand the server icon for the SQL Server on which you want to automate the OLAP cube processing task.

3. Right-click the server's Data Transformation Services folder, and then click New Package.

4. In the DTS Package window, on the Task menu, click Analysis Services Processing Task.

5. In the Analysis Services Processing Task dialog box, select the cube that you want to process. In the right pane, click the update process type and then click OK.

6. On the Package menu, click Save, provide a package name of your choice, and then click OK.

7.   In the Enterprise Manager window, in the Data Transformation Services folder, click the Local Packages icon.

8.   Right-click your package icon, customize the settings in the Edit Recurring Job Schedule dialog box, and then click OK to begin the automatic OLAP cube processing schedule.

Additional Reading

You can find additional information about maintaining Microsoft data reporting and analysis systems in the following Microsoft Press books:

■   *Microsoft SQL Server 2000 Resource Kit*

■   *Microsoft SQL Server 2000 Performance Tuning Technical Reference*

■   *Microsoft Access Version 2002 Inside Out*

■   *Running Microsoft Access 2000*

■   *Microsoft SQL Server 2000 Analysis Services Step by Step*

Summary

Creating database maintenance plans helps reduce wasted data collection efforts and makes database maintenance tasks easier overall. As part of any database maintenance plan, you should conduct an inventory of and document your data, take stock of your computer hardware, and plan for disaster recovery efforts in the event of natural disaster or theft.

Microsoft SQL Server 2000 provides graphical tools that can help you document, backup, restore, and optimize your SQL Server databases through automatic, scheduled maintenance. Microsoft Access provides graphical tools such as the Table Analyzer Wizard, the Performance Analyzer, and the Compact And Repair command that can help you optimize and repair your Access databases. Microsoft SQL Server 2000 Analysis Services provides graphical tools to help you archive, restore, and process OLAP cubes on a regular schedule.

Appendix A

Data Analysis Quick Reference

This appendix lists the steps you follow for many of the data analysis tasks described elsewhere in this book. You can use this quick reference to get started on specific data analysis tasks. For brevity, the steps in this appendix commonly use command names and menu options from Microsoft Office 2002.

Microsoft Excel

Sort a List of Data Records

1. Select the cells you want to sort.

2. On the Data menu, click Sort.

3. Select the field or fields you want to sort by, the sort order, and other options in the Sort dialog box.

4. Click OK.

Filter a List of Data Records Using Simple Criteria

1. Click any cell in the list of records.

2. On the Data menu, point to Filter and then click AutoFilter.

3. Select an item from the AutoFilter list for one or more fields, or use the Top 10 or Custom items to enter criteria for the filter.

Filter a List of Data Records Using Advanced Criteria

1. Insert at least three blank rows above the list of data records.

2. In separate cells in the first blank row, type the name of each column by which you want to filter.

3. In the second and subsequent rows, type the advanced filter criteria.

4. Click any cell in the list of records you want to filter.

5. On the Data menu, point to Filter and then click Advanced Filter.

6. In the Advanced Filter dialog box, identify the group of cells you want to filter (List Range) and the cells that define the filter criteria (Criteria Range).

7. Click OK to apply the filter.

Run a Worksheet Function

1. Click the spreadsheet cell in which you want the function's result to appear.

2. On the Insert menu, click Function.

3. Select the function name and click OK.

4. In the Function Arguments dialog box, enter the data values, cell addresses, or other arguments that the function requires.

5. Click OK to insert the function into the cell and see the results.

Format Cells Based on Certain Conditions

1. Select the cells to which you want to apply conditional formatting.

2. On the Format menu, click Conditional Formatting.

3. Enter the formatting conditions in the Condition 1 area. If you want to add more cell formatting options, click the Add button and provide formatting conditions in the Condition 2 area. Click the Add button again to add cell formatting options for the Condition 3 area.

4. Click OK to apply the conditional formatting.

Create a Chart

1. Select the cells containing the data values that you want to include in your chart.

2. On the Standard toolbar, click the Chart Wizard button.

3. Step through the Chart Wizard and select the chart type, the data range, chart formatting options, where to place the chart, and other options.

4. Click Finish to create the chart.

Import External Data into a Workbook

1. Click the cell in which you want the first item of the external data to appear.

2. On the Data menu, point to Import External Data and then click Import Data.

3. If you know that the data file or data source connection file already exists, locate and select the file, click Open, and then follow the directions Excel provides to finish importing the data. To create a new data source connection file, click the New Source button.

4. On the wizard's first screen, select a data source and then click Next.

5. Depending on the type of data source you want to connect to, follow the steps to specify connection properties.

6. After you have specified connection properties, click Finish. The Select Data Source dialog box reappears.

7. Click the data source connection file, click Open, and then follow the instructions to finish importing the data.

Query Data in an External Data Source

1. On the Data menu, point to Import External Data and then click New Database Query.

2. If your data source is visible on the Databases tab, double-click the data source and go to step 9 in this procedure. Otherwise, select the Use The Query Wizard To Create/Edit Queries check box, click New Data Source on the Databases tab, and then click OK.

3. In the What Name Do You Want To Give Your Data Source box, type a name for the data source that's descriptive yet easy for you to remember.

4. In the Select A Driver For The Type Of Database You Want To Access, select the type of database in which you want to query data.

5. Click Connect.

6. In the ODBC Setup dialog box, provide the information required to connect to the data source. (The information varies depending on the type of database you want to query.) Click OK.

7. In the Select A Default Table For Your Data Source list, select the table that contains the data you want to include in your query and then click OK.

8. Click OK to return to the Choose Data Source dialog box, and then click OK in the Choose Data Source dialog box to start the Query Wizard.

9. In the Available Tables And Columns list, double-click each column that you want to include in your query to move the column to the Columns In Your Query list.

10. Click Next.

11. Filter the data to be displayed by clicking a column in the Column To Filter list and specifying filter conditions in the Only Include Rows Where area. Click Next.

12. On the Sort Order page, specify columns to sort by and the sort order. Click Next.

13. Select an option to return the data to an Excel worksheet, view or edit the data in Microsoft Query, or create an OLAP cube from the data that the query returns. Click Finish.

Query Data in a Web-Based Data Source

1. Click the cell in the spreadsheet where you want to insert the first item of data.

2. On the Data menu, point to Import External Data and then click New Web Query.

3. In the Address box, type the address for the data and then click Go.

4. Click the arrows next to the data tables that you want to query.

5. Click the Import button.

6. Click OK. The results are inserted into the spreadsheet.

Subtotal a List of Data Records

1. Select the data for which you want to insert subtotals.

2. On the Data menu, click Subtotals.

3. Provide the subtotal settings in the Subtotal dialog box.

4. Click OK. The subtotals are inserted.

5. Use the outline buttons and the plus and minus buttons to show or hide data and subtotals.

Run an Analysis ToolPak Function

1. On the Tools menu, click Data Analysis.

2. Select the tool that provides the information you need.

3. In the dialog box for the ToolPak function, enter the information required; for example, the input range, the output range, and so on.

4. Click OK.

Run the Solver Add-In

1. On the Tools menu, click Solver.

2. In the Solver Parameters dialog box, enter information required for the target cell, the cells whose values can change, any constraints, and so on.

3. Click Solve.

Working with OLAP Data in Excel

Import OLAP Data into a Workbook Using an Existing Query (.oqy) or Offline Data Cube (.cub) File

1. On the Data menu, point to Import External Data and then click Import Data. The Select Data Source dialog box appears.

2. In the Files Of Type list, select OLAP Queries/Cube Files.

3. Locate and select the .oqy or .cub file you want to import, and then click Open.

4. In the PivotTable And PivotChart Wizard, select an option for where to place the PivotTable report that references the OLAP data, in either a new worksheet or the existing worksheet (beginning at the cell referenced in the list directly below the Existing Worksheet option).

5. Click Finish. The OLAP data is presented as a PivotTable report in the current workbook.

Import OLAP Data into a Workbook Using a New Connection to an OLAP Database Server or an Offline Cube File

1. On the Data menu, point to Get External Data and then click New Database Query. The Choose Data Source dialog box appears.

2. On the OLAP Cubes tab, click New Data Source and then click OK.

3. In the What Name Do You Want To Give Your Data Source list, type a name for the data source.

4. In the Select An OLAP Provider For The Database You Want To Access list, select Microsoft OLE DB Provider For OLAP Services 8.0 (for data sources using Microsoft SQL Server 2000 Analysis Services) or Microsoft OLE DB Provider For OLAP Services (for data sources using Microsoft SQL Server 7.0 OLAP Services).

5. Click the Connect button.

6. Select the Analysis Server option if you want to connect to an OLAP server; select the Cube File option if you want to connect to an offline cube file.

7. If you selected the Analysis Server option, type the name of the OLAP server in the Server box, click Next, click the name of the database that you want to access, and then click Finish.
   If you selected the Cube File option, type the path and file name for the offline cube file and then click Finish.

8. If the cube is not already selected in the Select The Cube That Contains The Data You Want List, select the cube you need and then click OK.

9. Select the name of the data source that you just added, and then click OK.

10. In the PivotTable And PivotChart Wizard, select an option for where to place the PivotTable report that references the OLAP data, in either a new worksheet or the existing worksheet (beginning at the cell referenced in the list directly below the Existing Worksheet option).

11. Click Finish. The OLAP data is presented as a PivotTable report in the current workbook.

Open an Offline Cube File in Excel

1.   On the File menu, click Open.

2.   In the Files Of Type list, select All Files.

3.   Locate and select the .cub file, and then click Open. The OLAP data is presented as a PivotTable report in the current workbook.

> **Note**   The previous procedure cannot be performed with Excel 2000.

PivotTable Reports and PivotChart Reports

Create a PivotTable Report and PivotChart Report in Excel

1.   On the Data menu, click PivotTable And PivotChart Report.

2.   In the Where Is The Data That You Want To Analyze area, specify whether the data is in a group of Excel cells, an external data source, multiple cell groups in one or more Excel files, or another PivotTable report or PivotChart report.

3.   In the What Kind Of Report Do You Want To Create area, specify whether you want to create just a PivotTable report or a PivotTable report and a PivotChart report that uses the PivotTable report as its data source. Click Next.

4.   Depending on which option you selected in step 2, do the following:

❑   If you specified a group of Excel cells as the data source, click the Range box and then select the group of cells that you want to include in the PivotTable. (If the cells are in another Excel file, click the Browse button first to specify the file's location.)

❑   If you specified an external data source, click the Get Data button, select the data source, click OK in the Choose Data Source dialog box, and then follow the steps in the Query Wizard. When you've completed the wizard, click Next.

❑   If you specified multiple cell groups in one or more Excel files as the data source, select an option for the page fields you want and then click Next. Click the Range box and select a group of cells that you want to include in your PivotTable report. Click

Add to add the group of cells. Repeat this step for each group of cells that you want to include in your PivotTable report, and then click Next.

❑ If you specified another PivotTable report or PivotChart Report in step 2, select the PivotTable report name in the Which Pivot-Table Report Contains The Data You Want To Use list and then click Next.

5. Select an option for where you want to put the PivotTable report area, either in a new worksheet or in the worksheet that's currently displayed.

6. Click Finish. The reports are created.

7. To customize a PivotTable report or PivotChart report, do the following:

❑ Include a field in a PivotTable report or PivotChart by dragging a field from the PivotTable field list (the PivotTable toolbar in Excel 2000) to the drop area.

❑ Move a field in a PivotTable report or PivotChart report by dragging the field to another drop area.

❑ Remove a field from a PivotTable report or PivotChart report by dragging the field to a screen location outside the report.

Filter Data in a PivotTable Report or PivotChart Report

1. With the PivotTable report or PivotChart report active, click the arrow beside the field name in the report.

2. For page fields, select the item associated with the data that you want to display. For fields other than page fields, select or clear check boxes to display or hide data for the field and then click OK.

Create a Calculated Field or a Calculated Item for Use in a PivotTable Report or PivotChart Report

1. Click a field inside a PivotTable or PivotChart report.

2. On the PivotTable toolbar, open the PivotTable menu, point to Formulas and then click Calculated Field or Calculated Item.

3. Type a name and formula to use for the calculated field or calculated item.

4. Click the Add button to add the calculated field or calculated item to the PivotTable field list.

5. Click OK.

Microsoft Access

Import External Data

1. On the File menu, point to Get External Data and then click Import.

2. In the Files Of Type list, select the file type for the data you want to import.

3. Select the file with the data you want to import, and then click Import.

4. Follow the directions displayed by the file type's import wizard to finish importing the data.

Link to External Data

1. On the File menu, point to Get External Data and then click Link Tables.

2. In the Files Of Type list, select the file type for the data you want to link to.

3. Select the file that contains the data you want to link to, and then click Link.

4. Follow the directions displayed by the file type's wizard to finish creating a link to the data.

Perform a Simple Sort

1. Open the table or form containing the data you want to sort in Datasheet view or Form view.

2. Click a field name.

3. On the Records menu, point to Sort and then click Sort Ascending or Sort Descending.

Filter Data Using Filter By Selection

1. Open the table, query, or form with the data you want to filter in Datasheet view or Form view.

2. Click an instance of the value that you want data records to match to be included in the filtered data. Select part of the value if you want to use only that portion of the value as a filter.

3. On the Records menu, point to Filter and then click Filter By Selection.

    After the matching records are displayed, you can repeat steps 2 and 3 until you have the group of records you want.

Filter Data Using Filter By Form

1. Open the table, query, or form containing the data you want to filter in Datasheet view or Form view.

2. On the Records menu, point to Filter and then click Filter By Form. All of the records disappear and a blank record is displayed.

3. In the Filter By Form window, enter filter conditions in one or more fields. To add multiple sets of filter conditions, click the Or tab.

4. On the Filter menu, click Apply Filter/Sort.

Perform an Advanced Filter or Sort

1. With the table, query, or form open, point to Filter on the Records menu and then click Advanced Filter/Sort. The records disappear and the advanced filter window appears.

2. Enter the filter conditions in the grid by dragging field names from the field list to the Field cell, setting the sort order, and entering criteria.

3. On the Filter menu, click Apply Filter/Sort.

Create and Run a Select Query

1. On the Insert menu, click Query.

2. In the New Query dialog box, select Design View and then click OK.

3. In the Show Table dialog box, select the tables or queries that you want to base this query on and then click Add. Click Close.

> **Tip**   If the Show Table dialog box is not visible, on the Query menu, click Show Table. To remove a table from Design view, right-click the table and then click Remove Table.

4. From the field lists, drag the fields you want in the query to the query design grid.

5. Enter any criteria required for the results you want.

6. On the Query menu, click Run. The select query runs, and the results are displayed.

Create a Report

1. Create a table or query that contains the data you want to display in the report.

2. On the Insert menu, click Report.

3. Select Report Wizard, and then click OK.

4. In the Tables/Queries list, select the table or query that contains the data you want to include in the report.

5. Add the fields for the report, and then click Next.

6. Follow the wizard to define report groups, sorting, layout options, and report style.

7. Enter a title for the report, and then click Finish.

View a Table, Query, or Form in PivotTable View or PivotChart View

1. Open the table, query, or form.

2. On the View menu, click PivotTable View or PivotChart View.

3. Build the PivotTable or PivotChart with the data you want to see.

> **Note**   The previous procedure cannot be performed in Access 2000.

Microsoft Office Web Components

Publish Excel Data to a Spreadsheet Component

1. With the Excel worksheet open, click Save As on the File menu.

2. In the Save As Type list, select Web Page.

3. Click the Entire Workbook option to save the entire workbook as a Web page, or click Selection to save a worksheet as a Web page. (If you want to save only a group of cells, select the cells before clicking Save As in step 1.)

4. Select the Add Interactivity option to make the data available for editing in the Spreadsheet Component on the Web page. Click the Publish button and then select AutoRepublish Every Time This Workbook Is Saved if you want changes made to the data in the original workbook to be published to the Web page.

Sort Data in a Spreadsheet Component

1. On the Spreadsheet Component's toolbar, click the arrow next to the Sort Ascending or Sort Descending button.

2. Select the field by which you want to sort the data.

   Repeat these steps to sort by other fields.

Sort Data in a PivotTable Component

1. In the PivotTable Component, click the field name by which you want to sort.

2. On the PivotTable Component's toolbar, click the Sort Ascending or Sort Descending button.

Sort Data in a Chart Component

1. Select the detail items by which you want to sort.

2. On the Chart Component's toolbar, click the Sort Ascending or Sort Descending button.

Filter Data Displayed in a Spreadsheet Component

1. On the Spreadsheet Component's toolbar, click the AutoFilter button.

2. Click the arrow next to the field you want to use in your filter.

3. Select or clear the check boxes to display records matching the specified values.

4. Click OK.

Filter Data Displayed in a PivotTable Component

1. Click the arrow next to the field name by which you want to filter.

2. Select or clear the check boxes to display records matching the specified values.

3. Click OK.

Filter Data Displayed in a Chart Component

1. In the Chart Component, click the arrow next to the field name by which you want to filter.

2. Select or clear the check boxes to display or hide matching items.

3. Click OK.

Show the Top or Bottom Items in a PivotTable Component or Chart Component

1. In the PivotTable Component or Chart Component, click the field or detail item for which you want to show top or bottom items.

2. On the component's toolbar, click the Show Top/Bottom Items button.

3. Point to the Show Only The Top or Show Only The Bottom.

4. Click the number of items you want to show.

> **Note** This procedure cannot be performed with Office 2000 Web Components.

Insert a Summary Function into a PivotTable Component or Chart Component

1. In the PivotTable Component or Chart Component, click the field whose values you want to summarize.

2. On the Web component's toolbar, click the AutoCalc button.

3. Click the summary function (Sum, Count, Min, Max, and so on).

Insert a Subtotal into a PivotTable Component

1. In the PivotTable Component, click the field whose values you want to subtotal.

2. On the PivotTable Component's toolbar, click the Subtotal button.

Insert Calculated Totals and Detail Fields into a PivotTable Component

1. On the PivotTable Component's toolbar, click the Calculated Totals And Fields button and then click Create Calculated Total or Create Calculated Detail Field.

2. Enter a name and formula for the calculated total or calculated field.

3. Drag the calculated total or field from the PivotTable field list to the PivotTable Component.

> **Note** This procedure cannot be performed with Office 2000 Web Components.

Microsoft Data Analyzer

Create a View File

1. In Data Analyzer, click New on the File menu.

2. Click Next, and then click Add.

3. In the Name box, type a descriptive name for the view that is easy for you to remember.

4. In the Connection Type area, do the following:

   ❏ If the data for the view is stored on a Microsoft SQL Server 2000 Analysis Services server computer, select the Server option and enter an OLAP server name.

   ❏ If the data for the view is stored in an offline cube file, select the Local Cube option and type the full path to the offline cube file.

❑   If the OLAP data is stored on a Microsoft SQL Server 2000 Analysis Services server computer that's accessible over the Web, click the HTTP option and enter the Web address for the server. Click the Advanced button if you need to provide additional Web connection details.

5.   Click the Connect button to connect to the OLAP data.

6.   Select the OLAP catalog name in the Catalog list and the OLAP cube name in the Cube list.

7.   Click OK to close the Connection Properties dialog box.

8.   Click Next.

9.   Select the check box next to each dimension you want to initially display in a corresponding dimension pane in Data Analyzer. Click Next.

10.   In the Display Type list, select the format in which measures will be initially displayed, either Bars or Grid.

11.   In the Length list, select an item that the bar lengths or pie slice sizes will represent.

12.   In the Color list, select an item that the bar and pie slice colors will represent.

13.   Click Finish. The view file is created, Data Analyzer connects to the source data, and the data view is displayed according to the options you specified.

Reset the View's Lengths and Colors

■   Do one of the following:

❑   Close and reopen the view file.

❑   Click Default Members on each dimension pane's toolbar.

❑   Right-click a blank area of each dimension pane, point to Go To, and then click Default Members.

Navigate Up and Down a Dimension's Levels

■   Do one of the following:

❑   Click the Drill Up or Drill Down buttons to navigate to the next highest or next lowest level.

❑ Double-click a member to show the member's child members.

❑ Right-click a blank area in a dimension pane, point to Go To, and then click the specific level's name.

Change the Bar and Pie Slice Colors

1. On View menu, click Color Scale.

2. If you do not see four buttons at the bottom of the Color Scale dialog box, click the Color Scale dialog box's Manual button.

3. Click Reset Values According To Data to reset the colors based on the current color scheme settings.

4. Click Automatic Mode. Switch to Manual Goal Settings to display the Min, Mid, and Max boxes. In these boxes, you can specify the minimum, midpoint, and maximum values on which to base the colors. To switch back to having Data Analyzer decide on the meanings of the colors, click the Manual Mode. Switch to Automatic Goal Settings button.

5. Click Change The Meaning Of Green And Red to determine whether low, middle, or high values are "good," or green.

6. Click Change Color Scheme to determine whether colors are based on filtered members (click Use Highest And Lowest Values Of Significant Selected Members Only) or whether colors are based on all members in all of the dimensions (click Choose Absolute High And Low Values).

Change Which Dimensions Are Displayed and Change What the Colors Represent

1. On the Edit menu, click Change View.

2. To include or remove specific dimension panes, select or clear the appropriate check boxes on the Dimensions tab.

3. Use the controls on the Measures tab to change the type of display and what measures the view's bar lengths, pie slice sizes, and colors represent.

Define and Use a Template Measure

1. With a view open in Data Analyzer, on the Edit menu, click Change View.

2. On the Template Measures tab, click Add.

3. In the Measure Name box, type a name that is easy for you to remember.

4. Click the Show Internal Syntax option.

5. Construct the custom measure by dragging dimensions, members, tokens, and functions listed in the lower half of the dialog box to the expression box just below the Measure Name box. When you have finished, click OK.

6. On the Measures tab, if the Display Type list is set to Grid, check the box containing the name of the new custom measure. If the Display Type list is set to Bars, select the name of the new custom measure in either the Length or Color list, depending on whether you want the bar lengths or colors to represent the new custom measure.

Use the Business Center

1. Right-click a member or dimension pane, and then click Business-Center.

2. Follow the BusinessCenter's directions to customize a built-in question.

3. When you want to run a BusinessCenter question, click the BC icon next to the question.

Export a Copy of the Information in a Data Analyzer View to an Excel Worksheet

■ With the dimension panes and members you want to export visible in Data Analyzer, click Export To Microsoft Excel Workbook on the Tools menu.

An Excel workbook is created with a worksheet for each visible dimension pane.

Export a Data Analyzer View as a PowerPoint Slide

■ With the dimension panes and members you want to export visible in Data Analyzer, click Export To Microsoft PowerPoint on the Tools menu.

A PowerPoint slide is created and a snapshot of the view file is placed on the slide.

Appendix B

Additional Tools and Resources

This appendix provides a brief description, installation steps, and usage guidelines for the tools provided on the companion CD-ROM. These tools and samples are installed by default to the folder C:\Microsoft Press\Excel Data Analysis\Extras. (For more information about the companion CD-ROM, see the section "Using the Accompanying CD" in the introduction to the book.) This appendix also describes tools and add-ins available on the Microsoft Web site (*http://www.microsoft.com*). You can download these tools from the Web pages listed to augment the data analysis capabilities of the Microsoft Office applications you use in your organization.

CD Extras

The following data analysis samples and learning tools are available on the book's companion CD-ROM.

Data Analyzer 3.5 Tutorial

This interactive tutorial introduces the concepts behind Microsoft Data Analyzer version 3.5 and teaches you how to become a proficient user. (The tutorial is also available at *http://office.microsoft.com/downloads/2002/datutor.aspx*.)

Installation and Use

1. Double-click the file datutor.exe in the Extras folder.

2. Click Yes to accept the license agreement.

3. Enter or browse to the location at which you want to copy the tutorial's installation file; for example, C:\DATutor. Click OK.

4. Click Yes if prompted to create the folder.

5. Click OK.

6. Open the folder you designated in step 3, and then double-click the file datutorial.msi.

7. Click Next three times through the installation wizard.

8. Click Close after the installation is complete.

9. Assuming a default installation path, open the folder Program Files\Microsoft Data Analyzer Tutorial and then double-click the file tutorial.hta to run the tutorial.

Sample PivotTable Reports

These four Excel workbooks contain 25 PivotTable reports and 4 PivotChart reports that you can experiment with. (These samples are also available at *http://office.microsoft.com/downloads/2002/Reports.aspx*.)

Installation and Use

1. Double-click the file reports.exe in the Extras folder.

2. Click Yes, and then click Yes again to accept the license agreement.

3. Enter or browse to the location at which you want to place the PivotTable reports and PivotChart reports; for example, C:\PVRpts.

4. Click Yes if prompted.

5. Click OK.

6. Open the folder you designated in step 3, and then open any one of the four Excel workbooks.

The article *25 Easy PivotTable Reports* referred to in the Excel spreadsheets can be found at Microsoft Office Tools on the Web at *http://office.microsoft.com*.

Microsoft Office XP Web Component Toolpack

The Office Web Component (OWC) Toolpack includes walkthroughs of Office XP Web Component features, a library of code samples for common OWC tasks, links to the documentation that comes with Office XP, and advanced PivotTable code samples (such as for conditional cell coloring using an add-in and conditional cell coloring using built-in functionality). The OWC Toolpack also includes a drillthrough sample, a server actions sample, and a sample for printing via Excel. The toolpack requires SQL Server 2000 Analysis

Services and the Office XP Web Components to be installed on the local computer. (The toolpack is also available at *http://msdn.microsoft.com/downloads/default.asp?url=/downloads/sample.asp?url=/MSDN-FILES/027/001/681/msdncompositedoc.xml&frame=true.*)

Installation and Use

1.   Double-click the file offpack.exe in the Extras folder.

2.   Click Next, and then follow the installation wizard to set up the OWC Toolpack on your computer.

3.   Click Close when installation is complete.

4.   By default, the installation wizard creates an item for the toolpack on the Programs menu. Click Start, All Programs, and then Office XP Web Component Toolpack to see a list of options.

Online Data Analysis Resources

This section lists some of the tools and add-ins available on *http://www.microsoft.com* that you can use to perform data analysis tasks in Microsoft Office. You can find these tools at the Web pages referred to for each tool. These pages also include instructions for installing and using the add-ins.

OLAP CubeCellValue for Microsoft Excel 2002

Available at *http://office.microsoft.com/downloads/2002/CubeCellValue.aspx.* This add-in allows you to retrieve a single value from an online analytical processing (OLAP) data provider and enter it into a single cell in a spreadsheet. The add-in also provides the CubeCellValue Formula dialog box (available from a command on the Data menu after you install the add-in) to help you construct the formula required to retrieve the data. To install and use OLAP CubeCellValue, follow the instructions on the download page.

Access Links for Microsoft Excel 2002

Available at *http://office.microsoft.com/downloads/2002/acclnk.aspx.* This add-in allows you to convert an Excel list to an Access database, create an Access report from Excel data, and use an Access form to enter Excel data. (This add-in is already included with Excel 2000.) To install and use Access Links, follow the instructions on the download page.

Report Manager for Microsoft Excel 2002

Available at *http://office.microsoft.com/downloads/2002/rptmgr.aspx*. This add-in allows you to combine Excel 2002 worksheets, views, and scenarios into reports that can be printed. After you add a report, it is saved with the workbook so that you can print the report later. (This add-in is already included with Excel 2000.) To install Report Manager, follow the instructions on the download page. After you've installed Report Manager, follow these steps to create a report for printing:

1.   On the View menu, click Report Manager.

2.   Click Add.

3.   In the Report Name box, type a name for the report.

4.   In the Sheet box, click the worksheet you want to use for the first section of the report.

5.   In the Section To Add area, do one of the following, repeating this step until you've created the sections you want in the report:

   a.   If you want to select a view to use for the first section of the report, select the View check box and then select the view.

   b.   If you want to use a scenario for the first section of the report, select the Scenario check box and then select the scenario.

   c.   If you want to add a section to the list in the Sections In This Report box, click Add.

To edit a report for printing, do the following:

1.   On the View menu, click Report Manager.

2.   In the Reports box, click the report you want to edit and then click Edit.

3.   Do one or more of the following:

   a.   To add a new section, click the sheet, view, or scenario you want under Section To Add and then click Add.

   b.   To delete a section, click the section in the Sections In This Report box and then click Delete.

   c.   To change the order of the sections, click the section you want to move and then click Move Up or Move Down.

   d.   To number the pages of the report consecutively, select the Use Continuous Page Numbers check box.

To print a report, follow these steps:

1. On the View menu, click Report Manager.

2. In the Reports box, click the report you want to print.

3. Click Print.

4. In the Copies box, type the number of copies you want to print.

Template Wizard with Data Tracking for Microsoft Excel 2002

Available at *http://office.microsoft.com/downloads/2002/tmplwiz.aspx*. This add-in sets up a database in which to store data entered from an Excel form. When you install the add-in program, the Template Wizard command is added to the Data menu in Excel. (This add-in is already included with Excel 2000.) To install and use Template Wizard with Data Tracking, follow the instructions on the download page.

XML Spreadsheet Converter for Microsoft Access 2002

Available at *http://office.microsoft.com/downloads/2002/msxmlss.aspx*. This add-in provides an easy way for you to format Microsoft Access 2002 data so that it can be recognized and used by Microsoft Excel 2002 or any application that recognizes the XML spreadsheet format. To install and use the XML Spreadsheet Converter, follow the instructions on the download page.

Index

Symbols and Numbers

About the Author

Paul Cornell works as a writer and an editor for the Microsoft Office Help team. He has worked on several Office Help projects, including the Microsoft Office Visual Basic Language Reference, Office XP Web Services Toolkit Help, Microsoft Office XP Primary Interop Assemblies Help, and the Microsoft Data Analyzer Tutorial.

In addition to writing and editing technical articles for the Microsoft Developer Network (MSDN), Paul contributes to the Office Power User Corner column at the Microsoft Office Assistance Center (*http://office.microsoft.com/Assistance*) and the Office Talk column at the Microsoft Office Developer Center (*http://msdn.microsoft.com/office*).

Paul lives with his wife and two daughters in Washington State.

The manuscript for this book was prepared and galleyed using Microsoft Word. Pages were composed by Microsoft Press using Adobe FrameMaker+SGML for Windows, with text in Garamond and display type in Helvetica Condensed. Composed pages were delivered to the printer as electronic prepress files.

Cover Designer:	Patricia Bradbury
Interior Graphic Designer:	James D. Kramer
Principal Compositor:	Dan Latimer
Interior Artist:	Joel Panchot
Principal Copy Editor:	Patricia Masserman
Indexer:	Shane-Armstrong Information Systems

Graduate
to the next generation of Visual Basic
at your own pace
with the proven
Microsoft Step by Step method.

U.S.A. **$39.99**
Canada $57.99
ISBN: 0-7356-1374-5

This primer is the fast way for any developer—new or experienced—who uses Microsoft® Visual Basic® to begin creating professional applications for the Microsoft .NET platform. The best-selling author shows you in easy-to-understand chapters how to unleash all the power of the new, Web-integrated version of Visual Basic. Learn core skills for programming in Visual Basic .NET at your own pace with the proven, modular, Microsoft STEP BY STEP training format. Select just the chapters you need— with expert code, optimization tips, advice, and samples straight from the experts.

Microsoft®
microsoft.com/mspress

Get a **Free**
e-mail newsletter, updates,
special offers, links to related books,
and more when you
register on line!

Register your Microsoft Press® title on our Web site and you'll get a FREE subscription to our e-mail newsletter, *Microsoft Press Book Connections.* You'll find out about newly released and upcoming books and learning tools, online events, software downloads, special offers and coupons for Microsoft Press customers, and information about major Microsoft® product releases. You can also read useful additional information about all the titles we publish, such as detailed book descriptions, tables of contents and indexes, sample chapters, links to related books and book series, author biographies, and reviews by other customers.

Registration is easy. Just visit this Web page and fill in your information:

http://www.microsoft.com/mspress/register

Microsoft®

- -

Proof of Purchase

Use this page as proof of purchase if participating in a promotion or rebate offer on this title. Proof of purchase must be used in conjunction with other proof(s) of payment such as your dated sales receipt—see offer details.

Accessing and Analyzing Data with Microsoft® Excel
0-7356-1895-X

_____

CUSTOMER NAME

Microsoft Press, PO Box 97017, Redmond, WA 98073-9830

MICROSOFT LICENSE AGREEMENT

Book Companion CD

IMPORTANT—READ CAREFULLY: This Microsoft End-User License Agreement ("EULA") is a legal agreement between you (either an individual or an entity) and Microsoft Corporation for the Microsoft product identified above, which includes computer software and may include associated media, printed materials, and "online" or electronic documentation ("SOFTWARE PRODUCT"). Any component included within the SOFTWARE PRODUCT that is accompanied by a separate End-User License Agreement shall be governed by such agreement and not the terms set forth below. By installing, copying, or otherwise using the SOFTWARE PRODUCT, you agree to be bound by the terms of this EULA. If you do not agree to the terms of this EULA, you are not authorized to install, copy, or otherwise use the SOFTWARE PRODUCT; you may, however, return the SOFTWARE PRODUCT, along with all printed materials and other items that form a part of the Microsoft product that includes the SOFTWARE PRODUCT, to the place you obtained them for a full refund.

SOFTWARE PRODUCT LICENSE

The SOFTWARE PRODUCT is protected by United States copyright laws and international copyright treaties, as well as other intellectual property laws and treaties. The SOFTWARE PRODUCT is licensed, not sold.

1. **GRANT OF LICENSE.** This EULA grants you the following rights:

   a. **Software Product.** You may install and use one copy of the SOFTWARE PRODUCT on a single computer. The primary user of the computer on which the SOFTWARE PRODUCT is installed may make a second copy for his or her exclusive use on a portable computer.

   b. **Storage/Network Use.** You may also store or install a copy of the SOFTWARE PRODUCT on a storage device, such as a network server, used only to install or run the SOFTWARE PRODUCT on your other computers over an internal network; however, you must acquire and dedicate a license for each separate computer on which the SOFTWARE PRODUCT is installed or run from the storage device. A license for the SOFTWARE PRODUCT may not be shared or used concurrently on different computers.

   c. **License Pak.** If you have acquired this EULA in a Microsoft License Pak, you may make the number of additional copies of the computer software portion of the SOFTWARE PRODUCT authorized on the printed copy of this EULA, and you may use each copy in the manner specified above. You are also entitled to make a corresponding number of secondary copies for portable computer use as specified above.

   d. **Sample Code.** Solely with respect to portions, if any, of the SOFTWARE PRODUCT that are identified within the SOFTWARE PRODUCT as sample code (the "SAMPLE CODE"):

      i. **Use and Modification.** Microsoft grants you the right to use and modify the source code version of the SAMPLE CODE, *provided* you comply with subsection (d)(iii) below. You may not distribute the SAMPLE CODE, or any modified version of the SAMPLE CODE, in source code form.

      ii. **Redistributable Files.** Provided you comply with subsection (d)(iii) below, Microsoft grants you a nonexclusive, royalty-free right to reproduce and distribute the object code version of the SAMPLE CODE and of any modified SAMPLE CODE, other than SAMPLE CODE, or any modified version thereof, designated as not redistributable in the Readme file that forms a part of the SOFTWARE PRODUCT (the "Non-Redistributable Sample Code"). All SAMPLE CODE other than the Non-Redistributable Sample Code is collectively referred to as the "REDISTRIBUTABLES."

      iii. **Redistribution Requirements.** If you redistribute the REDISTRIBUTABLES, you agree to: (i) distribute the REDISTRIBUTABLES in object code form only in conjunction with and as a part of your software application product; (ii) not use Microsoft's name, logo, or trademarks to market your software application product; (iii) include a valid copyright notice on your software application product; (iv) indemnify, hold harmless, and defend Microsoft from and against any claims or lawsuits, including attorney's fees, that arise or result from the use or distribution of your software application product; and (v) not permit further distribution of the REDISTRIBUTABLES by your end user. Contact Microsoft for the applicable royalties due and other licensing terms for all other uses and/or distribution of the REDISTRIBUTABLES.

2. **DESCRIPTION OF OTHER RIGHTS AND LIMITATIONS.**

   • **Limitations on Reverse Engineering, Decompilation, and Disassembly.** You may not reverse engineer, decompile, or disassemble the SOFTWARE PRODUCT, except and only to the extent that such activity is expressly permitted by applicable law notwithstanding this limitation.

   • **Separation of Components.** The SOFTWARE PRODUCT is licensed as a single product. Its component parts may not be separated for use on more than one computer.

   • **Rental.** You may not rent, lease, or lend the SOFTWARE PRODUCT.

- **Support Services.** Microsoft may, but is not obligated to, provide you with support services related to the SOFTWARE PRODUCT ("Support Services"). Use of Support Services is governed by the Microsoft policies and programs described in the user manual, in "online" documentation, and/or in other Microsoft-provided materials. Any supplemental software code provided to you as part of the Support Services shall be considered part of the SOFTWARE PRODUCT and subject to the terms and conditions of this EULA. With respect to technical information you provide to Microsoft as part of the Support Services, Microsoft may use such information for its business purposes, including for product support and development. Microsoft will not utilize such technical information in a form that personally identifies you.

- **Software Transfer.** You may permanently transfer all of your rights under this EULA, provided you retain no copies, you transfer all of the SOFTWARE PRODUCT (including all component parts, the media and printed materials, any upgrades, this EULA, and, if applicable, the Certificate of Authenticity), **and** the recipient agrees to the terms of this EULA.

- **Termination.** Without prejudice to any other rights, Microsoft may terminate this EULA if you fail to comply with the terms and conditions of this EULA. In such event, you must destroy all copies of the SOFTWARE PRODUCT and all of its component parts.

3. **COPYRIGHT.** All title and copyrights in and to the SOFTWARE PRODUCT (including but not limited to any images, photographs, animations, video, audio, music, text, SAMPLE CODE, REDISTRIBUTABLES, and "applets" incorporated into the SOFTWARE PRODUCT) and any copies of the SOFTWARE PRODUCT are owned by Microsoft or its suppliers. The SOFT-WARE PRODUCT is protected by copyright laws and international treaty provisions. Therefore, you must treat the SOFTWARE PRODUCT like any other copyrighted material **except** that you may install the SOFTWARE PRODUCT on a single computer provided you keep the original solely for backup or archival purposes. You may not copy the printed materials accompanying the SOFTWARE PRODUCT.

4. **U.S. GOVERNMENT RESTRICTED RIGHTS.** The SOFTWARE PRODUCT and documentation are provided with RESTRICTED RIGHTS. Use, duplication, or disclosure by the Government is subject to restrictions as set forth in subparagraph (c)(1)(ii) of the Rights in Technical Data and Computer Software clause at DFARS 252.227-7013 or subparagraphs (c)(1) and (2) of the Commercial Computer Software—Restricted Rights at 48 CFR 52.227-19, as applicable. Manufacturer is Microsoft Corporation/One Microsoft Way/Redmond, WA 98052-6399.

5. **EXPORT RESTRICTIONS.** You agree that you will not export or re-export the SOFTWARE PRODUCT, any part thereof, or any process or service that is the direct product of the SOFTWARE PRODUCT (the foregoing collectively referred to as the "Restricted Components"), to any country, person, entity, or end user subject to U.S. export restrictions. You specifically agree not to export or re-export any of the Restricted Components (i) to any country to which the U.S. has embargoed or restricted the export of goods or services, which currently include, but are not necessarily limited to, Cuba, Iran, Iraq, Libya, North Korea, Sudan, and Syria, or to any national of any such country, wherever located, who intends to transmit or transport the Restricted Components back to such country; (ii) to any end user who you know or have reason to know will utilize the Restricted Components in the design, development, or production of nuclear, chemical, or biological weapons; or (iii) to any end user who has been prohibited from participating in U.S. export transactions by any federal agency of the U.S. government. You warrant and represent that neither the BXA nor any other U.S. federal agency has suspended, revoked, or denied your export privileges.

DISCLAIMER OF WARRANTY

NO WARRANTIES OR CONDITIONS. MICROSOFT EXPRESSLY DISCLAIMS ANY WARRANTY OR CONDITION FOR THE SOFTWARE PRODUCT. THE SOFTWARE PRODUCT AND ANY RELATED DOCUMENTATION ARE PROVIDED "AS IS" WITHOUT WARRANTY OR CONDITION OF ANY KIND, EITHER EXPRESS OR IMPLIED, INCLUDING, WITHOUT LIMITATION, THE IMPLIED WARRANTIES OF MERCHANTABILITY, FITNESS FOR A PARTICULAR PURPOSE, OR NONINFRINGEMENT. THE ENTIRE RISK ARISING OUT OF USE OR PERFORMANCE OF THE SOFTWARE PRODUCT REMAINS WITH YOU.

LIMITATION OF LIABILITY. TO THE MAXIMUM EXTENT PERMITTED BY APPLICABLE LAW, IN NO EVENT SHALL MICROSOFT OR ITS SUPPLIERS BE LIABLE FOR ANY SPECIAL, INCIDENTAL, INDIRECT, OR CONSEQUENTIAL DAMAGES WHATSOEVER (INCLUDING, WITHOUT LIMITATION, DAMAGES FOR LOSS OF BUSINESS PROFITS, BUSINESS INTERRUPTION, LOSS OF BUSINESS INFORMATION, OR ANY OTHER PECUNIARY LOSS) ARISING OUT OF THE USE OF OR INABILITY TO USE THE SOFTWARE PRODUCT OR THE PROVISION OF OR FAILURE TO PROVIDE SUPPORT SERVICES, EVEN IF MICROSOFT HAS BEEN ADVISED OF THE POSSIBILITY OF SUCH DAMAGES. IN ANY CASE, MICROSOFT'S ENTIRE LIABILITY UNDER ANY PROVISION OF THIS EULA SHALL BE LIMITED TO THE GREATER OF THE AMOUNT ACTUALLY PAID BY YOU FOR THE SOFTWARE PRODUCT OR US$5.00; PROVIDED, HOWEVER, IF YOU HAVE ENTERED INTO A MICROSOFT SUPPORT SERVICES AGREEMENT, MICROSOFT'S ENTIRE LIABILITY REGARDING SUPPORT SERVICES SHALL BE GOVERNED BY THE TERMS OF THAT AGREEMENT. BECAUSE SOME STATES AND JURISDICTIONS DO NOT ALLOW THE EXCLUSION OR LIMITATION OF LIABILITY, THE ABOVE LIMITATION MAY NOT APPLY TO YOU.

MISCELLANEOUS

This EULA is governed by the laws of the State of Washington USA, except and only to the extent that applicable law mandates governing law of a different jurisdiction.

Should you have any questions concerning this EULA, or if you desire to contact Microsoft for any reason, please contact the Microsoft subsidiary serving your country, or write: Microsoft Sales Information Center/One Microsoft Way/Redmond, WA 98052-6399.